Smart Questions

Gerald Nadler

William J. Chandon

Smart Questions

Learn to Ask the Right Questions for Powerful Results

JOSSEY-BASS
A Wiley Imprint
www.josseybass.com

Published by Jossey-Bass
A Wiley Imprint
989 Market Street, San Francisco, CA 94103-1741   www.josseybass.com

Jossey-Bass books and products are available through most bookstores. To contact Jossey-Bass directly call our Customer Care Department within the U.S. at 800-956-7739, outside the U.S. at 317-572-3986, or fax 317-572-4002.

Jossey-Bass also publishes its books in a variety of electronic formats. Some content that appears in print may not be available in electronic books.

Library of Congress Cataloging-in-Publication Data

Nadler, Gerald.
   Smart questions : learn to ask the right questions for powerful results /
Gerald Nadler, William J. Chandon.
      p. cm.
   Includes bibliographical references and index.
      ISBN 0-7879-7137-5 (alk. paper)
      1. Problem solving.   2. Questioning.   3. Management science.
I. Chandon, William J.   II. Title.
HD30.29.N344 2004
658.4'03-dc22   2003026451

Printed in the United States of America
FIRST EDITION
HB Printing   10 9 8 7 6 5 4 3 2 1

~~~ Contents

To our wives,

Elaine and Bridget,

who support and inspire us,

and to our families, friends, and colleagues,

who encourage us

⟿ Preface

There is an easy solution to every human problem—
neat, plausible, and . . . wrong.

—H. L. Mencken

Nothing shapes our lives so much as the questions we ask.

—Sam Keen

These opening quotations from H. L. Mencken and Sam Keen aptly frame this book.

On one side, *Smart Questions* is about a "radical" new framework for solving problems and creating solutions. As Mencken points out, easy solutions are often the wrong ones. As consultants with over fifty years of combined experience in problem solving, we know this to be true. We have worked with scores of companies, national and local government agencies, institutions, and associations throughout the world on a wide range of situations, and we have seen how frequently people misjudge problems and create faulty solutions—or worse, solutions that just create more problems!

There are many reasons that business leaders, managers, and private individuals go about problem solving in the wrong way, and we explain them in detail in this book. But as an overview here, let us simply say that most people have learned to use the wrong framework or paradigm for working through the issues of a problem. In essence, they approach problems using a reductionist thinking mode, which leads them to excessive, if not pointless, data collection, analysis paralysis, and static solutions that tend only to patch up the situation for a short period of time.

Smart Questions proposes a "new" framework for creating solutions. The Smart Questions Approach (SQA) is unlike any other method of problem solving you were taught or have read about. The rationale and thinking behind the approach are completely different, the process is different, even the vocabulary we use to talk about problem solving are different (which is why we actually call it "solution creation," not "problem solving"). Everything about SQA diverges from reductionist thinking. More important, SQA works. We have developed SQA over many years of research and field experience. The research mainly involves learning how the leading creators of solutions in almost every profession and walk of life think and approach their assignments (which is why we put "radical" and "new" in quotation marks above; it is not radical or new to these leading solution creators). SQA has been applied to a wide range of simple and complex situations in business, government, education, and even in families.

The second side of this book, relative to the quotation from Sam Keen above, is that the SQA is also about learning how to create solutions by asking questions rather than assuming answers. In addition to the fallacies of the reductionist approach that make solution creation go wrong, people too often analyze problem situations and quickly assume they know what actions to take. In their eagerness to make the problem go away, they leap to conclusions and take premature actions without considering a wide range of variables and options.

As the title of this book suggests, SQA emphasizes another aspect of creating solutions that the reductionist approach does not. SQA teaches you how to ask smart questions every step of the way. In particular, you will learn about the three fundamental questions that every situation requires and how these three guiding questions will automatically lead you to think of many other corollary smart questions whose answers will help you work far more effectively and innovatively in any solution creation effort.

Smart Questions will completely retrain you to become a more intelligent thinker, a better creator of solutions, and, in all likelihood, a more productive person. As you learn to apply SQA to your business and personal life, you will emerge with a radical change in your ability to develop creative, purposeful, long-term solutions in a wide range of situations.

HOW WE DEVELOPED SQA

Our personal stories reveal a lot about how we came into the field of methods for planning, design, development, problem solving, and systems thinking. In addition, they explain in large part why we believe that SQA is a far more effective framework for creating solutions than anything else we have been able to uncover in our years of research and consulting experience.

Gerry's Background

My work in this field began in 1948, when I was a young industrial engineer and a graduate student working during the summer at a food processing plant in Wisconsin. After a couple of days of orientation, the president of the company called me into his office for my first industrial assignment. He explained that a logjam on the loading docks was killing the company. Freshness is critical when processing foods, so every second of delay from the fields to the cans or to freezing created costly waste and hurt quality. He asked me to study the problem and give him a one-page report about what to do.

I believed at that time that my academic training in engineering was precisely what the company needed. I rushed off to prepare flowcharts, statistical analyses, measurements of work and productivity. I flawlessly applied many techniques I had learned, and to be sure not to miss anything, I performed exhaustive analysis and put it all together into my first professional report. Why do just one page? I thought. I'd do even better to impress my boss with my first project. I crammed in everything—data, recommendations, the works—and eagerly turned in a ten-page report.

The next day, the president called me into his office. "Gerry," he said, "you know what I think of this report?" I waited for his lavish praise, but he took it gingerly in his hands, tore it in half, and pitched it into the wastebasket. "What I need to know is this: If you were in my shoes, how would you solve the problem?" After the shock wore off, I went back to the drawing board and completely rewrote the report. The next day, I handed in a one-page set of recommendations and their justifications, as ordered. My recommendations were adopted, and they worked.

More important, this experience planted the seeds for my work in the field of solution creation. Because he had asked me "to study the problem" and then give him "a one-page report about what to do," that is what I did. I didn't "hear" the important part of the president's request about "what to do" in one page and had instead focused on his request "to study the problem." Since he asked about studying the problem, I "knew" he would want all the valuable analysis I had made.

From this point on, I began paying attention to how the effective and creative people around me went about examining problems and creating solutions. Noticing that they seemed to do things differently from what they and I had been taught, I talked about my tentative conclusions with many colleagues at the university where I was now a professor. I found that an anthropologist, a management behaviorist, a philosopher, a psychologist, and a sociologist also wondered, "How do the most effective people you know go about being so effective? How do the best problem solvers solve problems? How do the best planners and designers go about planning and design?" In other words, "How do they get great and creative results?" The six of us initiated the beginning of the continuing research that has exposed the methods and thinking we describe here.

I have continued to observe managers, engineers, and many others whom I believed to be the most creative and effective to find out what they did differently from the rest of the people. What I discovered provided the same results as the research did: that the most effective solution developers threw out almost everything they had learned in school about how to plan, design, develop, improve, and create solutions. They used a different type of thinking and a methodology based on asking different kinds of questions—and lots of them. The decades of research, observation, and practice have led to the concepts and practices of the SQA.

Bill's Background

I became part of the research and work on the concepts that led to this book twelve years ago, but my experience learning about the real way to create solutions was similar to Gerry's. It began in the late 1980s, at the height of the Total Quality Movement, when I decided that I could make more of a contribution and help people by leaving the Jesuit seminary where I had been studying philosophy for a couple of years in order to get into the business world.

I took a position as a training and development consultant with a large high-tech electronics manufacturing company. One of my early assignments was as a facilitator in a high-tech firm whose rapid expansion was forcing the company to continuously move people to different facilities. The company had three computer teams—telecommunications, networking, and desktop—that were having a hard time getting the moved computer systems to work right. Users often suffered problems with their network, their e-mail, and the phone systems. In fact, users had reached a point where they could not get anything to work at all. Every computer problem fixed seemed to create a host of others.

My first reaction was to put together a team of leaders from all three groups to get at the root problems. We all assumed that if they could find and fix those, then the other problems would go away. Unfortunately, these leaders did not want to see that each of their problems was part of a larger problem. They each resolved to solve the problems themselves. The desktop team made their own list of things to deal with, as did the networking people, as did the telecom folks. They attended team meetings more from a desire to look like good team players rather than to share information and work together.

Although there were some minor improvements, the three leaders refused to see that their individual departmental problems were part of a bigger issue, which had to do with not working together. In hallway conversations, they located the blame on each other. It seemed that their real goal was to look good to their bosses so they could keep their jobs. The leaders wanted to make sure that they looked good to their boss, so they all developed solutions only within their own areas that they could address or solve. They managed to solve minor problems within their own areas but left the most significant problems unaddressed.

I tried every imaginable technique to break through the logjam. But I failed to make any real impact. Finally, realizing that I could do nothing more with this team, I left the role of facilitator for the team. The team continued and the problems remained, and eventually, this way of doing business damaged the company so much that it lost business and was finally sold.

I became driven to find a better way to solve problems on my next assignment. I scoured the literature on problem solving and found Gerry's previous book, *Breakthrough Thinking*. This was an "aha!" moment for me, and it radically changed my approach to problem solving. On one of my very next assignments, I used the ideas from

Gerry's earlier book, teaching everyone to ask smart questions about the problem and using the completely different framework that Gerry was teaching.

Ironically, a similar problem arose about customer service issues with computer installation and telecommunications. I used Gerry's approach, and the result and the experience of working with the team were dramatically different. The team dealt with the real issues, refused to blame one another, and developed a creative way of identifying and solving issues collaboratively. Customer service (as measured by regular surveys) improved dramatically at first and then steadily over time until the service became a nonissue.

Gerry and I met after I read his previous book and have been working together ever since.

HOW TO USE THIS BOOK

Smart Questions requires you to read the chapters sequentially because this book is largely about a process of thinking and action. The chapters build off of one another in presenting the SQA framework, so the book will not prove meaningful if you skip around from phase to phase. You need to learn all four phases in sequence in order to truly understand and assimilate the SQA process. Chapter Six on cases could be read early, but you may not get the full meaning of the process described in the earlier chapters.

Chapter One explains why most people go about problem solving in the wrong way. The chapter details the origin of reductionist thinking and why people believe it is the only way to solve problems. We point out numerous fallacies with this thinking process and show why the paradigm is more often than not ineffective in producing good results when you follow it to solve problems. We then contrast this with an explanation of holistic thinking, the approach we learned about by studying people who could be considered the leading solution creators of the world. We noticed that these people evaluated and acted on problems in a completely different manner, abandoning the traditional methods of reductionism and using a radically different paradigm.

We next lay out the precepts of the SQA based on holistic thinking. The first of these precepts is the use of three foundation questions—focusing on uniqueness, purposeful information, and systems—that must be explored for every problem. These three questions are an essential starting point for any work you do in creating solutions and exploring problems. We then provide an overview of the four phases of SQA—People Involvement, Purposes, Future Solution, and Living Solution—explaining what questions and actions each involves and why. We show how to go through each phase using three steps—list, organize, and decide—that are based on well-accepted practices of creativity and divergent and convergent thinking. This overview shows how creativity is sought throughout the SQA phases and provides you with the vocabulary of SQA, so you will likely immediately understand its significant benefits over reductionist thinking.

Chapter Two presents the first SQA phase: People Involvement. We discuss why getting a wide range of people involved from the start is critical in solution creation and how to ask smart questions about getting people involvement. Rather than the reductionist approach of getting buy-in usually in the last step of problem solving, SQA posits that problems are much more effectively and creatively solved and implemented when you tap into the knowledge and wisdom of the right people, using smart questions early in the solution creation process, who are affected by the problem or need to live with the solution. They are much more willing to get involved with SQA. We then go over the list, organize, and decide steps and show how to expand your thinking and asking questions about who to involve and how to select the right people.

Chapter Three presents the second phase of SQA, Purposes, which focuses on a concept unique to SQA, that of expanding your purposes. We explain why you need to explore the larger purposes of whatever situation you are dealing with. Organizations and individuals too often move ahead on problems without examining the larger purposes they are attempting to accomplish. We will teach you how to ask smart questions about purposes, and how to move from problems statements to purpose statements. Then we will walk you through the list, organize, and decide steps, showing you how to expand your understanding of your purposes and how to organize a "purposes hierarchy" from which you will select the most appropriate focus purposes for which you will then aim to create solutions.

Chapter Four discusses the third phase of SQA, Future Solution. The concept of a future solution for the selected focus purpose is unique to the SQA framework. It is a usable concept that we show goes far beyond the usual "flag-waving" admonition of traditional problem solving. A future solution is an ideal solution that you intentionally define in some detail. We explain the many benefits you obtain when you devise a future solution, including an enormous increase in creative solution ideas and a forward-looking mind-set that helps you avoid short-term patches in favor of proactive long-term thinking. We then go through the list, organize, and decide steps to show how to fashion the most creative future solution ideas and how to choose the best one to guide you for your situation.

Chapter Five explores the last phase of SQA, Living Solution. We explain why this concept is unique to the SQA and why it is called a living solution (because any solution must be implemented with an eye to how it lives on in the future). We then detail the three components of it: a detailed plan for change today, a plan for future stages of changes, and an installation plan. As with the other phases, we will go through the list, organize, and decide steps showing you how to create ideas for living solutions and how to narrow your choices down to one living solution plan and its three components.

Each of these chapters contains numerous case studies that exemplify the points discussed in the chapter. We have made this a highly practical book so you can truly get different results in whatever area of practice you are in. We believe it is important to show you how large, complex problems are solved with SQA, so Chapter Six contains two significant case studies—one from business and one from government. These two cases show how the SQA process was applied in the situations, phase by phase, with impressive results. In both cases, we show how the traditional reductionist approach had produced the wrong ideas or had failed to work.

Finally, Chapter Seven discusses the significant benefits of using SQA in organizations to provide people with a language for innovation, a systems orientation, and a sense of empowerment over their problems to create what we call a Smart Questions Organization. In our view, using SQA in organizations of all kinds can become a true strategic advantage, bolstering your organization beyond your competitors.

WHO SHOULD READ THIS BOOK

Smart Questions is an important book for leaders and managers in business and government. We have also used the SQA process with enormously successful results in businesses of all types, education (such as primary and secondary school curriculum design, teacher education, and classroom management), environmentalism, community work, and many types of personal and family problem solving and solution creation. As you read this book, we invite you to think about how you can apply SQA not just to your professional work life, but also to your marriage or other relationship, parenting, and community, association, and societal activities.

A NOTE TO READERS

The case studies and examples used in this book are drawn from our own and some of our colleagues' SQA practices. For simplicity, we discuss our cases using the word "I" without distinguishing which one of us worked on the case. When we talk about cases that other SQA practitioners have been involved with, we talk about the case in terms of "an SQA practitioner."

In order to avoid confusion, all cases and examples refer to using the SQA rather than to any of the other names from earlier versions of *Smart Questions*. Although the principles of the SQA in this book are similar to previous versions, the methods and techniques of the approach have been evolving. In addition, we continue to get smarter about the approach of using smart questions as an organizational change and development method.

Our use of the words "right questions" is to be interpreted as meaning "*significantly more* right questions" than those posed by using conventional reductionism.

January 2004

GERALD NADLER
Los Angeles, California

WILLIAM J. CHANDON
Gold River, California

Smart Questions

CHAPTER ONE

Introducing the Smart Questions Approach

Moving Beyond Problem Solving to Creating Solutions

The mind, once expanded to the dimensions of larger ideas, never returns to its original size.

—*Oliver Wendell Holmes*

Problems are an inescapable aspect of life. They are nothing less than impediments to the growth, happiness, and success of every individual and every organization on the planet.

We can't make all problems go away, but we must learn to deal with them. Businesses, governments, private associations, religious groups, and even families must be ready to solve the problems that interfere with their future. Whether it's what new product to develop, what new service to offer, what to do about global warming, how to fix a failing educational system, or how to resolve an international crisis, every person, organization, and institution has a constant need to know how to solve problems.

Solving problems may sometimes seem simple, but most personal, organizational, societal, and group problems are not simple. They are usually complex, involving numerous pros and cons, requiring difficult choices, and potentially affecting many people. As a result, many problems are not solved in an optimum manner and to everyone's satisfaction. Aspects of the problem remain: the new product fails to generate profits in the way you expected, the children don't increase their test scores, and peace eludes two warring nations.

In many instances, the attempted solution to some problems only begets other problems. Like the domino effect, each apparent resolution creates new problems, which when solved give rise to yet other problems, and so on in a never-ending cascade of incomplete or failed solutions.

THE PROBLEMS WITH PROBLEM SOLVING

Why do problems vex organizations and individuals? Why can't our business leaders, managers, politicians, workers, and parents find intelligent, cost-effective, and continuing solutions to their problems? Why can't you solve the issues that plague your life?

The main reason is that most people approach problem solving the wrong way. As researchers and consultants in this field, we know this because we have been studying, writing about, and performing problem solving for more than fifty combined years. We have witnessed firsthand the most common methods of problem solving used in business, government, and society at large.

Our research has been extensive, involving thousands of individuals and hundreds of different circumstances, including corporate, governmental, and personal. Our research indicates that the majority of the population—around 92 percent of people—goes about problem solving using ineffective and unproductive techniques and thinking. You may be wondering how it could happen that so many people could have learned ineffective methods. The main reason is that they are taught and almost all organizations use reductionism to solve problems.

The Reductionist Approach

The reductionist (or "rational") approach derives from the Cartesian scientific thinking paradigm that took root in European society in the 1600s. Named after French philosopher René Descartes, the Cartesian method of thinking was originally an attempt to expand human knowledge beyond the dogma of the Church, which dictated and controlled what people believed about everything, from astronomy and medicine to social relations and politics. The problem was that the Church's faith-based dogma was increasingly running counter to observations and learning in many fields. In an effort to create progress, particularly in science and math, Descartes and his compatriots—notably the English philosopher Francis Bacon (1561–1626) and the English philosopher and mathematician Sir Isaac Newton (1642–1727)—understood that a new paradigm of thinking was needed.

Descartes created an approach that relies extensively on the use of empirical evidence, logic, and reason. Problems in the reductionist approach are solved "scientifically," meaning through study aimed at identifying a key part or assumption, followed by collecting data about the part, then analyzing the data, proposing a hypothesis to explain what is "correct" about the part, testing the hypothesis, evaluating the results, and concluding what the "correct" knowledge about the part ought to be. The Cartesian method, which was developed to understand the smaller nature-based world that coexisted with the Church's heavenly based view, is based on four principles. First, everything can be divided into its component parts. Second, any of those parts can be replaced. Third, the solution of the partial problem can solve the entire problem. Fourth, the whole is nothing more than the sum of its parts. It sounds reasonable, doesn't it?

Most of us think and analyze problems according to this Cartesian scientific paradigm. We are schooled and trained in it exclusively as our analytic thinking style. We have been so steeped in this thinking style that we automatically gravitate to it like fish to water. As doctors, lawyers, politicians, businesspeople, educators, and even religious counselors, we use it every day to solve whatever problems we face in our organizations, institutions, and personal lives. Whenever there is a problem, we resort to reductionist logic.

Here's a little test to see if you are part of the 92 percent of the population who are reductionist thinkers. See if the following steps resonate with your current problem-solving approach (would you, for example, use this approach to improve an accounts payable system, set up a strategic planning process, fix a manufacturing problem, develop a community plan, or create a course syllabus?):

1. Something is not working right. The first thing we need to figure out is exactly what is broken.

2. We gather data about the current situation, especially the broken or missing element.

3. We analyze the data.

4. We model or chart the data in order for others to understand it also.

5. We attempt to determine logical conclusions about precisely what is wrong or what lies at the root cause of the problem, based on the data.

6. We try to be creative and develop a solution for correcting the root cause of the problem.

7. We implement the solution that best fits this problem.

8. We apply this solution efficiently and quickly.

9. We move on to the next problem.

How does this approach sound to you? Is it a similar sequence of steps you would likely use to solve a problem at your workplace or in your personal life or community? If it seems logical and comprehensive to you . . . sorry, you are one of the 92 percent who have been steeped in the traditional, reductionist approach that does not work. If it makes you feel any better, we were part of the 92 percent until we learned a different approach from studying the other 8 percent of problem solvers.

We have seen the reductionist pattern of logic over and over again as the one that most people automatically gravitate to. Most people cannot conceive that there might be another way. Almost all the professional literature on problem solving, planning, design, creativity, and related fields states that this logic is *the* way to proceed. They recommend that people begin their problem solving by seeking out what appears to be objective factual data, which then maps to some type of model of the situation and a representation of the solution. The solution is then finalized and implemented, and the problem is deemed to be over.

WHY REINVENT THE WHEEL? In addition to its reliance on rationality and logic, a corollary fallacy in the implementation of the Cartesian method of thinking is the notion that many problems or problem elements are identical or at least similar. This leads to the belief that many problems can be resolved in similar ways, usually by transferring, adapting, or grafting the solution used in one problem directly onto the solution of another problem. The thinking goes something like: "The elements of Problem B are similar to the elements of Problem A, so let's borrow [reuse, graft, transfer, slightly modify] the solution from Problem A and apply it to Problem B. After all, why reinvent the wheel? Why waste time redoing something that has already been solved?"

This thinking is precisely what causes so many fads to occur in the problem solving and organizational change fields, such as reengineering, total quality, empowerment, and team building. An idea that works in one company takes root and spreads like wildfire among other corporations and businesses, which believe they can reuse the same solution with no changes.

This urge to adopt management fads is also an outgrowth of the last principle of reductionist thinking: that solutions must be implemented quickly and efficiently. We find that the rush to fix problems with mass-produced techniques is increasingly a factor in modern business and government because our society pushes us to move faster and faster in developing solutions to problems. For simple problems, such as a leaking faucet, a noise in our car, or a lack of letterhead stationery in our office, a mass-produced solution is fine. However, most of us need to address problems and issues that are far more complex, where the decision making is far more difficult for an individual or group.

Here's an example from our consulting experience that illustrates precisely the flawed application of reductionist thinking in business. I once worked with a hospital that wanted to improve its massive medical record-keeping system. The system was overloaded, slow to respond to requests, and inefficient. Following the reductionist line of thinking, the hospital initiated a lengthy study that collected data on how the medical records were kept, the turnaround time for a request of a patient's record, how many files were added per day, and a multitude of other data points. The people involved in the study then dissected the problem into its component parts regarding warehousing space needed, speed of record transfer between departments, accessibility, and a zillion other data points. It was then determined that the cause of the problem—the "broken" elements—were related to speed and accessibility.

Meanwhile, the hospital had heard about another hospital where I had previously consulted that had adopted a high-tech and award-winning solution to its own record-keeping problems. That hospital's solution had involved extensive use of computers and software. Because of my work with that second hospital, the CEO of the hospital in question hired me and told me that he assumed I would simply adopt the same high-tech solution for their medical record keeping problem. In his mind, "there was no need to reinvent the wheel." He expected a quick solution to what he perceived as the same set of problems bedeviling his hospital.

However, my background with the research meant it would not be at all appropriate to assume that the two hospitals were the same with regard to the suitability of using the same high-tech solution. Although they were similar in size, medical services offered, socio-economic communities served, and financial condition, a great deal of time and effort might be wasted and resistance could be engendered if we immediately tried to graft the same technological solutions from my consulting job at the first hospital to this second one. As is so often the case, our research and previous practice indicated that the problem with their medical record-keeping system might require a very different solution, one tailored to their needs and to the capabilities of this hospital's staff. In fact, that turned out to be the case here: the medical records problem reflected much larger issues that had to do with several other processes within the hospital. This hospital's problem and the needed solution were not simply a matter of installing the technology-based system of the previous hospital.

As consultants, we see many businesses, institutions, and governments making the same mistakes: incorrect determination of what the problem is, incorrect development of what the solution is, and an impatient rush to implement a solution that is unsuitable, misleading, or inappropriate to that problem or creates significant resistance among the people involved because it was "not invented here." If you doubt this, just think about why so many management fads have come—and then gone. We think it is pretty clear: they didn't work because they cannot be applied in a mass-produced manner. Although most businesspeople try to be pragmatic, seeking out approaches that they think will work, it is usually too late that they find out that fad approaches don't work for their unique situation.

Clearly, the Cartesian method of thinking has contributed much to the world. Descartes' emphasis on analysis and empirical study led to the truly significant advances in the fields of medicine, architecture, engineering, astronomy, and life sciences that have brought us to our modern era. The reductionist method of thinking is so dominant today that most of us believe there is simply no other way to think about solving problems or even planning and designing solutions. In fact, if you are familiar with James Adams's classic book, *The Care and Feeding of Ideas* (1979), you will recall that it lists ninety-four types of thinking; however, those related to problem solving (for example, critical, rational, strategic, objective, analytical, market oriented, and efficient) are all described in terms of reductionism.

THE PROBLEM WITH REDUCTIONIST PROBLEM SOLVING. The reductionist thinking process was largely designed to solve scientific problems and to guide scientific research, but it is not the only mental model of thinking that humans follow. In fact, Gerald Nadler and Shozo Hibino in *Creative Solution Finding* (1995) describe how over twenty-five hundred years of different thinking processes guided planning, design, solution creation, and problem solving. They also show how the reductionist process of organizational and individual problem solving has significant limitations and flaws that need to be recognized.

This scientific approach seeks to simplify the problems, to eliminate variables and complexities by finding the root causes and trying to patch over them. But business and organizational problems have countless variables and are dynamic and constantly in flux. This makes the reductionist approach ineffective for problem solving in most situations, which in our view explains why so many problems are not fully solved and why some attempted solutions cause other problems downstream.

Our work has identified numerous major flaws with reductionist thinking for significant (nonroutine) personal, organizational, and societal problems:

• *Unrelated problems cannot be treated as being similar.* Reductionist thinking tends to look for and find false consistencies and similarities between problems, and our fast-paced modern world exacerbates this. But the truth is that no two problems are exactly the same. Our research has shown that far too often, people lump characteristics or design elements together among different situations, believing one is enough like the other that it deserves the same solution. But no two situations can be the same. The people involved are not the same, the organizations or institutions are not the same, and the circumstances are not the same. Given this, reductionist thinking will invariably fall short in implementing the right solution for a wide range of problems.

For example, in the business world, it's not uncommon for one company to attempt to imitate the solutions used in another company. The recent popularity of best-practice benchmarking, that is, studying and copying what is done in the "best" companies within an industry or even other industries, is nothing less than the wholesale erroneous adaptation of this philosophy. Trying to force the solutions used in one company onto another cannot produce optimal results, since the characteristics of the two companies cannot possibly be the same. Learn about those "best practices," but do not force their use.

• *Subdividing problems into their parts does not create effective solutions.* One of the fundamental assumptions of reductionist thought is that problems can be dissected into smaller parts and that a problem's solution can be accomplished by fixing or replacing just one or two of the parts. But just as problems are unique, they are also complex, with tight interdependencies among the various parts of the system. Solving problems by replacing just a few parts neglects the many interdependencies among the issues within a problem and often leads to solution failure and other "unanticipated" problems. The saying, "the sum of the parts is greater than the whole," identifies what creates the best solutions.

• *Data collection and analysis about "the" problem is always incomplete and far too often about the wrong issue.* Reductionist logic relies extensively on empirical evidence, which basically means data, data, and more data. Too many business managers and political leaders today solve problems by collecting data ad infinitum in a frantic attempt to "know everything" possible about the problem. The underlying belief is that once we are clear about what the current state and problems are, the solutions will be obvious and jump out at us. Unfortunately, rather than generating solutions, most data collection translates into analysis paralysis. Not surprisingly, data lovers are more comfortable with and become more skilled at problem analysis than they ever do in proposing and developing solutions.

The truth about data is that there is no such thing as perfect, total information about a problem. Complete information about a problem is unattainable regardless of how much information is collected. Data are always incomplete and time bound. Information is just a representation of any reality. There is no such state of being in which you can have all the hard facts about a situation. Regardless of how often people, and especially managers in large companies, insist on getting "all the data," even with the most advanced statistical techniques to supposedly smooth over any inaccuracies, there will always be a gap in knowledge about the problem, let alone the solution.

Furthermore, all measurements have some dysfunction, regardless of how much someone might proclaim they have accurate measures of the right things, because there is always an element of personal, group, community, or cultural bias that leads to inescapable discrepancies. Raw data are also time limited; what you collect today reports on tomorrow's past. In other words, information is always wrong, although some may be useful.

• *Problems almost always do not have just a single solution that will work forever.* Reductionist logic is shortsighted and impatient. In most cases, people who use reductionist thinking become so focused on solving their problem that they fix on one solution that appears to them fitting enough to resolve the immediate issue. But time marches on, and today's seemingly appropriate solution may not work tomorrow. Believing there is just one and only one permanent solution is erroneous logic. Technology changes, people change, and the circumstances of the problem and the solution change. There is no such thing as *the* answer.

• *Creativity is sought only while developing solution ideas.* In the reductionist approach, the type of creativity that inspires really big ideas is severely limited by all the data and critiquing that precede the search for solution ideas. But creativity is needed in all the other phases of solving problems, such as determining which people to involve, assessing what is actually the right problem to be working on, and ensuring that the intended solution is workable.

The vast literature on creativity techniques compounds this flaw by treating the quest for ideas only in solution terms. Almost all of the creativity literature about how to generate new ideas addresses just the one step in reductionism that says, "Okay, now be creative in finding solutions to ameliorate the difficulties or causes."

• *Solutions often overly emphasize "exciting" new technologies.* "When your only tool is a hammer, everything looks like a nail" is a well-known expression that applies to new technology. Too often, problem solvers resort to some type of new technology, thinking that this is the best or only way to fix what is broken. The consequences of the technology trap can be quite devastating.

In the 1980s, General Motors decided it was going to automate all production activities with the latest craze at that time: robots. The company spent nearly $40 *billion* to install robotic technology in its facilities, only to remove almost all of it within a couple of years as the quality of GM cars deteriorated. To make anything work, GM even had to rehire more real people than they had before they had installed the robots. As a result, the average GM car in the 1990s saw increased production costs in the range of $600 to $750 higher than its competitors to pay off this fiasco.

The only instance in which putting technology first makes sense is in an R&D setting, where it is logical to try to create brand-new products that exploit new technological hammers. For instance, Intel Corporation has an R&D unit that does ethnographical studies of families to discover what their problems are. The group has created a new chip product that senses movement and can be attached to the shoes or clothing on Alzheimer's patients who might wander or fall.

The flaws with the reductionist approach are serious and need to be recognized as impediments to effective and creative problem solving. Although the Cartesian method of thinking is behind many important contributions that have changed the world, it is also reasonable to speculate that reductionism may be equally responsible for the continued existence of so many political, economic, and social problems. In other words, we believe that the reductionist method has created as many problems as it has solved—and maybe more. To paraphrase Albert Einstein, you cannot solve a problem with the same system of thought that created it.

In its defense, we admit that the Cartesian method of thinking was not intended to solve all types of problems. The protean thinkers of the European Enlightenment such as Descartes, Bacon, and Newton developed their paradigm of thinking to overcome the inflexible theological dogma that ignored natural phenomena in favor of its faith-based view of the spiritual and supernatural. The Cartesian method of thinking ultimately led to the scientific revolution and the industrial revolution. For good or ill, rationalistic thinking created our modern society, the way of life as we know it today.

One further word about these flaws is needed before proceeding. Do not assume that these statements about the flaws of reductionist thinking reflect a head-in-the-sand outlook regarding the modern world. We firmly believe in learning new thinking and using whatever is new. As you will see, our method of solving problems encourages enormous creativity and the appropriate use of technology and solutions from elsewhere to their full advantages. Chapters Four and Five in particular show how learning is crucial to creating solutions, especially when it comes to using new knowledge when the need for it is identified.

The Unstructured Method of Problem Solving

Although it is the most common framework for thinking, the Cartesian paradigm is not the only problem-solving approach in use today. Many people prefer what has come to be called an unstructured approach.

Being unstructured, this approach is difficult to define or quantify, since it takes different forms for different people. However, the universal ingredient in the unstructured approach derives from a firm belief in human creativity—that we are talented, inspired beings who have enormous energy to find new solutions to our problems. Proponents of the unstructured approach believe that problem solving can be accomplished largely through sheer willpower to come up with creative ideas. The approach largely trumpets "the all-American can-do" spirit.

One company we know about that highly endorsed unstructured problem solving was attempting to fix an issue that plagued it. The CEO invited a group consisting of twenty-five of his best people and their families from around the world to come to one location, where they would begin analyzing and developing better distribution practices for the company. He exhorted them at the kick-off meeting to "be creative" and develop farsighted ideas. No other structure was set up for the project. All participants were encouraged to apply themselves to reach the goal.

After three months of work on their own, the project fell apart, with no results. The effort was canceled after over $1 million in costs, consulting fees (not ours), and uprooted families. Expecting cross-fertilization by allowing the team to float in an unstructured approach, however much the CEO emphasized the value of creativity, turned out to be fatal.

Our research has shown that unstructured problem solving is too often nothing more than a hit-or-miss, trial-and-error game. Although we endorse the creativity inherent in everyone, we have found that organizations, institutions, and individuals who problem-solve using any type of unstructured approach typically end up squandering large amounts of their energy going down useless roads, as well as creating frustration, confusion, and disorganization among those involved in the problem-solving exercise.

SEARCHING FOR A NEW APPROACH

As the experiences we both had convinced us, we believed that a new way of thinking or a new process with which to approach complex organizational and personal problems was needed. We found that the reductionist approach was too anachronistic and ineffective to solve the serious problems we were being asked to work on. Meanwhile, the chaos and randomness of the unstructured approach were equally unacceptable given the pressing need for good solutions implemented in cost-effective ways.

We spent many years investigating and studying the professional literature and work experiences on problem solving. Through the course of our research, conducted with many other people from a wide range of disciplines and fields, we experienced an important breakthrough when we began studying some people who were considered to be among the most successful solution creators. These were people who won awards and received peer accolades for their records as being exceptional creators of brilliant solutions.

As we studied this group of leading thinkers, we noticed that they all seemed to approach problems with a completely different mindset from reductionist thinking. We began researching their activities in depth through experiments, survey instruments, personal interviews, and reading the literature about them. We searched and reflected long and hard to identify and understand the intuitive reasoning they employed that made them so successful.

We eventually were able to synthesize what was a crucial distinction in how these people went about resolving the issues of their lives and businesses: *they intuitively employed a holistic, expansive thinking process rather than the rational, reductionist process.* Many of the leading solution creators told us they had to throw away what they had been taught as the approach to follow. Much of this research and synthesis is reviewed in Nadler and Hibino's *Creative Solution Finding* (1995).

You are probably wondering what we mean by *holistic* and if it is even possible for us to teach you to think holistically. But we can assure you that over our years of study of such thinkers, we have been able to identify numerous specific characteristics of the holistic thinking these leading thinkers drew on. Here are a number of characteristics that we notice are consistently present among holistic problem solvers:

- Holistic thinkers consider every problem individually and uniquely as a brand-new problem. They do not initially attempt to draw parallels or conclusions based on problems that they have seen before or to implement exact solutions borrowed from other situations.

- Holistic thinkers seek to understand problems in a broad context. Rather than parsing a problem into its smaller components and focusing on what is assumed to be a single broken element, they first try to expand their understanding to encompass the larger needs and purposes of solving each problem.

- Holistic thinkers use multiple mental styles of thought when considering problem situations. They often begin their exploration by asking open-ended questions of those who are involved in, affected by, or influential in solving the problem.

- Holistic thinkers are willing to use their own intuition as well as rational analysis of the situation. They understand that their own gut feelings about problems reflect a wisdom that cannot be quantified or rationalized.

- Holistic thinkers are highly concerned with the people involved in and affected by the problem and its solution. They recognize that acknowledging people's feelings and beliefs on the nature of the problem and its solutions—what would be called soft data— is as important to creating a successful solution as collecting the so-called hard facts and data.

- Holistic thinkers are able to tolerate ambiguity as they fashion their solution. They recognize that situations are not black or white. There are invariably areas of gray, that is, components that cannot be categorized or fixed perfectly, and they are willing to live with them.

- Holistic thinkers integrate many ideas into their recommendations. The answers they propose are not cookie-cutter solutions. Rather, they are highly customized to each specific circumstance.

- Holistic thinkers often seek out novel and creative solutions— stemming from internal and external sources—that go beyond the simple changes to a situation that people expected.

- Holistic thinkers view their solution ideas in a systems context as part of many interrelationships with other systems.

This list of holistic thinking characteristics is quite impressive. However, there is one more crucial distinction that we want to single out. We detected that holistic thinkers reverse the entire context of problem solving: *they see themselves not as solving problems but as creating solutions.*

We do not believe this is a subtle or superfluous distinction. It is an important, qualitative difference, though not something that can be quantified precisely. If you begin to use holistic thinking, you will soon understand the vast differences between the two approaches, which we might describe as follows.

Problem solving is oriented toward the past. It aims to analyze what existed in the past and pinpoint whatever is wrong with that. It seeks a single solution within a "fix-it" mentality. Once the problem is solved, the problem solving moves on to the next problem. Problem solving is fact oriented, cold, rational, and impersonal.

Creating solutions is oriented toward the future. It aims to understand situations in terms of where people want to be years from now before deciding what to do today. It recognizes that problems exist in time, and so solutions must be living solutions that are adaptable, flexible, and ready to change as needs change. Solution creation is innovative as well as people centered. It is warm, fluid, and effective.

People often ask us to cite an example that contrasts the difference between reductionist and holistic thinking. One of the best ones that captures the distinction is the difference between Western and Oriental medicine. In Western medicine, when someone is ill, the doctor aims to identify and isolate one specific agent as the cause of the disease, be it bacterial, viral, degenerative, psychological, or something else. Once the causative factor is determined, it is treated independently, usually with pharmaceutical drugs, and the patient is sent away assuming that the disease has been treated and he or she will heal.

In contrast, Oriental medicine takes what most would call a holistic approach to healing. When a person is sick, Oriental medicine considers the entire person as being ill because it recognizes that many factors may contribute to the illness. Oriental doctors therefore investigate a wide range of issues in an effort to treat not just the symptoms of the moment but the person's entire mind-body system. An Oriental doctor will examine and treat the person's energy level (which the Chinese call *chi*), but also the person's diet, state of mind, stress level, work and exercise habits, and perhaps sexual functioning. The Oriental philosophy believes that all of these factors need to be in balance; when they are not, they collectively contribute to illness. There isn't just a single culprit as in Western medicine. As a result, treating all of these factors is needed to heal the whole person. This is why modern Oriental doctors usually prescribe herbs, acupuncture, dietary changes, and perhaps several other treatments in an effort to reinvigorate the person's energy and to rebalance the systems.

Holistic Solution Creation	Reductionist Problem Solving
Employs many mental models: intuitive, analytic, creative	Employs rational, empirical thought process
Future oriented; focuses on creating solutions	Past oriented; focuses on solving each problem
People centered	Fact centered
Seeks out broad context in which to understand a problem and its potential solutions	Limits context to the problem itself
Aims to find unique, novel ideas that provide the basis for a living solution that can endure and change over time	Aims to find a single, immediate solution that "fixes" the problem
Recognizes that all information is soft	Emphasizes only hard data
Initially treats each problem situation as unique	Seeks similarities with other problems
Puts solutions in a system framework, recognizing interdependencies with other systems	Specifies changes only in terms of the parts of the problem

Table 1.1.   Comparison of Holistic and Reductionist Approaches

The two systems of medicine are vastly different in approach. As you might deduce, Western medicine employs fundamentally a reductionist paradigm and is strictly problem focused. It aims to heal the patient from one specific disease right now. In contrast, Oriental medicine is holistic and aims to heal the whole person. We are not suggesting that Western medicine is wrong and Oriental medicine is superior. But it is also true that Western medicine has been moving recently toward a far more holistic approach and is now incorporating many aspects of Oriental medicine in its increasing recognition that humans are integrated mind-body systems.

Table 1.1 summarizes what we have learned about the differences between reductionist and holistic problem solving.

INTRODUCING THE SMART QUESTIONS APPROACH

What we learned from the best holistic thinkers significantly inspired us in our work to create a more effective paradigm to handle the complex problems we were seeing in business and government. The challenge was how to translate their gift of intuitive precepts of holistic thinking into a repeatable process that others could learn and use in their daily lives.

To effect a paradigm shift in the way people go about solving problems, we recognized the need for both a set of concepts behind a new methodology and an easy-to-understand process with specific steps to follow. Over the course of many years, we synthesized our observations of these leading creators of solutions and their holistic thinking into a comprehensive new methodology for creating solutions. We refined our paradigm several times over and tested it in many real-life situations with a wide range of businesspeople, politicians, educators, and others.

Called the Smart Questions Approach (SQA), we propose this powerful new process of thinking for any type of problem solving, planning, and creating solutions, regardless of the field of endeavor. SQA can be applied to solving family conflicts, business problems of any size, large corporate strategic change, as well as local, state, and national political issues, and even large-scale international conflicts. There are many aspects of SQA that need explanation, so we will start at the top.

At the heart of SQA is the fundamental premise: *Ask questions.* This concept is rooted in what we learned from the leading thinkers: that the best way to begin approaching any problem is to ask questions to gain *appropriate* knowledge and wisdom. (Of course, we will teach you how to ask "smart" questions.)

Asking questions is actually one of the world's oldest techniques to think through an issue and arrive at a clear understanding of its truths. Perhaps the most famous questioner was the Greek philosopher Socrates, who developed his method of asking questions in the Greek forums of the fifth century B.C.E., where he challenged youth to question the deepest moral and social beliefs of Athenian society. His constant questioning ultimately infuriated the Athenian leadership, and they condemned Socrates to death by forcing him to drink hemlock.

The Socratic method of thinking has endured in one form or another for millennia among the greatest philosophers, scientists, and social thinkers. Its most powerful principle is that thoughtful questions disrupt our normal and mostly unconscious patterns of thinking. They are the first intervention in implementing a change. That said, not all questions are smart. Today's version of questioning is too often reductionist or based on assuming humans can be creative when simply told to do so.

Instead, smart questions serve several critical purposes. Smart questioning challenges you to examine the assumptions and knowledge you may think you have about the problem and its solution. We all have mental models or assumptions about ourselves and the world. These remain mostly unconscious, but they become the model or paradigm by which we view the world, and hence our problems. When you problem-solve, you automatically resort to your trusted mental models because they allow your brain to speed up decision making, without requestioning everything all over again each time you need to assess a problem.

The problem, of course, is that your assumptions are not always true or applicable to every situation. Your hidden assumptions can cause you to move in the wrong direction and, more important, miss gathering the right, or "smart," information. Unless you recognize the limits of your assumptions and are willing to expose them, and even to turn them on end, you will be doomed to getting the same limited results.

In our view, reductionist thinking especially locks you into accepting assumptions. Reductionist thinking adheres to the logic pattern, "If A and B are true, then C is true," but the result is that few people question whether A and B are true to begin with. Smart questioning forces you to seek the truth behind the relevant background assumptions that you automatically take into a situation.

Humankind's greatest revolutions have been based on great thinkers' questioning the accepted assumptions or models of the world. Copernicus refused to accept the paradigm that the sun revolved around the earth. The founding fathers of the United States refused to adhere to the accepted assumptions that a monarchy is the only way to govern a nation. Henry Ford refused to accept the notion that a new method of producing goods (cars) could not be accomplished in mass quantities. Ed Land developed the Polaroid camera by asking if there were a way of producing photographs you could see right away. Steve Jobs and Bill Gates believed that they could change the world by putting computers in the hands of regular people instead of keeping them for only big organizations.

Smart questioning inspires new idea generation and encourages the exploration of new arenas. Creativity is often thought of as the merging of two thoughts, stimuli, or old ideas into a new one: $A + B = C$. But this requires you to have many perspectives to prime the creativity engine. Asking questions is thus a useful technique to remind yourself of possible ways to find new combinations of old and new ideas.

A good example of how questioning fuels creativity is Einstein, who asked why space and time were separate "things." His question shocked the field of physics and provoked an astonishing shift in how the universe was perceived. It turned out that just because there were two separate words for them did not mean they were two different and unrelated things. You couldn't define one without the other; that is, they were related to each other (hence the term *relativity* theory). Einstein had to create a new word—*spacetime*—to describe that relationship. His creative insight suddenly solved many of the mathematical problems that had plagued astronomers for a millennium.

Smart questioning also gets people to open up. A question of the smart variety encourages people to become more willing to pursue new directions on what could be effective solutions. It boosts thought, imagination, and discussions about the future. It stimulates the search for new information and the ability to talk to different kinds of people. Furthermore, when you are the smart questioner, you can create momentum toward expansive thinking, and you become a very good listener rather than a seller of answers.

Smart questioning creates mindfulness. A manager who proposes, for example, that the company adopt a particular quality improvement system recommended by guru A that he or she learned about at another company is jumping on the bandwagon or trying to impose a fad. He or she is acting on automatic pilot. Instead, smart questions create a mindfulness that there could be more than one perspective or way of creating solutions. Mindful questions develop the mind-set that innovation and creativity can be continuing parts of an organization's culture. They motivate ongoing change and arouse the curiosity of people to seek out learning about what's new in other realms besides their own organization.

Consider such mindful or smart questions as the following ones, and see if you can feel how strongly they might trigger creative ideas:

- What do your customers want your products or services to accomplish?
- What is your leading product or service, and how can it be improved?
- What can we do to help poor people?
- How can the rampant crime in this country be reduced?
- How can two nations resolve their differences without war?

- What would your life be like if you lived every day with passion and purpose?
- What would it be like to work in an organization that used your desire to be creative and empowered?

Did any of these questions trigger ideas and thoughts in you? If so, can those ideas be recombined to form new ideas to improve your business, your family, or the world?

Asking questions is not a faddish management trend that we are seeking to foist on the world. It is a powerful and age-old mental process that pushes you to examine your thinking about an issue, seek out fresh understanding, and boost your creative potential. The type, form, timing, and orientation of the questions in the SQA differ from those posed in reductionism. For example, SQA asks, "What are we trying to accomplish with a solution to this problem?" whereas reductionism asks, "Why does this problem exist, and what causes it?"

Briefly, then, smart questions stimulate thinking, require smart answers, provide purposeful information, get people to be open and empower themselves, let you lead the process, and make you be a good listener and coach for others.

SQA is built on three foundation questions and a four-phase iterative process of questions that form the basis for the actions you take to explore and understand the problem, and to create living solutions. Here is an overview of the SQA process, which the remainder of this book explains.

THE FOUNDATION QUESTIONS OF SQA

The three foundation questions of SQA are intended to act as a North Star that you can use to navigate your way through any solution creation effort. They provide a constant reminder for actions you will take during the four phases of SQA. The foundation questions are as follows.

SQA Foundation Question 1: How Can We Treat Every Problem Initially as Unique?

This is one of the most critical characteristics behind the effective leaders and problem solvers we studied. These thinkers always began their work by considering each situation on its own merits. Each problem needs to be individualized because no matter how similar two situations may appear on the surface, they cannot be the same. There are several important reasons to accept this characteristic.

First, the people involved in every apparently identical situation or system are always different. No matter how similar the exterior facts of two situations may be, the diversity and values of the people involved differ. Cultural differences are always present, whether you are dealing with different nations, states, local organizations, or even among different departments or locations within a single organization.

Second, the purposes to be accomplished in every apparently identical situation are likely to be different. Even companies in the same industry are likely to have different purposes to achieve in solving problems for the very same activities with the exact same name, such as *medication administration, strategic planning, public works,* or *inventory control.*

And finally, the technology available and appropriate to the solution of problems in seemingly identical situations is likely to differ. Technology now changes so quickly that even today's solution may be outdated by tomorrow. More important, you can't impose technology on the people involved, and since the people are always different, the technology needed may be different.

This foundation question stands in sharp contrast with reductionist thinking, which tends to encourage a "let's not reinvent the wheel" state of mind. The uniqueness of each problem and its eventual solution must be recognized initially, especially at the outset, when you need to focus on understanding what distinguishes this problem from any other and therefore what unique solutions and results may follow.

In general, this means that you cannot resort to imitative or adapted solutions, or solutions that copy or borrow a process or technology from another situation. Solutions need to be tailored not just to the so-called objective facts, but also to the feelings and emotions of the people involved in the problem's solution and its implementation. Importing solutions almost never works because people often do not understand all aspects of a borrowed solution; it may be more or less than they need, or they may not trust the elements borrowed from outside their own environment. In addition, those familiar with the solution being borrowed often don't know why the solution did work, and so they can't explain it. The analogy of "If the Jones Company can do it, then so can we," like all other analogies, can never be certain and is far too often costly and damaging to invoke.

Human nature is such that people tend to reject solutions imposed on them from outside. Think how many times you have heard about employees who invoke the "not invented here" excuse when they resist a change or how, even in different divisions of the same organization, the best practice from one group cannot immediately be copied to another. Even in so-called standardized situations—such as fast food restaurants, grocery chains, gas stations, and national consulting companies—the slight differences from one location to another is usually enough to prevent standardized solutions to every process. Even McDonald's recognized this idea when they allowed for unique items on their "standardized" menu to account for local and regional differences.

Initially considering the uniqueness of each situation does not mean that many of the ideas and concepts in someone else's solution may not be used eventually in yours. SQA will show how important it is to keep learning about developments and solutions from elsewhere and provide a process for making effective and creative use as needed of such information.

Accepting the uniqueness of each problem at the outset helps avoid the ineffectiveness and extra costs that are so common in reductionist problem solving. The uniqueness foundation question thus explains why almost every attempt to adopt a great solution from the Joneses nevertheless takes a lot more time, costs much more, and engenders a lot of negative residual feelings among those forced to use the outside solution.

SQA Foundation Question 2: What Purposeful Information Do We Need to Create Living Solutions?

This question grows out of our observation that the leading creators of solutions seldom put a lot of stock in collecting large amounts of hard data about what exists or went on in the past. Three reasons support this concept: information is a human construct; it is always incomplete, inaccurate, and imprecise; and it is not wisdom. Let's examine these.

INFORMATION IS A HUMAN CONSTRUCT. Information is not real; it is simply a representation of reality, a human construct in an attempt to paint a picture of reality. As such, each individual has a different sense of information. That is the message of the oft-told story about three blind men coming upon an elephant for the first time and each one describing it based on the part of the elephant he touched and felt. In other words, each of us has information that we believe to be true, but we each walk around with our own construct of reality. Each one of us describes what we see in the world differently—even when we think we have seen the same thing.

Furthermore, we can be deceived by what we see. We may think we have seen or understood something, but it could very well be that the information we collected in our brain is incorrect. Consider the case of a crime victim, such as the one who wrote a poignant op-ed article I remember reading a couple of years ago in the *New York Times.* The article told of a victim who testified at several trials that a certain man she identified was her attacker, but she was later proved wrong by a DNA test. She stated that she had even made heroic efforts during her ordeal to memorize her attacker's characteristics so she could identify him with absolute certainty, if she ever had the chance.

The point is that if you believe in and rely on information, data, or so-called objective facts to analyze and solve your problems, it doesn't guarantee that you have correctly perceived the reality. Whatever you believe, based on the information you have, may not be true about the actual situation itself. You have simply translated whatever was there into some type of language that represents it and appears to be meaningful to you. Your language can be mathematical or statistical, expository or graphical, but it is no different from speaking Japanese or French to describe the problem.

I have done a simple experiment dozens of times with groups of people to illustrate this point. I write five words on an easel chart pad: *always, mostly, sometimes, rarely,* and *never.* Then I instruct the group to write down for each of the five words a number between 0 and 100 to represent the meaning of the word in terms of percentages. For example, if something "always" occurs, what percentage of time does that occur? Then I record each person's numbers assigned for each word.

You will be amazed by the variety of answers this exercise generates, reflecting how differently people interpret even these common words that we assume have an unambiguous meaning. For example, some people actually assign 0 percent to the word *always* because they believe that nothing *always* happens. Others assign *always* with 100 percent because they believe when people say this word, they must mean each and every time. Still others say 85 percent because they believe people say *always* when they really mean "most of the time," which to them correlates to roughly 85 percent of the time. I have also had people who associate *always* with odd numbers like 3 percent, because they believe events occur in a bell-shaped curve, with *always* and *never* at the ends of the bell-shaped curve. The answers are similarly disparate for the other words.

INFORMATION IS ALWAYS INCOMPLETE, INACCURATE, AND IMPRECISE. It is impossible for data to be completely comprehensive and accurate. Perfect information is unattainable. You cannot collect all the data about a problem because the issues are too complex and interdependent. Data are also time bound; any information collected today is out of date tomorrow.

In addition, data are not neutral. They are colored by those who collect and those who analyze the information, and so data can never be accurate from an objective standpoint. As the physicist Werner Heisenberg showed, the accuracy of data is even influenced by the sheer fact of doing the measurements to get it. At a macrolevel, if you try to take the precise temperature of a room, your own presence will influence the temperature. In the end, you cannot rely on raw data to model solutions to problems. Data require interpretation. Interpretation requires humans, and humans vary in their interpretations. Consider the case of eight witnesses to an automobile accident. There are usually eight different stories in the details of the data.

The fact is that information is people dependent. The quality and truth of information depend on the people who have collected it and the people who interpret it.

INFORMATION IS NOT WISDOM. Having information is sometimes confused with having wisdom. However, there are many types of information, most of which lie far below the level of wisdom. Consider the following levels of information:

• *Raw data.* Raw data are like what a police officer arriving at a crime scene finds. Raw data are collected using observations and the senses, and possibly the help of experts (like the coroner) and various technologies (like DNA matching). In terms of everyday situations, raw data include things like the outputs of a manufacturing line, level of accomplishment of a seventh-grade class, responses on a survey questionnaire, acres flooded by a river, and testimony of a trial witness.

Trying to represent any reality with raw data, however, is not possible. The ultimate validity of all such raw data depends on the way in which they were gathered and the context associated with them. If you measure room temperature by a heating vent, you will not get the average room temperature. If you assume that your temperature readings are the same throughout the room, you will be very cold or hot indeed. If you measure productivity by the number of items shipped, without regard for the number returned because they are defective, you will not get a very good idea. If you ask workers how morale is, you will probably get different "raw data" than you will get from asking management the same question.

In other words, both human observation and physical measurement criteria play a role in whether your "raw data" are data that inform or garbage that confuses them. This sounds pretty obvious.

But today the first question most people ask when faced with a problem is, "Can you get me the data?" Because data are so easily transmitted anywhere in the world with technology, this question leads to the flood that overcomes almost everyone. Instead, they should be asking, "What are the criteria that will allow us to collect the data that will actually inform us so that we can create a real solution to the actual problem?" Volumes of useless or irrelevant data do not add anything to creating solutions that work.

The questions that are posed before the data-gathering process is set up are far more important to a successful outcome than the volume of raw data collected. If you rush in with the wrong question, that is ask for action before determining what the purpose of collecting the data is, you will drown in pointless noninformation or raw data.

• *Real information.* Putting raw data together gets you to the next level of representation: real information. This is when you begin to make sense of the data. There are many techniques for putting data together in a way that helps you see the forest and not just the trees. The most popular ones are statistics, charts, and graphs (models that could range from descriptive to mathematical) that can be transmitted quickly around the world because of technology. These help, but such manipulation of raw data has to be done carefully, with attention to the underlying assumptions with which you collected the data in the first place as well as to any assumptions that underlie the statistical manipulation. Otherwise, you may corrupt the value of these raw data by ignoring the limitations of such manipulation imposed by the hidden assumptions. You must also be aware of how these models and information formats might be used and abused by others in discussing solution creation and problem solving.

For example, if you collected temperature data in a room during the summer months, you cannot assume that it will be the same during winter. If the room was empty of computers and people (both give off considerable heat), you cannot assume that the average temperature in the room will be the same when filled with your technology and staff as when it was empty.

Raw data are always about the past too. If El Niño strikes, your temperature measurement may be way off. You must always use care when drawing conclusions about what will be from what has been.

• *Knowledge.* Once you are informed by information, you are at the gateway to knowledge. In other words, being informed about current events does not mean that you know what happened. Only after digesting and putting together the relevant information yourself do you know what happened. Knowledge is complex and interactive. It has meaning to you. You can do something with it: make decisions, take action, or decide not to take action.

Knowledge is the next level of representation. To know implies that you have understood your purpose. You have been able to validate information from multiple sources or perspectives. You have been able to ask questions and get answers that provide real information that has been weighed, like evidence. You know that whatever information and knowledge you have are time related and will likely change. By combining different types of real information, knowledge adds interpretation, experience, history, and additional context to your representation of the issue. Standardized test scores, for example, are combined and manipulated in many ways with other information (such as essays and grade point averages) and individual perceptions by teachers to figure out what pupils know. Knowledge is personal; asking you to transmit your knowledge about something cannot be done, whereas requesting real information can. Even within one organization, many surveys show that only 10 to 12 percent of respondents felt that existing knowledge was transferred satisfactorily.

• *Understanding.* Knowledge is not understanding. To understand means that you not only know the real story told by your digested information, but that you know what it means and how it fits in the big picture. You have gained broad insight about the area of concern or reality, including its stories, moral, values, beliefs, implications, explanations, methods, and history. This lets you judge (as a jury and judge do during the first part of a trial) guilt or innocence based on the case put forward by the knowledgeable prosecutor.

Another popular word to describe this level of representation is *intelligence*. Many companies use this term when assessing their industry and competitors or in the military to provide a picture of the enemy. This is the level where you start asking, "How would a CEO, or the guy on the loading dock, or the competition down the street interpret these data, information, and knowledge?" Are these the people to involve in your solution creation activities? If they are, when should you involve them?

Integration of many types of knowledge, information, and raw data is the basis for understanding. Understanding provides some overall logic or reasoning about what is known about the reality and the forming of possible mental models and conceptual frameworks about it. Knowing the relative worth of different types of knowledge about any given problem is the essence of your understanding of it.

• *Wisdom.* Wisdom is the transformation of understanding into concrete action, the ability to put understanding to use. It is like being the judge in the second half of a criminal trial: deciding what sentence fits the particular crime.

Wisdom is pragmatic. It applies a sense of values and beliefs, like justice and compassion, to knowledge and understanding in particular circumstances to come up with desirable results. It is about making a decision and getting into action. It is the insight into what is called for by the absorption of the raw data, information, knowledge, and understanding. It is about asking the right questions.

Everyone possesses some amount of wisdom just to survive: they cope with daily life based on their ability to integrate and use the understanding of the reality in which they exist. The wiser you are, the better your ability is to cope with and handle unusual local, community, societal, and international circumstances.

Despite these distinctions, too many people spend enormous amounts of time, energy, and money collecting data about the status of a system or problem area when they start a project. Great quantities of effort are squandered in believing they can accurately learn "everything." People falsely assume that a problem can be solved by throwing data at it. Furthermore, excessive data gathering will often blind-side you to the discovery of the best solutions.

This SQA foundation question about information reframes data collection completely. We will suggest a different approach in *Smart*

Questions: it is better to spend time gathering data that can help create solutions, not analyze problems. The goal is to seek only purposeful information that contributes to knowledge about and understanding of solutions. Knowledge is personal and interactive. It has meaning to you and reflects the uniqueness of each situation and the people involved in it. Data are an impersonal and static representation of the situation. They have no meaning other than what you ascribe to them. Ideally, what you need to seek is only the minimum amount of essential information, identified with the SQA process questions, about what exists and what is needed to develop a living solution.

SQA Foundation Question 3: How Can a Systems View Ensure the Solution We Are Creating Will Work?

This foundation question derives from the observations we made of the best holistic thinkers who were especially gifted at finding the forest through the trees. It reinforces the holistic perspective that nothing exists by itself. Successful problem prevention and solution creation hinge on taking into account the various interrelated elements and dimensions that comprise every situation—in other words, making sure that everything fits into a system.

A system is a mental framework for understanding how something works and how the component parts of it work together. It recognizes the interrelations among the multitude of parts of a whole. Our system framework has numerous elements that make it a whole: its purposes, inputs, processes, outputs, an environment, and human, physical, and information enablers (enablers refer to the things that make the system work).

By exploring a systems view of your solutions, you ensure that:

- The solution has a framework for considering the recommended activities and events to occur.

- Everyone involved shares a language for discussing and describing what needs to be accomplished and how the solution will work.

- There is a shared vision that the solution will behave or operate as desired once it is installed.

- A documented structure exists for the solution after it is implemented and installed.

- All aspects of each element are considered, such as the values and beliefs of the organization, measures of desired performance, control of them as the solution is being operated, interfaces with other systems, and the future state of the solution.
- The odds of failure are greatly reduced.
- There is purposeful information available to help make the many decisions needed in crafting a solution.
- The basis for continued learning and change is established.

If the description of systems seems a bit sketchy, don't worry. The details of how systems and the other guiding concepts help in asking the smart questions will be provided in the phases of SQA, especially in Phase 4, when we discuss how to fashion a living solution, whereby your chosen solution must be concrete enough to account for how it fits into the system of which it is part.

THE FOUR PHASES OF SQA

The three SQA foundation questions are not an action plan but rather form the mind-set or background to the entire solution creation process you will now undertake. The foundation questions are kept as your guideposts or continuous reminders of questioning that you need to do along the journey toward creating solutions.

With that said, SQA does have an action plan. Any process for creating solutions requires a structure or action plan that provides the step-by-step pathway forward. The human mind can churn out ideas ad infinitum, but without a structure to the thought process, moving toward solutions will not occur except by happy accident.

SQA uses four phases in its action plan, as shown in Figure 1.1. Each phase reflects a series of both questioning and actions that you will take.

The path through the phases is generally linear, but as you will notice in Figure 1.1, we have bidirectional arrows between the phases. This is to remind you that SQA is not perfectly linear; you cannot always proceed from one phase to the next. Yes, there is some artfulness and creativity, which we will discuss, involved in practicing SQA. Given that the foundation questions behind these action phases are based on holistic thinking, you need to be open to having your

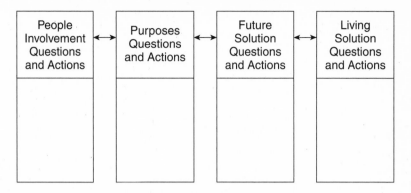

Figure 1.1.   Phases of the Smart Questions Approach

progress through the phases be as iterative as needed. The value of the phases is that they provide a structure for the work of asking questions, seeking information, and making decisions.

Here is an overview of what is involved in each of the phases.

Phase 1: People Involvement—Who Are the Possible Stakeholders and Resource People to Involve?

The best holistic thinkers understand that no problem or solution exists without people. People are the cause of a problem or the recipients of its effects. People's intelligence is the only way to understand the problem. People are needed to implement the solution. People are the ones who must live with the solution.

As a result, Phase 1 of SQA begins with people. In this phase, you need to ask questions that will lead to better solution creation actions that represent the interests of all relevant stakeholders. These could be the workers, managers, leaders, family members, community members, customers, customers' customers, suppliers, shareholders, decision makers, "experts" in potential solution areas, and any outsiders who can contribute to or affect the effectiveness and implementation of the solution.

Keeping the SQA foundation questions in mind, questions in this phase are aimed at eliciting information that helps you understand what is unique about the people involved in this situation, what unique information they have that will help the situation, and what role they play in the creation of the solution. The three foundation questions lead you to expand your thinking through Smart Questions about who is involved or affected by the problem, who is best qualified to be part of the solution-finding and decision-making process, and who has the talents and resources needed to implement and maintain the solutions.

Through questioning in this phase, you will seek an outcome composed of two specific actions: to get the right people involved and to ensure the future buy-in and acceptance of the solution from everyone involved.

Recognizing the need for people involvement at the very start of SQA is critical to the success of any solution creation endeavor. Too many solutions are devised by a few people in power without regard for those who need to live with the solution or those who need to implement it. It is often said that change is difficult for people. This is a misconception because what is actually difficult is change when people have not been consulted or asked for their thoughts, when they have not seen the future. Numerous studies have shown that when people participate in change, they embrace it.

Involving people early, especially with Smart Questions, serves many valuable purposes that facilitate the change. It allows everyone to:

- Share meanings and interpretations about what needs to change.
- Develop champions of change.
- Foster a winning attitude among all individuals involved.
- Develop capabilities for change among participants.
- Build a network of change agents and resources.
- Create teamwork and sharing.
- Produce creative ideas.
- Overcome resistance and arrogance.
- Avoid past mistakes that people know they have made.
- Overcome emotional, cultural, and environmental blocks.
- Avoid the tendency to overcontrol the change effort.
- Establish agreement and acceptance.

Yet another reason to begin with asking questions about the people is the increasing recognition that change does not always come from the top. Organizations are becoming more like spider webs of interconnected people. The designations of top, middle, and lower levels are increasingly less meaningful. People in all parts of an organization experience problems and blockages to creativity and improvements. It is more useful to think of people as having various roles, each requiring creativity and decision-making power. As a result, all people in an organization are the trigger point for proposing change, as well as the resource for implementing it.

Phase 2: Purposes—What Are Our Many Possible Purposes to Achieve, and Which One Should Be Our Focus Purpose?

Once you have started to work on the people involvement issues of your situation, this phase invites you—and the people selected to work with you—to delve deeply into the real purposes to be accomplished. Instead of the conventional exhortation, "Be sure you are working on the right problem," given without any concrete instruction on how to find this, Smart Questions show you how to identify the focus purpose. This purpose reflects the ultimate needs, desires, or intentions of the issue and its larger context.

The effective leaders we studied always placed every problem in a larger context. They sought to understand the relationship between the effective actions implemented to solve a problem and the purposes or context into which the solution is to be implemented. This led them to develop some sort of hierarchy or ever expanding set of purposes for each issue they encountered. This expansion of purposes is a critical element in effective and creative problem solving, because it allows you to understand clearly the wider context of the situation and to open the door to many more possible solutions. Stated simply, it expands your creative thinking space.

Many businesses misperceive or misjudge the purpose of solving their problems, and so they end up making the wrong decision to alter a product, build a new factory, move a warehouse, or fire employees when in reality they have incorrectly identified their real purpose. Governments too are notorious for spending money wastefully as they seek to fix a so-called problem and then fail to fully correct the entire problem because the real issues or needs were not truly identified. Even families can become trapped in perpetual conflict because they have misidentified the issues between their members.

Phase 2 therefore gives you the opportunity to ask a chain of questions that delve into identifying your bigger purposes. Your questions need to be aimed at understanding not just the specific goals behind fixing the problem, such as "decrease processing time by 25 percent," but the larger purposes that you more likely want to achieve behind the surface goals. These larger purposes are often unstated, and so in this phase, we help you bring them out. We teach you to keep asking about purposes until you finally get to the largest purposes. By doggedly pursuing this chain of questions until, at an extreme, your purposes are something like, "To achieve the roles of human beings," you eliminate many hidden assumptions, while building a deep awareness of what purposes you truly need to fulfill in your solution creation.

Phase 3: Future Solution—What Is the Ideal Solution That Will Allow Us to Achieve Our Focus Purpose Not Just for Now, But for the Future?

Phase 3 gets you to look further down the road to what we call the future solution. This phase is modeled after the leading thinkers who understand that finding solutions for today is not good enough. The more effective process to pursue is to seek out tomorrow's solutions for achieving the focus purpose—and then build backward from it. It is far more effective and efficient to paint the long-term picture of where you would really like to be in an ideal world rather than to simply go for the quick fix. Again, this is a crucial distinction between problem solving and creating solutions.

Another important distinction in SQA is that this phase seeks solution ideas for purposes that need to be achieved rather than just for the immediate issue that may have initiated the problem-starting effort. I was asked by the president of a medium-sized company to help design a factory that would double the company's capacity. This was the issue I was given after the president and eight of his executives had been studying how to eliminate the late delivery of almost all orders, reduce the high costs of and number of damaged products, and "clean up the confusion" in the factory. Before I started on what they considered a dream assignment to design a state-of-the-art factory, I asked the team what the purposes of the project were. Their decision was "to develop management control systems." But as we developed an ideal solution to achieve this end and its larger purposes, we ended up designing new systems for the current factory rather than a brand-new facility. The reductionist approach would have developed a great new factory solution—but for the wrong problem.

In this context, Phase 3 teaches you to ask questions that help you develop a model of the ideal solution. You aim to define and describe the ideal situation in which the problem may no longer exist. You will be amazed at how embracing this long-term solution-after-next view can change the way you go about making decisions, increasing your efficiency, and affecting the willingness of others to accept the solution.

Phase 4: Living Solution—What Ideas Can We Install Today That Stay as Close as Possible to the Future Solution?

One of the major precepts of holistic thinking is that there is no one perfect, permanent solution. Given that the world constantly changes, no solution can possibly endure forever. As a result, the ultimate goal in using SQA is to create what we call a "living solution." Whatever solution you implement, you must be prepared for it to be continuously altered, modified, and upgraded from one day, week, month, and year to the next, leading to the use of the future solution.

In Phase 4, you therefore continue to ask Smart Questions aimed at eliciting how you intend to keep the solution you are implementing as close as possible to the future solution developed in Phase 3. You set up a time line of expected changes to today's solution that keeps moving toward implementing the future solution within the time frame it encompasses. This may be one, two, three, or more years. Many organizations also build in a later review, say, two years after initial installation, for developing a new future solution. There needs to be a constant effort to evaluate the success of the solution you implement and a willingness to update or alter it as the purposes, goals, mission, and technology change.

THE DIVERGENT-CONVERGENT STRUCTURE OF THE SQA PHASES

You now have an overview of the three foundation questions and four phases of SQA. There is one additional perspective that we need to explain: how to go about asking Smart Questions. SQA is not about a free-form lovefest of questions, such as you might perform when using a creativity game or an unstructured problem-solving approach. You do not simply ask questions willy-nilly, without rhyme or reason, ad infinitum.

We have synthesized a specific structure behind the method of asking questions, eliciting ideas, and choosing an action. This structure is based on the basic mental process described in the literature of the creativity field, in which the development of truly creative solutions requires you to expand the range and number of ideas and options as far as possible during the initial stages of any creative work. One of the major precepts of creative thinking is the idea that the universe of potential solutions is improved if you generate as many ideas as possible for each phase rather than targeting just one or two that come immediately to mind.

In the creativity field, this process is known as divergent thinking. You diverge, or enlarge your field of thought as wide as possible. You seek to make connections in your mind between and among often unrelated matters. Your goal is to generate numerous new ideas without prejudging or assigning value to them. You are probably familiar with the creativity technique known as brainstorming, which is actually a specialized technique to encourage divergent thinking and has become very popular among business and creativity consultants. But there are other techniques that foster divergent thinking as well that we teach in this book.

Naturally, divergent thinking cannot continue ad infinitum when you have problems to solve. At some point, you must begin whittling down the ideas, evaluating and weighing them to select those that appear to offer the most promise given the situation. This honing process is known as convergent thinking. As in a funnel, you begin to converge the ideas into an integrated solution. In the process, you might also take aspects of several ideas and combine them with yet another idea to devise a single best approach.

Aspects of divergent and convergent thinking are also used in reductionist thinking, but only in the sense that you divide a problem into its component parts so you can quickly narrow the focus to identify a single part that is wrong or faulty and replace it with a new one. So although reductionist divergent and convergent thinking may prompt you to think expansively and flexibly when you are supposed to consider how to correct what is wrong, the real benefits are significantly reduced because your mind-set has been limited by becoming so knowledgeable about the problem.

In contrast, SQA uses divergent and convergent thinking to expand your perception of the people to be involved, the purposes to be achieved, and the potential solutions. SQA requires you to open up to broad vistas of purposes and solutions as you ask all aspects of the foundation systems question in the four phases of SQA.

Given the importance of divergent and convergent thinking, we have adopted specific techniques to accomplish them directly into SQA. In addition, we added another component that the leading creators of solutions pointed out is critical: putting the many ideas generated in divergent thinking into several cohesive options or alternative options to consider as you move into convergent thinking.

Thus, in each of the four phases of the Smart Questions process, your questions follow the three-step process shown in Figure 1.2. Here is a brief description of what occurs in each of these steps.

The List Step: Divergence—What Are Many Alternatives for the Phase?

The goal during this step is to ask Smart Questions that help generate as many ideas and topics as possible that are relevant to the phase you are in: People Involvement, Purposes, Future Solution, and Living Solution (PPFL). The nature and type of your questions will be slightly different from phase to phase. However, what unifies the list step across all four phases is the principle of divergent thinking. How many ways can I develop to accomplish the ends of this phase? In all cases, the goal is to fuel discussion and idea generation. We will present and discuss several divergent-thinking techniques to use during the listing step in each phase.

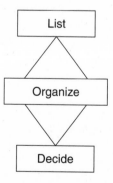

Figure 1.2.   Steps of Each Smart Questions Phase

The Organize Step: Organize—How Can We Organize the Alternatives into Possible Options to Consider?

Think of this step as the middle of the pendulum swing between divergent and convergent thinking. Given that the divergent thrust of the list step produces a large number of often random and disconnected ideas, this step encourages you to begin organizing, refining, and adapting the ideas into some type of pattern. The format for identifying the pattern or making sense of the list ideas will vary depending on the phase of SQA you are in.

This level of organizing is not to suggest that you now revert back to a reductionist way of thinking, applying Cartesian logic to the ideas that you have generated to see which idea can be eliminated as being faulty or which can be substituted for a broken part in your problem. Rather, you continue to apply intuition and creativity to organize the ideas you have generated into relatively cohesive options, and even combining parts of ideas into new ones. An important part of SQA is always to have options to consider before making a choice of what to do.

The Decide Step: Convergence—Which Option Is Most Effective and Creative for This Phase?

This step, as the name implies, is the point at which you start making decisions about which option or options to select. You begin to draw conclusions that lead you toward action. However, again, the decision making done through SQA is not the same as what occurs in a reductionist approach. Your decisions are, and should be, drawn from the wide range of options you created in the PPFL phases. In SQA, the expanded divergent and convergent thinking has guided you in a far more holistic and integrated manner than what occurs in reductionist decision making, where decisions are usually based strictly on data, mathematical analysis, and empirical evidence. Each chapter covering one of the phases provides a framework for evaluating the phase's options during the decide step.

WHAT IS A SMART QUESTION?

Each phase of SQA gives rise to many questions as you proceed through the list, organize, and decide (LOD) steps. We will illustrate the types of questions you will be asking as we detail the four phases.

However, the operational word here is *illustrate.* It is impossible to present all the questions you or your group should learn to ask. The questions we provide as examples are meant to stimulate you to invent and ask your own Smart Questions based on SQA and holistic thinking.

Nevertheless, you may be wondering, "How will I know the question I'm about to ask is smart?" Unfortunately, there is no black and white answer. Sometimes intuition takes the driver's seat and knows the best route. Nevertheless, here are some guidelines to ask yourself about any question you are considering asking. These questions will point the way to helping you know whether you are asking a smart question:

- Does the question I'm asking align with the three foundation questions?
- Does the question I'm asking open up and expand look-to-the-future responses and possibilities?
- Does the question I'm asking create new smart question–type metaphors and information sources?
- Does the question I'm asking feel like an interesting question or one that adds to the perceptiveness of others?
- Does the question I'm asking spark creative responses (in the sense that the question can yield many options), or other smart question–type questions?
- Is the question I'm asking likely to provide a way to empower individuals to use Smart Questions for creating solutions on their own?
- Is the question I'm asking likely to bring people together enthusiastically and with commitment to focus on building a desired future and getting results?

SUMMARIZING SQA

The entire SQA of holistic thinking is diagrammed in Figure 1.3.

THE BENEFITS OF HOLISTIC THINKING IN SQA

The problems facing businesses, institutions, and governments today are enormous. They tend to involve many complex issues and can affect large numbers of people—employees, association members,

Ask Smart Questions

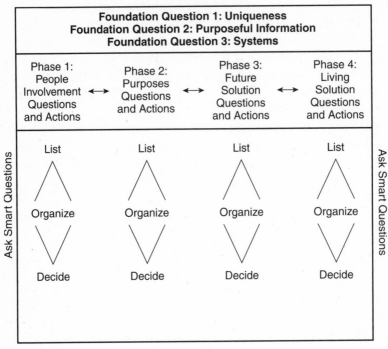

Figure 1.3.   The Smart Questions Approach for Creating Solutions

citizens, family members, and others. We live in a highly interdependent world, where we are all increasingly connected in unknown ways. One organization's or one person's problem can soon become another's if it is not solved correctly, efficiently, and fairly.

Consider what happens when one factory goes bankrupt due to its inability to solve its problems. It causes several of its upstream suppliers to close down too, leaving even more people unemployed. Or consider when one nation's economy experiences a high level of inflation. It puts pressure on other nations to bolster their currencies, creating economic havoc for millions of people.

At a more personal level, we are all interdependent. Think about what happens when a family does not take care of its children, who may then end up in poverty or committing crimes. On the positive side, think about the lone entrepreneur who knows how to create brilliant solutions and so manages to create a successful business, employing dozens, if not hundreds, of other people.

The complexity of our individual and societal problems raises important questions. How are we going to solve them? What operational model of thinking and problem solving can we follow to settle our issues in the most effective, efficient, and creative manner? In our experience, there are only three major paradigms to follow: reductionism, unstructured creativity, or our proposed SQA process based on holistic thinking. Each may have its pros and cons, advantages and disadvantages. Table 1.2 summarizes what we see as the leading substantive differences among the three methods of problem solving.

The choice is clear: it is time for a paradigm shift away from the old Cartesian rationalistic thinking process, which was never intended to be the sole mental process humans use to understand and resolve their problems. The old reductionist approach to problem solving is rife with flaws that frequently fail to solve the problems at hand or create additional problems downstream. The unstructured approach is too chaotic and unpredictable in its ability to produce results. Holistic thinking is the only mental model that can deal with today's economic, business, social, and political challenges in effective and enduring ways.

SQA is far better adapted to the types of problems that organizations and institutions face today because it emphasizes the use of holistic thinking that embraces a wide range of issues around any given problem, rather than the reductionist approach that tries to understand problems as just small pieces of a pie. It is a disciplined and comprehensive way of getting powerful results with these benefits:

- It recognizes that there are always options to consider before making a decision.
- It gets people involved and moves them naturally out of their current comfort zone.
- It develops a willingness for paradigm shifts and delving into the unknown.
- It empowers people and gives them the courage to state their convictions in a "smart" way.
- It gives people a unified language for developing solutions and solving problems.
- It leads to a friendly environment for change (the Smart Questions Organization).

Smart Questions Approach	Reductionist Approach	Unstructured Approach
Provides a semistructured approach to problem solving that is human centered, warm, flexible, and innovative	Provides a highly structured approach that is data centered, cold, inflexible, and bureaucratic	Exists as a free-form approach that emphasizes creativity but lacks organization, structure, and focus
Recognizes and respects the uniqueness of every situation as being different, independent, and deserving of its own solution	Attempts to find similarities among situations, reusing and adapting solutions that do not fit because the problems are unrelated	May or may not recognize uniqueness of a situation or may find answers by adapting supposed creative solutions from other problems
Gets people involved extensively in the entire problem-solving task, fostering ownership and investment in the outcome	Relies extensively on data and empirical evidence, often disregarding the needs and wants of the people involved	Usually involves people extensively in the solution process but emphasizes the search for "creative" people, which may not include the right people
Questions the assumptions behind the problem and the proposed solutions to ensure that the correct problem is being solved in the largest way	Accepts many assumptions as being true	May or may not examine the assumptions behind the problem or the proposed solution
Integrative approach seeks to find the largest context for understanding the problem and its solution	Divisive approach that attempts to dissect problems into small component parts; no sense of a holistic rationale behind the problem solution	May or may not succeed in recognizing a holistic solution
Accepts the possibility that there is more than one solution	Targets only one solution	May or may not develop multiple solutions or multifaceted solutions
Encourages organizations to give continuous attention to living solutions that ensure long-term success	Encourages a view on fixing "the problem" and short-term success	May or may not contain continuing focus on long-term issues and problem solving
Emphasizes an iterative process that constantly monitors the success of its own movement	Emphasizes a linear process that has a clear beginning and end point, even if the problem is not fully solved	May be linear or iterative

Table 1.2.   Comparison of the Three Methods of Problem Solving

- It supports different forms of creativity during all phases of creating a living solution.

- It recognizes that life is not static and there is no such thing as THE solution.

- It provides everyone with a systems perception.

- It makes change normal and expected because people know where it is going.

- It manages team conflicts and turf wars.

- It takes less total time and uses fewer resources to develop effective and creative living solutions that are very likely to be installed.

ADOPTING THE SQA FRAMEWORK AND VOCABULARY

SQA presents a new framework for holistic thinking about problems and solution creation. Everything about this framework will seem new to most of you at first, so you may have difficulty in changing your conventional thinking habits. You may wonder why you need the three foundation questions and how they relate to your learning to ask Smart Questions. You may not understand why the four phases that define the approach do not appear to be linear or why they cannot simply correspond to the type of analytic thinking you automatically do now when solving problems. The concepts of divergent and convergent thinking embedded in the LOD steps may seem overly expansive or time-consuming for the type and pace of creative work you are asked to do. The process of asking questions along the entire path to solution creation may make you feel impatient, eager to find answers rather than waste your time asking questions. Even the specialized vocabulary of SQA—*uniqueness, purposeful information, systems, people involvement, purposes, future solution, living solution, list, organize, decide*—may seem unclear or unnecessary when all you want to do is learn how to solve problems in your personal life, business organization, or community quickly.

We ask that you withhold judgment until you have read this book and begin to use and master the approach. Quash any resistance you feel to adopt a new framework. Instead, indulge your intellectual curiosity to find out the inner workings of SQA. As you will see, we have more than ample reason—and years of solution creation experience—to explain how and why we have synthesized the four phases of the SQA framework. We will explain clearly how the specialized vocabulary of SQA helps you internalize the new concepts for developing solutions that will serve your goals far more effectively than other problem-solving paradigms you know. We will ultimately convince you that SQA can work for you regardless of the type of problem you are facing.

Teaching people to adopt SQA often raises a paradox because accepting the SQA means that you must release your reductionist thinking in order to accept the very precepts of SQA. But do not worry; SQA is not a Trojan horse in the problem-solving business, aimed at fooling you to let down your reductionist thinking guard. SQA is a well-conceived, highly practiced, and successful paradigm for making the world a better place.

DON'T WAIT TO FIND THE RIGHT PROBLEM

We have one final point to make at this time. We have often taught people about SQA, and their uniform response is to praise the approach. However, some of these same people then tell us that they head back to their offices with SQA in their pocket, eagerly awaiting the right problem they can use it with. This is a misunderstanding of SQA.

We want to make it absolutely clear that what you learn in this book about SQA is ready to use anywhere and at any time. The three foundation questions, the four phases, and the divergent and convergent LOD steps can be applied to any problem of any nature and size you face in your world. The case studies in this book are just a sampling of problems we have worked on. Many other scenarios can be resolved by following SQA. So don't procrastinate about using SQA because you believe you need to find the right situation for using it. Every problem is the right situation.

In the following chapters, we illustrate phase by phase how to use SQA to identify and understand the unique problems you face, the true purposes you have in solving them, and the enduring, cost-effective, and creative long-term solutions you can implement. For each phase, we will teach you how to ask Smart Questions that elicit constructive, creative, and innovative ideas to develop creative solutions for your situations.

We invite you to join the ranks of those who create solutions rather than solve problems.

CHAPTER TWO

SQA Phase 1
Getting People Involved

People are the common denominator of progress. No improvement is possible with unimproved people.

—John Kenneth Galbraith

Getting people involved is the starting point in any process for creating a solution. After all, there would be no reason to create a solution if there were no people. There would be nobody to cause any problems, nobody to complain about anything, nobody to attempt to create solutions, nobody to implement changes, and nobody for whom the solution would matter.

This mental exercise points to the myriad ways that people can be involved in problem situations. They can be:

- The cause of the problem
- An input into its solution
- Bystanders in the environment in which the problem exists
- A participant in the process of creating a solution for the problem
- A data point in the information about the solution
- Implementers of the solution
- Recipients of the solution

- The initial identifier of a problem, issue, policy, or need
- Users or customers of the outputs of the problem area
- Suppliers to or vendors for the problem area
- Users, customers, or recipients indirectly affected by the problem or solution

People can play any number of these roles in creating a solution, or they can be included in most or all of them. That is why people involvement stands as the first phase of SQA. In addition to the insights we gained from studying the leading creators of solutions, our consulting clients recognized (and thus reinforced what our research had shown) that it is critical to know who will be involved at every phase of the solution-creating process. You want to plan as much as possible which people to involve in defining the purposes of the effort, who might contribute to the possible future solution, who might be able to implement the living solution, and who has to exist amid the results. This phase thus covers the process of determining which people need to be involved to play the many roles throughout the entire solution creation process.

We assume throughout this book that the policies and management attitudes, especially in larger organizations, respect people and encourage them to think. SQA (or any other solution creation paradigm) cannot be effective in an autocratic organization where people have no effective participation (as in, "You are paid to work, not think") or where it is unacceptable for people to even suggest that a problem exists, let alone respond proactively to a problem-solving request from the boss. The conditions of low pay, excessive overtime, a harsh work environment, no training and development activities, and frequent job firings do not engender the type of environment people need to help the organization solve its problems or create solutions. In fact, SQA can be used to significantly ease the task of a newly enlightened management to engage people in creating effective living solutions, as well as to handle the usual operational problems that arise.

THINKING HOLISTICALLY ABOUT PEOPLE INVOLVEMENT

Reductionist problem solving, particularly in repressive organizations, may involve people right at the start, but most often it does so in a negative context, in the sense that the first step in the reductionist approach is frequently finding out who caused the problem. This approach creates a blame game in which the first outcome is to find the individual or a group who must have been doing something wrong. Extensive efforts are made to identify a guilty party and "fix" him or her.

In addition, the reductionist approach to problems often downplays people's ideas and involvement, preferring to collect data and analyze information first. Implicit in the reductionist approach is often a greater trust of hard data over soft data, which are stored in people's heads. Leaders or those in charge of the problem focus their efforts on data in a misguided effort to figure out what the problem is and how to fix it. In some cases, the people involved with the problem—such as the workers on the shop floor, the inhabitants of the community, those who have personal firsthand knowledge and wisdom about the problem, possible technology, marketing, or financial expertise who might stimulate ideas, or who are users of or suppliers to the area of the problem—are completely neglected.

Even when the people involved may be consulted, it is often by an "expert" outsider who has been put in charge of the investigation because they can be "objective." The questions these experts ask are frequently self-serving to polish the image of their expertise, as they dwell on collecting data and investigating causes rather than figuring out how to create a desirable living solution that everyone involved has contributed to and can accept. The worst cases are those when an expert is delegated with the final decision and then does exactly the opposite of what the people involved have suggested.

The lack of authentic people involvement and respect for their opinions explains why the reductionist approach often contains a last step entitled something like "sell the solution" or "get buy-in for the solution" or "convince the boss to use the solution." Since the experts or task force has not fully involved the right people in the solution creation process, they must now seek to overcome the inertia, resistance to change, and not-invented-here reactions of the people who must implement and use the solution. According to Ohio State professor Paul Nutt in his book *Why Decisions Fail* (2002), one of the main reasons that the implementation rate for so many solutions is so poor is this lack of people involvement.

Nutt also points out that some executives hesitate to involve many stakeholders because they add a level of uncertainty in the process of developing a solution. He goes on, though, to note that not involving them may produce a recommendation that has not been thoroughly examined by the stakeholders, thus engendering negative feedback or action from them, which can cause a significant increase in the likelihood of failure for the change or a threat to the organization's long term success.

In contrast, SQA begins immediately with a different mode of being and acting. First, it demonstrates respect for what the people involved can contribute. People have an amazing capacity to share their knowledge and creativity when they are invited in a positive way to do so. SQA posits that it is impossible to determine in advance who can or will contribute to creating a solution. Any assumptions about an individual or a group of people can be easily shattered when they are given the opportunity to get involved in creating solutions. We have seen it in our consulting experience too many times not to believe this is true.

SQA also does not need a last buy-in step. It recognizes that people are willing and motivated to accept change if they have been involved in the process of developing a future they can see. Numerous studies have proved that people will enthusiastically endorse change when they recognize through their involvement that something is in it for them. Their reward can be either intrinsic, meaning an inner reward such as a feeling of pride, or extrinsic, such as money, a new office, or a better product. What matters is that they sense that they are part of the change rather than victims of the change. (Just to clarify, our living solution phase includes a step for getting approval for resources that need to be allocated for installation. Getting approval is much easier when the affected people support the request, but this step is not the same as the mental and emotional buy-in step that reductionist problem solving so often requires.)

Andy Van de Ven (1991), professor of management at the University of Minnesota, summarized the relevant social science research on this, saying, "[People] resist change when the need is not well understood, it is imposed from above, perceived as threatening, seems to have risks that are greater than the potential benefits, or interferes with other established priorities" (p. 7).

In short, SQA requires you to think holistically about people right from the start in the context of the three foundation questions. Asking each foundation question prompts you to think about numerous important issues regarding people involvement and leads to many valuable corollary questions in the list, organize, and decide steps. We begin with some general insights to help you recognize the underpinnings of these foundation questions for people involvement.

SQA FOUNDATION QUESTION 1: WHAT IS UNIQUE ABOUT THE PEOPLE IN THIS PROBLEM?

One bumper sticker we like to quote reads, "Remember you are unique—just like everybody else." Of course, this cleverly stated bumper sticker ridicules the fact that several billion of us have the same uniqueness characteristic. It's a paradox. In the grand scheme of life, it seems ludicrous to draw such fine-line distinctions among us. We are all human; we are born the same way, and we die the same way. Modern psychology generally confirms that we all operate roughly along similar lines of thought, in having generally similar wants and needs. How could we possibly be unique?

But the answer is that we are. The veneer of our similarities as humans is far overshadowed by the deeper core of our uniqueness. No matter how alike two people may seem, each is unique. The odds are basically zero that two people can possibly be alike. It is impossible that they have the same biological makeup or genetics, mental model, family experiences, life experiences or memories (which change daily), or larger community cultural mind-set (or zeitgeist, as sociologists would say). Not even identical twins think the same, and that is about as close to identical in genetics and environment as people are going to get.

Each of us is a unique individual because our reactions to our experiences and choices that we make are different. No two of us have the same mix and sequence of life events or the same likes and dislikes and the same thoughts. Figure 2.1 illustrates this concept that each person is surrounded by an enormous number of life factors. Since no two people can possibly share the same experiences and feelings of all these influences, they cannot be alike.

Our uniqueness also stems from the cultural differences among our birth and childhood places. People behave in ways that reflect both the huge cultural habits of their country, and the subtle cultural differences embedded in their region or city or town. A culture is nothing but a collection of learned assumptions. Each culture imparts its assumptions to its people, and those assumptions live on in each individual.

For example, in the United States, we have a noble tradition of rugged individualism borne of our frontier beginnings. Most Americans honor and respect bold individuals who stand out and make a name for themselves. Such people are held in esteem in businesses and organizations, and many of us strive to act and think this way. In

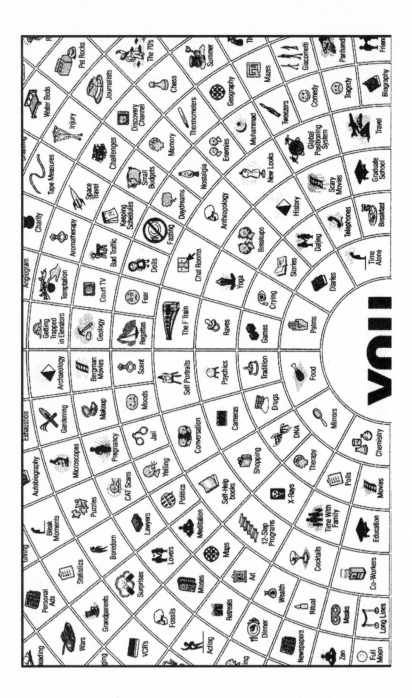

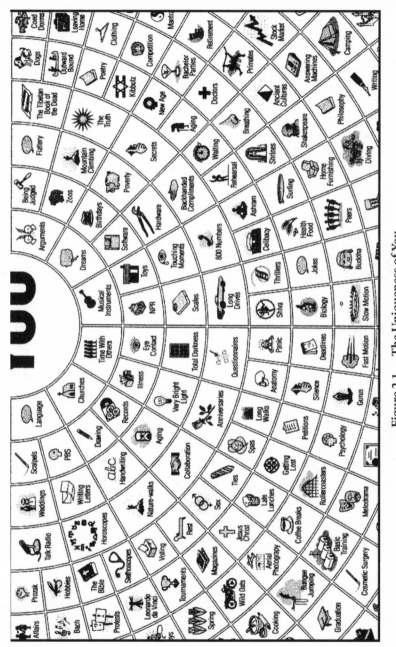

Figure 2.1. The Uniqueness of You

Source: Reproduced with the permission of Jesse Gordon and Natasha Tibbott.

Japan, however, individualism runs counter to deeply held cultural attitudes. The Japanese have a saying, "The tall nail gets hammered down." This speaks to a very different tradition in Japan: standing out is not a virtue but a bad reflection on a person. In Japan, being a humble member of a successful team is preferable to being known for individual achievement.

Even countries that appear to be close culturally to the United States can have subtle differences that will influence how people behave and feel. Canada is culturally close to the United States in many ways, but it is nonetheless unique. No one should decide to move a factory to Canada because the value of their dollar is lower than ours and then expect the workers to act the same as American workers. Canadian workers are different.

Our uniqueness is also a reflection of many other variables: age, gender, demographics, and even personal attributes like hair color or height. Despite generalizations like "ditzy blondes," "dumb jocks," or "forgetful seniors," such categorizations are clearly misguided. Even accepted categories such as "veterans," "baby boomers," and "Gen Xers" can be dangerous to apply to a specific individual in a group because that person may share none of the same values of the supposed categorization.

In our experience, too many management gurus neglect this uniqueness factor. Considering people to be roughly the same, they make predictions about worker behavior that turn out to be far from reality. Statistical gurus often calculate the likelihood that something will happen based on assumptions about general human behavior. It may comfort them to look at graphs of productivity and profits, but the graphs, though they might look polished and definitive, do not mean a thing because their basic assumption that people will act identically in all situations is false. There is simply no such thing as a person having average human behavior.

Given this premise, asking uniqueness-oriented questions about people is critical. SQA posits that getting many different people involved and respecting their differences is a necessary first step. Any preconceptions about who can contribute to solving the problem or situation should be dropped. Everyone has some creativity, as Alan Rowe demonstrates in his book *Creative Intelligence: Our Hidden Potential* (2004). You simply cannot tell who may have ideas that would benefit the situation. And the vast differences among individuals, groups, and cultures should make you extremely wary of any attempt to impose a successful approach from somewhere else.

Here is an example of the erroneous belief that people everywhere are the same or can be made to perform in the same way. In the 1970s and 1980s, the huge financial success of Silicon Valley companies emblazoned the world of high technology. Given the armfuls of money others were making in Silicon Valley, numerous development gurus and venture capitalists invested heavily in an attempt to spawn copycat initiatives throughout other parts of the United States as well as in other countries. What they failed to consider were the significant cultural differences among the areas. As a result, many of these efforts—such as those in Taiwan, Singapore, India, Indonesia, several European countries, and in many research and technology parks in the United States—failed or had little success because they could not imitate the unique cultural characteristics of Silicon Valley.

Although technology has made location and distance a seemingly inconsequential factor, Silicon Valley at that time offered a unique combination of attributes. It had proximity to some of the top higher education institutions and research facilities, a plethora of influential people, hearty competition, access to venture capital, and a host of burgeoning new technologies—all factors that the other cultures did not have to the same degree. The closest successes occurred in Silicon Alley in New York City, Route 128 outside Boston, and the Triangle Research Park in North Carolina, where the cultural conditions were more similar to Silicon Valley.

Intelligence and Creativity

Our uniqueness expresses itself in a very clear way. The study of intelligence and creativity has shown that people differ greatly in the types of intelligence they have. Some people are repositories of knowledge about a particular topic (gatekeepers), while others have an idea a minute without concern for possible utility (creatives), and still others have strong political and contextual insight into situations (street smarts). Some people like to jump right into taking action (do anything, but do it now types), while others like to think and think and think (reflectives).

Noted Harvard psychologist Howard Gardner (1993) has advanced the theory that there are several types of intelligence—linguistic, logical-mathematical, kinesthetic, musical, interpersonal, intrapersonal, and spiritual—and that each of us differs in the various combinations we have of these. People are usually dominant in one of these intelligences, but they also combine elements of the other intelligences in certain situations and types of problem solving they may do. The variety of intelligence combinations is thus enormous, further explaining the uniqueness of each of us.

Psychologists have come to share a sense that knowledge is subjective and fluid and that it evolves as it is used. Learning occurs all the time and is situated in the everyday life experiences of individuals. Knowledge can never simply be transferred because it does not exist in transferable form. The context of knowledge, in both its acquisition and its application, is always unique.

When this complex fabric of experience, culture, intelligence, and knowledge is woven together, it creates a tapestry that cannot be duplicated. Each one of us is unique and cannot be replaced. Our uniqueness is vital to keep in mind, because it means that no one can predict the type of thinking, reasoning, or creativity that a person might use when talking about purposes or contributing an idea to its solution. No one can make assumptions about who has an answer to an issue; the janitor, for example, may have just the creative idea needed to fix an operational problem. In a sense, you have to become a Sherlock Holmes and figure out over time who holds the keys to creating a solution. Anyone has the potential to become a valuable contributor.

SQA thus suggests that first efforts need to focus on creating an atmosphere that fosters optimal contributions from the right individuals. To do that, you must throw away any preconceptions about who is qualified to offer solutions and really listen to what each person has to say.

Reaction to Change

Another reason to involve people in solution creation right from the start is related to the fallacy that people resist change. There has been a long-standing image in conventional thinking that people are nothing but "hands," objects to be manipulated at management's desire, available for physical rather than mental activities, unable to participate in change. Douglas McGregor in his classic *The Human Side of Enterprise* (1960) called this Theory X and defined it as the "assumption of the mediocrity of the masses" (p. 34).

Logic (as well as our own studies of successful people) tells us that this is false. People want to be involved in making decisions that influence their lives. We all tend to accept and feel good about implementing solutions that we helped to devise. Getting people involved and respecting their potential to contribute allows you to maximize their participation and secure their creativity and commitment to the solution—even before it is fully known.

One study on change provides a compelling reason to involve people as early as possible in any change effort. The authors, Robert Kegan and Lisa Laskow Lahey (2001), professors at the Harvard University Graduate School of Education, studied how people often have hidden commitments and assumptions that prevent them from accomplishing change, however much they may claim to favor it. For example, one manager discovered he was committed "to not learning about things I can't do anything about," based on his assumption that he "should be able to address all problems [or] be seen as incompetent if I can't solve all problems that come up."

This is precisely where SQA can be helpful. By getting people involved through the process of asking smart questions, you can help them surface their assumptions in a way that avoids their feelings of embarrassment. The key is to get people involved and committed to the change effort right away, providing them with genuine opportunities to contribute without the fear of exposing what they may feel are their weaknesses.

Getting people involved in the problem also serves another important purpose: creating champions of change. In the conventional reductionist model of problem solving, it takes unusual energy and commitment by one or two people to overcome the usual barriers to change because of the potential consequences of failure. People fear potential blame if their ideas go wrong. But with SQA and its emphasis on people involvement, many individuals become willing to take on roles of champions of change, in the forefront of carrying the ball.

In many instances, the benefits of involving people in creating solutions outweigh whatever solution is developed. For example, one company we worked with was in the process of improving its cost allocation system. Using SQA, the executives set up teams from their regional offices as well as headquarters to work on the problem. Previously, the offices had been feuding over the cost allocation system; the new team got more people involved and created a new camaraderie that the company had not seen before. According to the vice president of human resources, the most important benefit to the company was the team building that had occurred. In other words, whether intentional or not, using the SQA can be an organizational change strategy.

Creating a Learning Environment for Yourself and Others

Getting people involved in creating a solution sets up a virtuous cycle that helps organizations learn to solve future problems more effectively and quickly. Sharing your solution creation process, especially SQA, with others teaches them the specialized terminology to use and the strategic thinking skills of solution creation. It also encourages them to have positive attitudes about problem solving and change.

Unfortunately, many people have learned bad habits by which they underestimate themselves and their abilities. You can see this in the wide range of negative characteristics people unconsciously reveal about themselves: apathy, fear, self-doubt, isolation, impatience, faulty evaluation of ideas, tentativeness, and failure to listen to others. Conventional models of how to tackle new challenges and solve problems tend to reinforce and exacerbate these negative characteristics; examples are the reductionist tendencies to find a "guilty" party, to blame people for mistakes, and to bring in outside "experts" who are supposed to know more than the people involved.

In contrast, the high degree of people involvement required under SQA can reverse these tendencies. SQA encourages people to participate and reduces their self-negativity. Learning new skills and being creative are especially critical today as more and more organizations become increasingly complex webs of roles, relationships, and constantly changing environments. No longer does change always start from the top. Many of the case studies in this book demonstrate that people holding all roles and levels of responsibility in an organization can get involved in working on operational issues and in learning to develop strategic thinking skills to improve their organizations. Conversely, studies of unsuccessful change programs trace their failures to inadequate involvement of people or to a lack of management commitment in training people to think effectively.

The world is becoming increasingly complex, and the demands of modern life are fundamentally different from even just a few years ago, when computer usage by individuals was rare and the Internet was used only by scientists and academics. The human response to the complexity is to become more complex ourselves, more capable of dealing with the demands of modern life. The capability that we need is not physical capability—the capability to work longer hours, to lift heavier objects, to dig deeper ditches. The capability that we need to increase is intellectual. We need increasing levels of intellectual development.

SQA creates precisely the type of learning environment that the passage above refers to. Involved, active, participatory people learn to understand the solution-creation process, start to understand each other better, and become more flexible and adaptive for future activities that call for them to work together.

SQA FOUNDATION QUESTION 2: WHAT PURPOSEFUL INFORMATION DO PEOPLE HAVE?

Chapter One pointed out several erroneous assumptions about the value of extensive information collection that reductionism tends to overlook: that information is incomplete, inaccurate, and imprecise; that it is a human construct; and that it does not offer the benefits obtained from knowledge and wisdom. Given this, the People Involvement Phase reframes data collection in three important ways:

- It values how people interpret information differently rather than deriding it.
- It takes advantage of the wisdom people offer as well as the information they have.
- It uses information sharing as a way to boost interpersonal interaction.

The Value of Different Interpretations

Recall that we said that information is determined in the eye of the beholder. Although many people may see the same situation, how they interpret that same information is most likely to be significantly different.

Rather than letting multiple points of view be a conundrum, SQA turns this to an advantage. Because each individual involved interprets the problem and its potential solution differently, SQA intentionally seeks out multiple perspectives from many people. Obtaining multiple viewpoints boosts knowledge and understanding about a problem. Each person you talk to or ask questions of will reflect back to you the type of intelligence he or she uses to understand the issue. One person may have a logical perspective of the situation, another a mathematical formulaic understanding, and yet another a spiritual vision, and all three can become part of the living solution.

The Wisdom of People

As we emphasized in Chapter One, knowledge and wisdom are much higher on the scale of valuable information than are raw data and information. Knowledge is far more complex than data. Even the most advanced technology cannot transmit the knowledge embedded in the brain of a human. Furthermore, knowledge is not separate from the person who knows it. You can ask, "Where is the information?" or "Who has the knowledge?" but you cannot ask "Where is the knowledge?"

According to John Seely Brown, director of the Xerox Palo Alto Research Center, and Paul Duguid, social and cultural studies research specialist at the University of California at Berkeley, there are three key differences between knowledge and information:

> First, knowledge usually entails a knower. . . .
>
> Second, given this personal attachment, knowledge appears harder to detach than information. . . . Someone [can] send you or point to the information they have, but not to the knowledge they have.
>
> Third, knowledge seems to require more by way of assimilation. . . . While one person often has conflicting information, he or she will not usually have conflicting knowledge [2000, pp. 119-120].

Knowledge develops in people like a large puzzle. The pieces interlock in complex patterns that make sense only to the person who can see the whole puzzle rather than just the individual pieces.

Solution creation requires knowledge and wisdom more than raw data and analysis. Knowledge and wisdom exist only in the minds of people. Involving many minds is therefore a major objective of this phase. Involving many types of wise people can only help to generate effective and creative living solutions.

Here is a case that illustrates the superiority of seeking wisdom and knowledge rather than data. The executive vice president of a large retail distributor of magazines and books wanted to reduce delivery time in order to provide better service and decrease operating costs. She told us that her goal was "to get all the facts about what's going on so I can make inroads on our objectives."

Rather than jumping to her demand to investigate the facts, we began by asking her questions to obtain her views on the purposes of solving her company's problem and her vision of its future. By directing our efforts at her own wisdom and knowledge, we were able to show her that the most valuable data we could be collecting was information about the new system she eventually needed, not the humdrum facts about what had been going wrong in the past. Through this discussion, we ended up installing an advanced technology system to suit her future needs, and the project was done in less time and for less money than originally allocated. In addition, many personnel from the previous system were involved and became committed to the new one quickly. Our client was so enthusiastic that she put a poster on her wall, "Facts = purposes, ideal solutions, and implementable solutions."

Information Sharing as a Way to Boost Interpersonal Interaction

Creating a living solution acceptable to everyone involved requires essentially a team-building, organization-building, or community-building effort. SQA recognizes that an important aspect of collecting information is to surface and share the information that people carry around in their heads. Through the open sharing of information, viewpoints, ideas, and solutions, people come to understand each other and accept what others have to offer. In this way, SQA uses information as a link between people rather than as a divider in the way reductionist problem solving often does, where people hoard data for territorial status or proprietary purposes.

Sharing information and its interpretations can be especially useful in situations where people and ideas are at odds. For example, assume there are community activists who have always opposed the implementation of an expansion of your company purposes (or mission). Rather than bypass these people in your solution creation effort, it will prove far more useful to get them engaged early on with the task. Both sides will gain an understanding of the information the other side has, as well as how each interprets the data. This early sharing can eventually form the basis for a living solution that meets the needs of everyone, thus saving a great deal of the time and money and avoiding the potential for lingering antagonism that would occur after a solution has been proposed and implemented solely by your group.

We worked with one nonprofit organization that had a number of watchdog groups that had traditionally been at odds with the organization. We involved the watchdog groups from the very beginning of the project. It turned out that they were valuable contributors of ideas and support. Everyone was surprised except us. We have seen this happen many times. Some companies—not too many, though—hire presumed misfits and weird people to goad organizations and projects.

So What Valid Information Do You Really Need?

Finding a balance in the search for truly necessary, purposeful information versus getting many points of view and interpretations on that information is a learned skill. Information is instrumental in creating solutions for complex problems, but wisdom and the types of knowledge and understanding that a variety of people can bring to the table are also critical. In the end, we have developed several guidelines about collecting information from people that we recommend for any effort:

• *Focus your efforts on collecting only the necessary solution-oriented information for a particular project.* Too much information obscures important issues and does not help make the most effective decisions.

• *Seek to provide meaning to the existing information.* Groups develop cohesiveness and effectiveness through shared meanings and interpretations of the real world. Since information is just a representation of reality, this encourages mutual understanding.

• *Encourage networking for obtaining information, contacts, and results.* Achieving a breakthrough depends far more on the interaction of people than on the amount or accuracy of the information.

• *Avoid disorganization.* The second law of thermodynamics holds that all entities tend toward disorganization, called entropy. Combating this natural tendency requires energy. An overload of information saps energy.

• *Reduce the preparation of many unnecessary and never-to-be-read documents and the arguments over their differing measurements, interpretations, and analyses.* Surveys and questionnaires are especially suspect techniques for information collection because so many of them are improperly worded or ambiguous.

• *Avoid the institutionalization of information collection as an end in itself without regard to purposes.* For example, many corporate data gatherers attend seminars to find out what competitors are doing, what new products they are offering, what facilities they are building, and so on. But how valuable can such programs be for most problem prevention and solution? If your competitors have new products, services, and facilities, you are already behind.

• *To maximize the use of your time and resources, aim to limit infor-mation collection.* The search for failures or their symptoms and root causes of problems is seldom worthwhile. Often people will agree to this only after they recognize the syndrome in themselves.

SQA FOUNDATION QUESTION 3: HOW CAN WE THINK SYSTEMATICALLY ABOUT THE ROLES THAT PEOPLE PLAY IN CREATING THE SOLUTION?

The key to getting the right people involved in creating a solution is to think systematically. This is best accomplished in the context of exploring and understanding the roles that people will play in the future solution system you are creating.

This foundation question requires you to explore the wide world of systems in which an assortment of people will be needed to play many roles in your effort. A systems approach helps you begin to see the connections between your various stakeholders and the solution you are going to create. We use *stakeholders* as the general term for the people who need to be involved. *Stakeholders* can include anyone who may affect your potential solution or on whom the solution may have an impact. This might include financial shareholders in a profit-making company; those who supply the inputs to your system; those who receive, distribute, use, and dispose of the outputs from your system; those who constitute the organizational, physical, and external environment surrounding your system solution; and those who prepare and provide the people, information, and physical devices needed to have your living system work. The level of people involvement may also be determined by your schedule, budget, or other constraints.

Roles Stakeholders May Play

The number of people who might be involved varies by role, position, and timing. Some people may participate throughout the project, while others play a role during certain steps or phases. For instance, you may need to distinguish among the people who will play various roles during each of the LOD steps in the four phases of SQA, which we will discuss in each chapter. In general, the variety of roles and skills needed for a project should be identified before individuals are considered. Here are some of the roles that people can play:

- Administrator
- Adviser
- Advocate
- Analyst
- Champion
- Change agent
- Client or owner
- Coach
- Conciliator
- Consultant expert
- Consumer, purchaser, or user
- Customer's customer
- Decision maker, source of power
- Designer or innovator
- Educator or expert
- Evaluator
- Executive sponsor
- Facilitator
- Financial and accounting expert
- Lobbyist
- Manager
- Organizer
- Owner
- Representatives of affected groups (for example, union, community activist, environmentalist)
- Researcher
- Stimulator of creative ideas
- Trainer

These are not necessarily pure roles; the boundaries of each are flexible, and some people may assume more than one role at a time or you may ask others to take on multiple roles. The fact that some people may fulfill many roles should be taken into account when considering them for participation.

Ways to Get People Involved

Getting many people involved in a solution creation effort does not necessarily mean that you need to waste inordinate amounts of time in meetings. Numerous technologies and techniques exist to facilitate nontraditional meetings, such as telephone conferencing and Web conferencing, that enable people to meet without the expenditure of time required in face-to-face meetings, particularly when individuals are not co-located. In addition, e-mail can be a powerful technology for sharing ideas and making decisions quickly. However, at least one face-to-face meeting may make the technological tools used later more effective and productive.

There are literally dozens of methods and ways you can involve people in the various phases and steps, including these:

- Hold informal team meetings during a lunch hour to ask questions.
- Set up a one-time meeting with people who might constitute a good long-term project team.
- Set up a one-time meeting to plan the problem-solving process.
- Involve different people individually by asking questions.
- Set up e-mail lists or networked discussion groups.
- Use existing groups or teams.
- Set up formal meeting times for a project team.
- Arrange several town hall meetings.
- Any combination of the above.

Getting people to take part in meetings or any of the other methods listed can be a disaster without the appropriate methods and techniques of conversation. Table 2.1 lists many potential techniques you can use to work with people either individually or in groups.

GROUP VERSUS SOLO WORK. There are vast differences in how people operate when it comes to working in groups or alone. Many people find that being in groups is stimulating; for them, group work increases their creativity and productivity over what they would accomplish if they were asked to work alone. Other people find groups to be stifling and much prefer to go solo.

Keep in mind that it takes time for groups to gel and learn how to work as a team. We will discuss various issues related to team work as we go through the four phases of SQA. If a group does not work well, you can always follow up by talking to people individually later so as not to waste their creativity.

Finally, do not be disappointed if a group does not or cannot stay together, even if they are working well. Some people express high initial interest about getting involved but later run out of steam, change their minds, or discover they are not needed in the way they assumed.

Brainstorming and blue-sky imagining	Stakeholders openly discuss and exchange ideas on an improvement problem to come up with a combined solution that best suits the situation.
Brain writing	This technique is basically the same as brainstorming, except that each person writes each idea on a separate card. The cards are either passed to the next person seated at the table or placed in the center of the table for distribution to other members. Each person who gets a card adds ideas and suggestions to make the idea more workable.
Debate	Two groups formally debate proposals. A committee of decision makers assesses and rates each group's performance to determine the best proposal.
Decision worksheet	Crucial characteristics of alternative solutions are ranked by the participants on a decision worksheet (discussed in Chapters Four and Five) to arrive at the best one.
Delphi method	Questionnaires are sent to respondents for the generation of ideas; the responses are summarized by a staff group. Subsequently, a second questionnaire is sent to the same participants, who independently evaluate earlier responses and vote on priority ideas included on the second questionnaire. The staff team makes a new summary of the evaluations and votes, and a decision-making group decides on the most suitable ideas.
Game or simulation	Computer programs simulate the possible processes that follow implementation of each alternative. Outcomes of simulations determine the final decision.
Idea writing	Ideas are developed and their meanings and implications explored using four steps: initial organization of problem-solving subgroups of a large group, initial written responses, written interaction among the participants, and analysis and reporting of the written interaction.
Interacting	A group meets to discuss problems in an unstructured way. There is minimal direction by the leader, although a trained leader can provide increasing degrees of structure.
Interviews of individuals in groups	Ideas and decisions are facilitated by interviews of individuals who offer their opinions independently without interacting with other members of the group.
KJ method (person card)	Each person in the group writes one idea per card. The group places all the cards on a board or face-up on a table. The members sort the cards into piles, each one representing "one person" in the "family." The result is a chart of relationships of the "persons" or groups of cards in whatever structure or order the group decides: hierarchy, balloon diagram, outline, or something else. ("K" and "J" are the initials of the two people who developed an initial version of the technique.)

Media-based balloting	Balloting through media (such as TV or conference calls) allows decision making through voting and avoids direct interaction among the participants.
Multiattribute utility assessment	The utilities of various attributes of different alternatives are assessed mathematically to reach a decision.
Nominal group technique	Individuals meet and silently generate in writing ideas that are subsequently reported, one idea per person, one person after another, and recorded on a flip chart. Discussion of each individual idea follows, and each individual prioritizes the ideas. The solution selected is mathematically derived through rank ordering or rating.
Opinion poll	Individuals express ideas and preferences of a problem situation through a poll of opinions without having to interact directly.
Pay for performance	Individuals are rewarded based on the performance results of their team rather than individual results.
Quality circles or work teams	Small informal groups of employees meet voluntarily to discuss and provide solutions for productivity improvement problems. Quality circles are part of the Japanese participative management philosophy.
Questionnaires and surveys	Participants respond to questionnaires and surveys to provide ideas on problems without interacting.
Role playing	Individuals role-play various roles in the decision-making process, thus becoming aware of their attitudes and effects on others and learning how to become more effective problem solvers.
Sensitivity training	This process helps individuals develop self-awareness whereby they can become more sensitive to their effects on others and can learn by interacting with other participants of the group.
Shared participation	Group members are encouraged to share opinions and ideas openly in a shared participation manner. Everybody participates in the decision-making process.
Suggestion system	Individual suggestions for improving workplace productivity and quality are obtained. Suggestions are often dropped in boxes. A committee assesses if the recommendations are worthy of implementation.
System matrix	A solution framework guides the problem-solving group through the development of its solution. The system matrix forces members to think holistically and thus consider interfaces and future dimensions of the recommendation.
Telecommunications	Voice messages, e-mail, or video images are sent back and forth among participants, allowing the exchange of ideas without direct face-to-face interaction of ideas and decision makers.

Table 2.1. Group Process Techniques

Other people may have joined the effort because they felt threatened by a planned change and wanted to protect their turf. They later realize they have nothing to worry about and so they resign. Groups also naturally change as people transfer jobs or terminate employment or as new people are hired who get involved.

CHARACTERISTICS OF GROUPS. Following are some characteristics of groups to consider when getting people involvement ideas for designing a solution-creating effort:

- The purposes and objectives of involving particular people or groups
- To whom the group is responsible and its degree of autonomy
- What group authority each member desires and the relationship of each member to others
- Whether the group operation is formal or informal
- The friendliness, frankness, and freeness of the discussion atmosphere
- The cohesiveness of the group and the comfort level of each person in the decision-making process
- The degree of control of the facilitator and the source of the decision making
- Physical resources available, such as computer terminals, telephones, and meeting rooms
- Information resources such as Web access and the availability of databases

MEETING CONDITIONS. Because working conditions can make a big difference in the success of a group, face-to-face meetings should be held on neutral turf, in a nonconfrontational seating arrangement to avoid subgroups seated by rank or faction. Many other factors need to be thought about and determined before the meeting, such as lighting, heat, and ventilation.

Here are some guidelines for holding meetings, which we offer based on our experience of working with hundreds of groups:

- Stick to a previously distributed agenda with topics that are purpose oriented.

- Err toward covering too little rather than too much for the available time on the agenda.

- State on the agenda how long the meeting will last.

- With each agenda topic, control only the process, not the content of the meeting. Give everyone a chance to contribute, call on those who don't typically speak up, and use techniques that ensure everyone's participation.

- Start with a statement of achievements anticipated in this meeting; inform the group of developments since the previous meeting and have others participate.

- Use majority voting only when consensus appears not to be possible.

- Be enthusiastic about the group's work if you expect the group to be interested and enthusiastic.

- Put any decision that narrowly achieved a majority on the agenda for the next meeting as a means of gathering new information by obtaining ideas from outside experts and other persons with interest in the situation from your company.

- Emphasize purposes for all deliberations and decisions. Check and summarize to ensure broad understanding.

- Avoid spending too much time on obvious workable ideas or the first alternative. Seek out other alternatives and broadening information. Avoid the dangers of groupthink mentality toward conformity and uniformity.

- Maintain some flexibility so informality is not cut off when group members seem to need it for building openness, creativity, and trust. Discussion can be encouraged if a hot topic arises that affects the project, even if it is outside the agenda or from outside the group.

- Maintain a positive tone. Ask questions rather than give answers, rephrase ideas positively, offer one or more interpretations, cut off name-calling, and establish civility and respect among members regardless of differing viewpoints.

- If the status (organizational level, experience, power, reputation) of those in the meeting varies greatly, talk with the high-status people before the meeting to get expressions of willingness for equal treatment of all in the group. Aim for a first-name basis for the entire group, and avoid introducing any status words such as *expert* or *doctor*.

- Avoid criticism of ideas during idea-generation activities. Seat people at random or alphabetically rather than by position or their functional work categories.

- Conflicts that arise should be put into a win-win form that aids rather than divides the group. Positive conflicts, such as tempered challenges to the status quo, questions about illegal or immoral activities, or voicing an opinion, can benefit the outcomes of all phases of SQA. Creativity can emerge from conflicting viewpoints by moving to larger and larger purposes. Focus on achieving the purpose and results rather than on defeating a person.

- Give everyone all the information to avoid coalition formation.

- Be alert for and appropriately responsive to problems and all difficulties. Some people may act bored or may attack the chairperson, attendance may be low, time may always seem to run out, the team may lack skills and mutual respect, and so on.

- After asking a question, wait at least three seconds, even if there is complete silence, before saying anything.

- Be neutral in responding to ideas. Avoid saying "okay," "good," "nice idea," "fine," and so on. Instead try a phrase such as, "Does this way of stating your idea agree with what you meant?" or "Let's expand that idea." The additional questioning and probing stimulates more and better ideas.

THE LIST, ORGANIZE, AND DECIDE STEPS

We are now ready to apply the holistic thinking concepts of the foundation questions to setting up an action plan for people involvement. The list, organize, and decide (LOD) steps of the People Involvement Phase will move you toward the choice of an action plan regarding who should be involved, the purpose of each stakeholder's involvement, how each person might be engaged, when their involvement will be needed, and what the scheduled time line and resources for the whole effort might be. The issues raised by the three foundation questions will inspire your ability to ask smart questions as you perform the LOD steps.

Deciding on what people to involve, in effect, starts the implementation of whatever solution emerges. *Implementation starts from the beginning.* This is a key component of SQA. Whether a project will be successful depends primarily on people-related issues—your internal people's competencies and skills and customer perceptions. Other contributing success factors will be introduced in the purposes, future solution, and living solution questions you will learn about later.

The People Involvement Paradox

Before we begin reviewing the LOD steps, we must comment on a seeming paradox for some readers, especially for anyone in a large organization, association, or community group. This paradox is best framed by the question, "Who selects the people who select the people?"

In other words, who should be appointed to lead the People Involvement Phase and perform the LOD steps to set up an action plan for selecting people? Should it be only the management of the organization? Should it be the individual who originally identified the problem or someone who is willing to champion its cause? Do you appoint a committee? Do you hire an outside "objective" observer? Do you bring in an SQA facilitator to lead the group and help set up the action plan?

The answer to this paradox is not to make it too complex. The answer depends on the situation. You might initially resort to having a champion be the leader for this phase, or you might use an outside consultant or facilitator trained in SQA. (However, we are not advocates of using only senior management or executives to be in charge of the people involvement LOD process.) But if you follow the SQA process, the paradox should not become a major issue in your organization. As you work through the steps of this phase and ask smart questions, you will automatically involve increasing numbers of people in the process of setting up a people involvement action plan. When you use SQA, you will more effectively choose people to lead when they are appropriate for the role that needs to be performed rather than in reference to their particular role in the organization as a whole.

Another people involvement paradox is how you can involve everyone when that "everyone" may include thousands of people whose work will be affected by any change. The answer is that you cannot involve them all directly in a time-intensive face-to-face approach. Consider selecting people representative of your entire spectrum: functional, geographical, organizational responsibility, customer, supplier, and so on. In addition, part of how they are involved ought to include having each representative report to and get feedback from as many others as possible in their cohort group.

Nevertheless, large groups of people can be at least minimally involved by providing them information about the project even from the early phases. Projects that are shrouded in secrecy cause people to make up their own stories about what is going on. Be proactive, and share purposeful information liberally. Even if you do not know specific outcomes early on in a project, it is better to be clear about it and tell people when you expect to know something that you will be sharing with them.

The List Step

Listing is a simple process, and the goal is exactly as the term sounds: to compose lists of ideas—in this case, about the people who need or ought to be involved in creating the solution. Remember that the objective of the list step is to expand your thinking, not to analyze the problem and focus on a narrow component. This is the divergent thinking we referred to.

When you make up lists, you need to refrain from the temptation to judge ideas and the people who propose them. The best way to do this is to use the three foundation questions as the basis for asking more smart questions about people. The box provides examples of the types of questions you might ask as you explore people involvement.

Effective list questions such as the ones in the box are meant to open up possibilities and help you begin listing ideas regarding the types of people to consider for involvement. As you ask these smart questions, avoid the temptation to be judgmental about answers. You never know who has what ideas to offer at this point, so keep all ideas open. It is better to get someone involved initially even if the person's background and role may seem tangential to the issue at first. These people may be pleased about being asked and will drop out if they sense they are not contributing anything.

Above all, do not make any decisions at this time about who "should be" involved based on false premises such as organizational hierarchy, titles, degrees, or experience in other situations. Just include the names on the list as possible participants. Since each problem is unique, there is no guarantee that their past success is an indication of their role in this situation.

SMART QUESTIONS FOR THE PEOPLE INVOLVEMENT PHASE

List Step

As you begin considering stakeholders to involve, here are the types of questions you need to be asking yourself and others. We provide these as examples of the types of questions you may wish to ask, based on the concepts in this chapter: stakeholders, roles of people, wide world of other systems, and so on. Use these sample smart questions to stimulate your own development of other questions that may be better for your circumstances. Each of the following questions and those you develop are not independent of the others. Because of the uniqueness of people, it is better to try to capture the same meaning in two slightly different but overlapping questions that might lead to better understanding than not asking the second question.

Uniqueness

- What is unique about the culture of the people involved in this problem that I need to consider?
- How might the unique cultural norms be integrated (or modified) into our solution creation efforts by getting people from those cultures involved?
- Who are the people who might contribute information about the possible impacts of the whole range of conditions from which a prediction of a future solution is created?
- What potential buy-ins for my idea can I obtain by considering initially every situation as unique?
- What unusual stakeholder groups (for example, environmentalists, the government, religious communities) should be represented in creating a living solution?
- Who should be involved to provide maximum assurance that whatever living solution is developed can be implemented?
- What stakeholders should we involve to help determine the real issue?
- What individuals might be involved who are considered the go-to person for answers or who are looked to for "crazy" and "zany" ideas about many issues?
- Who might be involved to provide signals about what may be future issues, technology, customer wants, and societal and legislative changes that could be relevant to our solution creation recommendations?

Continued

Continued

Information

- Who might have insights into pertinent types of data we may need to gather, and how do we minimize messing up collecting that data?
- Who would have the ability to best convey the information that may need to be presented?
- Do any people have information about relevant measures that might be helpful?
- What people might provide perspectives about the situation that we should consider beyond the information we have?

Systems

- What types of stakeholders and people in related and outside systems ought to be included to help determine what system we ought to be creating?
- What different roles do we need represented to make the whole effort effective?
- Who are the people motivated and committed to developing future and living solutions for the issue?
- Who are the human resources (recorders, researchers, information technologists, accountants) to involve for purposes of assisting the group in the solution creation process?
- What environment do we need to set up for the solution creating effort?

INVITING ANTAGONISTS, FOES, AND ENEMIES. Anyone who is connected to or affected by any future solution proposed is a potential valuable contributor to involve. Even people antagonistic to your cause (those with the power to slow or stop you) should be involved as early in the process as you can invite them. It is better to know and learn right at the beginning about the stance that they may take and how their opinion might influence your potential results. More important, though, getting antagonists, foes, and even enemies involved early lets them contribute to the purposes to be achieved and future solutions to the extent that they can become equally committed to the recommendations that are developed as you.

Here is an example of the positive benefit of involving people who are supposedly on the other side. Reggie White, the outstanding former defensive end of the Green Bay Packers, donated $1 million to his home town to set up a Knoxville Community Investment Bank to assist with the economic development of the inner city. The city then added $250,000 to the gift.

One of Reggie's colleagues knew about SQA and suggested that he arrange for me to facilitate an all-day planning meeting to determine how the investment bank should be organized and operated. When the people in Knoxville were asked about who should be involved in the meeting, they mentioned many of the obvious stakeholders: educators, health care providers, residents of the inner city, commercial bank leaders, ministers, and social workers, to name a few. But they also specifically disinvited an urban activist who gave talks about the inner-city problems and presented petitions to the city council and government officials on behalf of the residents. They did not want him included because he had filed suit against the three major commercial banks that would likely have representatives at the meeting. However, I asked the associates if the activist could affect and influence the implementation of the meeting's outcome. They said he could—and he would. My reply was simple: "Of course, he has to be included."

The resulting work group for this project contained twenty-six people, including the presidents of the three banks and the activist. There was polite hostility between them at the beginning of the meeting, but I focused everyone on the People Involvement and Purposes phases. By the end of the day, after going through dozens of smart questions covering the entire PPFL process, everyone agreed about the manner in which the bank ought to be set up, the time line, the milestones for activities needed to implement the first release, and who would be responsible for each activity. The activist had an assignment to accomplish, just as the other group members did. He quickly became an essential part of the entire process rather than an antagonist to it, even as he presented his perspectives. The other people listened, and several of his points were considered and affected the outcome. Contrast this positive outcome with the negative reaction that the activist would have had to any plan developed by a group that he was not part of.

Of course, life would be far more pleasant and productive if people could be somehow committed to the same solution for an issue or, if conflict occurred, if they were willing to enlarge their comfort zone and creative space to come to the same conclusion. It would also be nice if everyone could think at a systems level and was always eager to be positive and constructive in discussions. That will never happen.

People are unique; they think differently, and they carry many differing views. In addition, involving antagonists can have the valuable benefit of avoiding groupthink, the tendency of a group to agree with a particular answer even though some group members do not really believe the answer is correct; they just "go along" and "do not rock the boat." At this point in the solution creation process, it is crucial not to pretend otherwise or to shy away from potential conflicts. Engaging everyone forthrightly, even those who do not have the desirable participant characteristics in the process, usually results in bringing people together and ultimately producing agreement and commitment. We have seen it happen too many times not to believe it.

HELPFUL SOURCES FOR ASKING SMART QUESTIONS IN THE LIST STEP. When asking people involvement smart questions, it can be useful to tap into the following additional references and sources of ideas to ensure that you are identifying all the possible people and roles you may need or want to involve:

- Organizational charts—Who is in a position that could contribute to your effort?

- Job descriptions of positions and functions—Is there someone with a particular job function that ought to be involved?

- The system of your problem—Who works in the wider system of the problem where the issue has arisen (customers, suppliers, customer's customers, others)?

- Mailing lists used for notices sent to those not in your organization (for example, customers, suppliers, shareholders, regulators)—Should any of them be considered?

- Community groups—Are there people in any of these groups who would or should be interested in the project?

- Experts—Are there experts in this field who could be used to stimulate creativity or help lead the effort (but not make decisions in the reductionist manner)?

- Employee lists—Are there retirees or previous employees who have something to offer to the effort?

- Unions—What union representatives might have an impact? Are there union personnel who would want to participate?

SMART QUESTIONS FOR THE PEOPLE INVOLVEMENT PHASE

Organize Step

Here are some questions you can ask as you organize the people and ideas you have generated in the list step. These are only a few samples of questions we have used in our own work that we hope will stimulate you in developing your own smart questions more specifically related to your circumstances:

Uniqueness
- Are there unique features or circumstances in my organization that need to be considered in setting up options of people involvement and action plans?
- Who has a high level of the unique skills used in my organization?
- Who has a particularly relevant unique talent or skill that is required at a particular phase in the process of creating a solution?
- Without whom will the effort likely fail?

Information
- What information do we have that makes sense to us to help put together a broad-based functional group?
- Who has information that will help provide a wide range of perspectives for the issue?
- Who can help us validate the reliability of the sources of that information?
- Who can provide any other impressions that make sense to us and would add value to the information we have collected?

Systems
- What purposes are we expecting each person to contribute to the effort?
- Who are the specific people to suggest for a particular possible solution, and who are the contingency backup people?
- Which individuals are suggested for involvement in all phases of the smart questions process, and which ones are best used in particular phases?
- How will we engage the people in the whole effort?
- What are the time line and milestones for the action plan?
- What resources will we need to put our action plan in operation?

- Peers—Are there peers in your field at other organizations who could suggest other people to involve?

- Specific individuals—Who has been named employee of the month? Recognized as an information gatekeeper? Identified as someone who keeps having unusual ideas? Taken part in past successful solution creation efforts? What people have a broad background in various organizational functions who might be able to supplement current team members who have backgrounds in only one function?

The Organize Step

The organize step is about finding ways to put together the potentially disparate or large number of people, stakeholders, resources, methods of involvement, timing, and other random thoughts that you created while listing. The process of this step is to continue asking smart questions that allow you to begin arranging your ideas into several options or alternatives in preparation for the decide step.

This step also helps you pinpoint more details about what people who are invited to work on the problem need to know. People who are asked to be involved usually want to hear such details as the time line for the effort, who else will be participating, what their roles are (and everyone else's), when they will need to be involved, how much of their time it will take, what they will be doing, how they will be involved, and so on.

The organize step thus begins specifying these details so that each option developed reflects a realistic plan of action for involving people to begin creating a solution. By the end of this step, you may end up with a few different groupings of people, time lines, and methods of involvement, all leading to possible different action plans for involvement. Even within each option, you may want to include alternate people to take the place of those desired individuals who may not be able to participate.

Keep in mind as you go through this step that you are still not making any decisions. The gate is still open on people involvement at this time, and you can shuffle, rearrange, reclassify, and revisit any ideas you developed during the list step.

When you organize the two or three options that are likely to emerge from the list ideas, avoid judging the options based on the people who proposed them. The best way to do this is to use the three foundation questions as the basis for asking more smart questions about how to organize the involvement of people. The box provides examples of the types of questions you might ask as you explore ways to organize the people involvement options.

TECHNIQUES FOR ORGANIZING PEOPLE INVOLVEMENT OPTIONS. You can handle the answers to the organize questions for people involvement in a couple of ways. You can use an informal or intuitive process. Simply review the options you have developed during the list and organize steps, and then begin to pick out the people who seem to offer the best talent, or are the most available and supportive, or are likely to help lead you to success.

Or you can follow a more structured approach, using a worksheet such as the one we created: the People Involvement Worksheet shown in Exhibit 2.1. This worksheet will make more sense as we discuss each of the phases of smart questions.

If you prefer this more structured approach, use a worksheet for each option or alternative grouping of people you are considering. You might have a "perfect world option" in which you identify the best people you could hope to involve, and another option of people you can't live without, and another option of the best people available, and so on. Having several options can help refine your thinking.

"Who to Involve?" Column. The worksheet lets you sort out the list of stakeholder alternatives and group them in the "Who to Involve?" column. Remember that the group will almost always lose some of its members to job changes, retirements, or departure from the company. For this reason, it is useful to identify some contingency people. There is some value to this turnover, as a replacement newcomer to a group often motivates the continuing members to review their past decisions and develop new options and methods for doing the group's work.

For projects of any scope and complexity, the information provided in this column could identify a possible team leader if the project's authorizing agency has not already tapped this person.

"Purposes of Their Involvement" Column. As each stakeholder group is considered, ask about the purposes each would serve. See the list of purposes people can play on page 60 as a reminder about all the purposes people can serve. Because the living solution resulting from this

Issue: _____

Alternative Number: _____

Phases and LOD step	Who to Involve?	Purposes of Their Involvement?	How Will They Be Involved?	When to Involve Them?
Purposes—List				
Purposes—Organize				
Purposes—Decide				
Future Solution—List				
Future Solution—Organize				
Future Solution—Decide				
Living Solution—List				
Living Solution—Organize				
Living Solution—Decide				

Exhibit 2.1. Smart Questions People Involvement Worksheet

effort will affect others not involved now, another value in identifying the purposes of involving certain people is knowing who can provide legitimacy behind the proposed changes to those not involved. This can be important because many studies have shown that people want shared values in their work settings as a basis for doing their tasks most effectively and productively—values such as truth, trust, openness, honesty, and caring. Another advantage of asking questions about purposes in this initial phase is that it sows the seeds for the importance of purposes and initiates the move away from problem analysis to what needs to be achieved.

"How Will They Be Involved?" Column. This column allows you to list methods of getting people together. A face-to-face meeting is not always the best way to get people involved initially or on a continuing basis. Some people may be at different sites, others have busy schedules, still others hesitate to speak up in large meetings, and some feel they do not want to use their position as a way to influence the group. Furthermore, because each person has a preferred learning style (auditory, visual, kinesthetic), you can tailor the contacts to allow different modes of presenting the questions and recording responses: tell stories, use graphs and charts, have a way to try things out, use scribble pads, and so on. In addition, this column helps you begin developing a sense of the environment in which the involvement will take place—for example, will there be a separate meeting room? Should music be piped in? What meals will be served?

Virtual teams are a growing phenomenon in many organizations. They can be exceptionally effective with SQA because the process is specific about what needs to be done in each phase, with little wasted time. This is particularly important when groups are geographically dispersed and do not all gather around the same conference table every day for organizational meetings. Our experience of working virtually ourselves and coaching virtual teams is that the organization and assignment of responsibilities in virtual teams is critical for success. Ad hoc organization is a formula for failure.

One issue that may affect how people will be involved is group polarization—the tendency of members of a group to move toward a decision based on a persuasive member or two, social influences based on the people's conception of themselves, and the influence of those with extreme views who are certain they are right. Overcoming such polarization depends on maintaining an effort to promote diversity, implementing a system of checks and balances that continually inserts competing alternatives and views, and engaging members who are "low-status" people in a group to prevent them from remaining quiet during deliberations.

Some techniques that can be used for determining how they will be involved are conducting one-on-one interviews, holding team meetings or small group breakfast or lunch meetings, having each individual privately list stakeholders and people who might be involved and then one person at a time gives the group one item until all items are listed, mailing minutes and asking for comments, sending questionnaires, working by e-mail, and setting up a Web site (which theoretically lets everyone be involved). Review Table 2.1 to select other appropriate techniques. Which technique to use with which people should be based on the purposes for which the person is involved, his or her preferences and attributes, and where you are in the SQA phases.

You can also tap into unusual and creative methods to engage people in addition to the standard. Robert Tucker, author of *Driving Growth Through Innovation* (2002), suggests such techniques as involving customers in new ways (such as surveying the needs of the customers' customers—for example, home builders instead of home supplies retailers), focusing on the unarticulated needs of customers (such as listening to their frustrations and finding ways of eliminating them, or asking them to consider hypothetical products or even prototypes), and getting competitors' customers, former customers, and anyone not yet a customer to respond to inquiries.

"When to Involve Them?" Column. This column puts a time frame on the whole effort, thereby helping to provide guidance to the people involved, giving them a sense of the approximate amount of their involvement and the timing of it. The column might indicate milestones or deadlines for the various LOD steps of each phase. Although most motivated people work hard to meet a deadline, an unrealistically short deadline tends to burn out people or cause them to cut corners. In addition, the amount of budget for the effort or requested by the team affects the resources available for the estimated time.

One advantage of SQA is that you can easily allocate an overall time frame based on the LOD steps of each phase, along with clear milestones. Such a time frame can be far more concrete than time frames done under the nonspecific nature of the reductionist approach, whereby people often guess at the time line times: "two weeks to gather data, three weeks to model it, one week to analyze the models, two weeks to be creative to come up with a solution," and so on. What typically happens is that the "be creative" step is compressed near the deadline date, with an accompanying lack of concern because it is often believed that people develop their most creative ideas when the time pressure is intense.

Unfortunately, this is too frequently not the case, so there is a tendency to adopt any idea that meets the deadline. In contrast, SQA incorporates creativity into every step of LOD in all four phases rather than being left to only one step at the end where ideas are supposed to be generated.

Some techniques that can be used for deciding the details about schedules include Gantt charts, project management software, program planning method, scheduling model, doing a system matrix to describe the whole project, preparing work schedules for team members, and simply asking people to estimate what the time allocation should be for each phase. (A system matrix is discussed in Chapter Five.)

KEEPING AN OPEN MIND. Keep in mind as you organize the people involvement ideas from the list step that there is no way to predict who will contribute what at any time. Without the opportunity to contribute, people will feel snubbed. Worse, they may let negative feelings rule their attitudes toward the whole project. When offered an authentic invitation to participate, a previous decision not to take part is no longer an obstacle to the individual's future contributions. All of us know people who do not speak up until the third or fourth meeting, while others dry up after the first one.

The Decide Step

In the decide step, you begin to whittle down the options you have created and to devise a draft or sketch plan indicating the people necessary for creating a workable solution. How do you ultimately decide who should be involved?

We adhere to making decisions by considering the four major components of any decision:

1. The *purpose* of the decision—in this case, the need to identify the people to involve, how, and when in this phase.

2. *Alternatives* or *options* to consider for achieving that purpose— in this case, the options or alternative scenarios for people involvement from the organize step.

3. *Criteria, factors,* or *considerations* to use in evaluating the alternatives. Factors might include time availability of the individuals, willingness of those outside the organization to take part, costs of the resources needed, impact of the deadline date for completion on when people can participate, fairness and compassion in dealing with noninvolved people, and inclusion of all stakeholder perspectives. The factors used in this step are most often general, intuitive, and based on management desires. However, such factors are necessary for decisions about people involvement; the factors in the decide step of the following three phases become progressively more specific than in people involvement.

4. An *assessment method* for selecting among the alternative options in terms of the criteria. Assessment methods might include such techniques as randomly selecting one option "out of the hat," using an intuitive way of tossing the options around in your mind and then selecting one, assigning levels of importance to each criterion so the most critical ones are used more thoroughly, or asking colleagues each to identify the best option so the one most frequently selected becomes what you decide to use.

This basic decision framework is used by everyone to some degree, consciously or not, in making a choice for any situation—whether it's what movie to go to tonight, which car to buy, when to enroll in a continuing education program, or where to work. Although the framework remains the same regardless of the situation, the amount of detail and thoroughness needed varies widely dependent on what the critical nature of the decisions involves. The movie decision will not need much detail at all, the car might warrant a little more detail, the continuing education might need some more thought and detail, and where to work might deserve still more.

—~~~— **SMART QUESTIONS FOR THE PEOPLE INVOLVEMENT PHASE**

Decide Step

Here are sample questions to ask in the decide step to help your intuitive sense or provide information for making the most effective choice of people to involve.

Uniqueness

- How can we include consideration of our uniqueness (particular situation, constraints, deadlines, available resources, priority of the project, and so on) in deciding on what people to involve and the action plan to use?
- Are there any unique criteria, factors, or considerations we need to use in evaluating the options?
- Does the organization require a specific way of using the criteria for selecting options?

Information

- How accurate does the information about stakeholders need to be in order to make a decision about who to involve?
- How long might we have to wait until reasonable information would be available?
- What purposes are we seeking to achieve in the solution creation process with these questions about information collection? (the wisdom of deciding what's relevant)

Systems

- What system elements (purposes, inputs, outputs, process, environment, and enablers) of the possible future and living solution options does each person considered in a people involvement option provide the best insights to?
- How does each prospective participant prefer to be involved?
- Can a local or wide area information network help an option be effective?
- Which option represents the broadest range of other people systems (organizational functions, customers, suppliers, community interest) with which our living solution will likely have to interface?

We present this framework in its simplest form here to provide you with at least a bare-bones structure for deciding whom to involve. Since you already have a purpose for this decision and you have likely developed some alternatives or options, your decision depends on the criteria, factors, and considerations that are important to you, as well as whatever assessment method works best for your situation. Using the decision framework for choosing which alternative option for people involvement does not need to be complex or create headaches. In most cases, it is not difficult to select which people to involve in a solution creation process. In many cases, the individual or group responsible for people selection probably reviews the options in the same relative cursory way you might select, for example, the car to buy. As you will see though, the decide step in the purposes, future solution, and living solution phases can require successively more formal decision-making tools that we will describe.

While going through the decision framework, however, we recommend that you continue asking smart questions such as those shown in the box. Do not be surprised if your answers to these types of questions cause you to modify your options for involving people. Even at this step, you might end up combining some aspects of a couple of options into one or even more than two options, changing criteria, modifying your assessment methods, or adding people or resources to one or more of the options.

Although the decisions you need to make regarding people involvement are highly dependent on your unique situation, we offer a few general observations from our experience working with clients in the decide step of the People Involvement Phase:

• There may be times when you need to settle for people who are not from your best available option. This happens because sometimes the group of people to get involved is self-selected because no other people are available to take part in the project or the interest level is too low.

• It can be very useful to get the eventual decision makers or groups that need to give approval for your solution recommendations involved in deciding which option or alternative for people involvement to use. Their having participated in selecting the people often gives them greater confidence in whatever living solution is proposed.

- We always recommend that technical people never outnumber all the other stakeholders. Some technical people tend to want to move back into reductionist thinking, analyzing the problem, collecting data, insisting on a technological solution, and so on. Avoid this at all costs in order to maintain the benefits of SQA.

GUIDELINES FOR ASKING SMART QUESTIONS

We have provided numerous examples of smart questions related to the three foundation questions throughout the LOD steps in this chapter. As you go about learning to ask your own smart questions, you may wonder how to know if the questions you want to ask are truly smart. In fact, there is no recipe book for asking smart questions. Asking questions is an art, not a science.

We can, however, offer a framework as a starting place for your unique journey. Here is a reminder from Chapter One of some useful guidelines to help you develop the skills of the smart questions art:

- Does the question I'm going to ask align with the three foundation questions and the four phases of SQA?
- Does the question I'm going to ask open up look-to-the-future perspectives (rather than the present or past), as well as new responses and possibilities?
- Does the question I'm going to ask create new smart question–type metaphors and information sources?
- Does the question I'm going to ask feel like an interesting and wholeness-enhancing smart question?
- Does the question I'm going to ask spark creative responses, that is, responses that offer many options or lead to other smart question-type questions?
- Is the question I'm going to ask likely to provide a way to empower individuals to use smart questions for creating solutions on their own?
- Is the question I'm going to ask likely to bring people together enthusiastically and with commitment to focus on building a desired future and getting results?

THE ITERATIVE NATURE OF THE LIST, ORGANIZE, AND DECIDE PROCESS

Keep in mind that the entire LOD process (in each phase) is iterative. You may need to return to asking people-based questions while you tackle the Purposes, Future Solution, and even Living Solution phases once you recognize that other stakeholders may need to be involved in the problem analysis or solution implementation. For example, you may find in the Purposes Phase that you need to refocus your efforts at a different level from the one that initiated the project, and thus you need to involve different people than you planned on. In our experience, the Smart Questions People Involvement Worksheet is almost always updated throughout a project.

THE BENEFITS OF DIVERSE PEOPLE INVOLVEMENT

Getting people involved and understanding the roles they play in creating solutions is critical to the success of any venture. We have seen this over and over again. Human nature is such that you cannot force people to adopt solutions to which they have not participated in formulating or committed to accomplishing. Doing otherwise is like treating people as prisoners who have no say in their lives.

When people become involved, they:

- Are motivated.
- Take advantage of the opportunity to contribute.
- Find a sense of meaning in what they do.
- Are challenged to release their creativity.
- Are willing to implement the solutions they develop.
- Develop trust in the process and with others.
- Learn how to see the whole picture.
- Find a way to communicate easily with others.
- Understand that change is always going to occur. That's why we use the term *living solution* as the code words for a *change for today that has built-in seeds of continuing change.*

These ideas stem from the wisdom of the leading solution creators we have studied and our own experiences in positively motivating individual, organizational, and societal performance. These concepts can transform any levels of change activity, moving it to a higher level of solution creating performance.

HIGHLIGHTS OF THE PEOPLE INVOLVEMENT PHASE

- Implementation of the solutions starts at the beginning of a project by getting related people involved. Each individual is one in an almost infinite number of combinations of characteristics that form the person's life, and thus each person has something unique to contribute. Individuals with diverse cultural backgrounds and different kinds of intelligence in design and solution creation should be consulted.

- Each person is unique by virtue of having a different creative intelligence and potential; there is no way to know what transpires in each person's mind, and so each person affected even tangentially by a problem, or who could influence a solution creation effort, must be involved in some way in its solution.

- Bringing people actively into solution creation is a need, not just a social value. Conventional approaches assume that as you work on a problem, it is possible to separate the technical aspects from the human, social, or learning aspects. It is an erroneous supposition that experts should design the best economically justifiable technological solution and then get management and workers to accept it.

- The need for creative and innovative solutions in organizations is matched by the need for fast implementation and use of the solutions. Installing change requires the active involvement of those who will operate it. Their commitment is built by understanding what the solution is and how it was developed.

- Everyone touched by the efforts to create or restructure solutions and affected by the results should be given continual opportunities to participate in SQA.

- People are the source of information. Much less information needs to be collected when it's right there in the room with you. Bringing people in secures information from a wide variety of resources. People need to be considered as the purveyors of wisdom rather than just baskets of mindless information collection that serves little purpose.

- People can understand intricate techniques and complex situations. There is no reason to claim that those affected cannot grasp the sophistication, beauty, or elegance of a proposed solution.

- People enjoy working on and accepting responsibility for projects.

- Bringing people in creates champions of change, builds teamwork capabilities, and increases creativity in planning, design, improving, and problem solving.

- Involving people significantly increases the possibility that the solution devised will fit those who operate the system.

- Getting people involved early provides a creative and effective path through the remaining three phases to ensure powerful results with lasting solutions.

CHAPTER THREE

SQA Phase 2

Selecting a Focus Purpose

Never solve a problem from its original perspective.

—Charles "Chic" Thompson

he word *purpose* has many connotations. It can
mean *utility,* as in the purpose of pliers is to squeeze things. It can mean
intent, as in "his purpose was to raise questions." It can mean *mission,*
as in "the purpose of our company is to provide high-quality consulting services in the area of tax planning and strategic tax savings," or
it can mean *function,* as in "the purpose of the fundraiser was to raise
money for research into muscular dystrophy." In this book, the word
purpose encompasses all of these connotations.

This phase focuses on helping you discover the larger purposes
(meaning all the connotations above) that might be behind your
desire to solve a problem and create a solution. The smart questions
you ask and the work you do are aimed at exploring and expanding
the rationale for your issue, situation, or problem to ensure that you
end up working on the right issue.

We learned to question purposes through our research studying
and also watching the leading creators of solutions in action. Whenever they approached a problem, they did not accept the problem
statement in the way it was initially framed. Instead, they always asked
themselves and the people involved to explore and redefine their

issues, expanding them into a larger context. This usually led them to identify many possible other purposes that ought to be accomplished, which they then organized into a hierarchy of purposes that pointed to a larger context within which the living solution they were developing would fit.

Expanding purposes is analogous to what happens in the medical arena. A patient comes into the doctor's office complaining of a certain symptom, called the presenting problem. The smart doctor does not accept the patient's statement as the only possible problem. The doctor is likely to explore many other options through questions and tests in order to discover and treat the "real" problem.

The same is usually true with personal, business, organizational, community, and social problems. The presenting problem—the problem as initially stated—is only the tip of the iceberg. You need to expand your questioning to identify the larger purposes you want to work on.

PROBLEM STATEMENTS VERSUS PURPOSES

A problem statement is not the same as a purpose statement. A problem statement identifies something that is broken or not working properly—for example, "We are having late deliveries." The purpose statement identifies what you desire to accomplish—for example, "to deliver software that has been ordered." The advantages of purpose statements are that you know *what* needs to be accomplished and you can easily explore what the *what* is supposed to accomplish, both of which may have one measure, such as delivery timeliness, among others of how well you accomplish them.

This phase of SQA reframes the initial problem statement into an extended list of purposes statements in order to expand your creative space for creating solutions. By *creative space,* we mean the mental flexibility and permission you give yourself to question assumptions and think creatively. The key point here is that the SQA does not accept the initial problem statement as the real purpose for solving the problem. It is only the starting place for creating a solution.

SQA practitioners go beyond the initial problem statement and start to examine the problem from different perspectives. They explore the purposes of solving the problem and consider a number of purposes in a process we call purpose expansion to make sure that the real need is addressed. Expanding purposes often shows that you should be creating a solution to achieve a different, and usually larger, purpose from the one implied in the originally identified problem statement.

THE PURPOSES HIERARCHY

A good way to visualize the SQA focus on purposes is to imagine an unusual ladder (it's sort of like Alice in Wonderland, where things work differently) that expands upward, with each successive step wider than the last, as shown in Figure 3.1. The bottom rung is the smallest-purpose statement for the problem situation, such as "to make widget A" or "to resolve the disagreement between A and B about who to hire for a position." As you enlarge the scope of your thinking, considering larger and more global purposes for achieving the initial purpose, you climb the ladder in widening successive rungs. This represents the expansion of your thinking. As you move up the ladder, asking smart questions that lead to bigger purposes, you may eventually identify one purpose to achieve that invites possibilities for far more effective and creative solutions, such as "to produce holding device X" where widget A may not even be needed, or "to have A and B develop a complete human resource system for hiring personnel."

Here is a good example of how examining purposes enlarged the scope of thinking in one business and led the company to a larger,

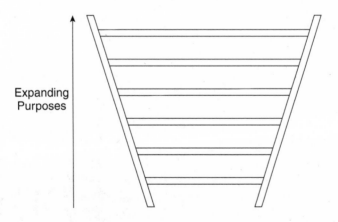

Expanding Purposes

Figure 3.1. The SQA Ladder of Purpose Hierarchy

more efficient, cost-effective living solution. This case occurred at a manufacturing firm that had a problem with a stamping machine whose function was to die-cut an opening in a sheet of cardboard to be used in product packaging. The stamping machine did not work right, creating about 25 percent poor-quality or waste cardboard, so the company defined the initial problem as "decreasing waste from the machine."

In a reductionist approach, the company would likely have proceeded as follows: gathered as many data as possible about the machine, prepared graphs and statistical analyses on the frequency of the error rate and waste, determined the root cause of the machine's problem, changed the die cuts, rerun the machine and measured the new error rate, and so on. This approach implicitly accepts the initial problem statement as *the* purpose for taking action.

Instead of following that approach, the manager of manufacturing, who had been trained in SQA, set up a team to talk about the purposes of the stamping operation. They began by identifying the smallest purpose (the first rung of the SQA ladder) as "to stamp an opening in the cardboard." The team then asked what the purpose of that purpose was, and came up with "to be an opening in a box formed from the sheet of cardboard." Continuing this line of questioning led them to successively larger purposes, which formed a hierarchy:

- To stamp an opening in the cardboard
- To be an opening in a box formed from the sheet of cardboard
- To package and dispense plastic bags
- To deliver one bag at a time to customers
- To provide customers with plastic bags
- To provide customers with a flexible, waterproof container

From this list, the group decided that the actual purpose for which they needed to develop a living solution was not the first purpose but rather one of the larger ones: "to deliver one bag at a time to the customer." Now spending their time and resources working on *that* purpose, they ended up redesigning a completely new box with a different kind of opening that did not even require the stamping machine. This solution more than solved the initial problem: it gave them a better manufacturing process and saved them time and money fixing the wrong problem. In addition, their new box design gave them a strategic competitive advantage for getting new customers because their bids for business to potential customers were lower as a result of reduced manufacturing costs.

Cases like this are typical of many problem situations. For us, they suggest five critical lessons to learn:

1. Always explore the larger context of your purposes because it allows you to get into a larger thinking and creative space.

2. Each bigger purpose you recognize has potentially more possible solutions to consider.

3. Developing a solution for a bigger purpose may completely eliminate the need to find a solution for the situation that you thought was the initial problem.

4. You are likely to discover a solution that can have much broader beneficial results for the whole organization.

5. The solution developed for whatever purpose you select will fit within and help accomplish a context of larger purposes.

We are firm believers, based on what the leading creators of solutions do, in the value of expanding your creative space. Large, creative spaces lead to more ideas and better thinking. In expanding the purposes of solving a problem, you also tend to move toward higher-level strategic thinking that increasingly identifies bigger issues of your situation. In the stamping machine case, for example, the marketing, product design, manufacturing, engineering, corporate executive, and accounting functions of the company all had to work together to bring the living solution to fruition, converting a humdrum operational issue with a stamping machine into a significant strategic change for this company.

Purposeful thinking is powerful. If you want to become a strategic organization, begin to think in terms of expanding purposes rather than always accepting problem statements as defined.

As Bill George, retired chairman and CEO of the $7.7 billion Medtronic, states in his book *Authentic Leadership* (2003), "...[T]he best-kept secret in business is that the mission-driven [*mission* and *purposes* are synonyms] companies create far more shareholder value than do financially-driven firms" (p. 61). Similarly, Larry Bossidy, retired CEO of Honeywell, and Ram Charan, a management consultant, in their book *Execution: The Discipline of Getting Things Done* (2002), equally point out the power of thinking about purposes and creating solutions in the way that SQA does:

> We see three major flaws in the budgeting or operations processes at most companies. First, the process doesn't provide for robust dialogue on the plan's assumptions [what the concept of purposes does]. Second, the budget is built around the results that top management wants, but it doesn't discuss or specify the action programs that will make those outcomes a reality [what a living solution does]. Third, the process doesn't provide coaching opportunities for people to learn the totality of the business, or develop the social architecture of working together in common cause [what SQA provides] [pp. 228–29].

THINKING HOLISTICALLY ABOUT PURPOSES

To initiate thinking about purposes, begin with the three foundation questions. The holistic perspective encompassed by these three questions will significantly improve your ability to focus on purposes. Each foundation question leads you to important distinctions and insights that move you up the ladder toward seeing the larger global purposes behind whatever solution creation you are doing.

SQA Foundation Question 1: What Is Unique About Our Situation and Its Purposes?

Asking purpose questions reinforces SQA's emphasis on uniqueness. Because your organization, community, and values are unique, the problem or issue that started you on the solution creation path and the expansion of its purposes will be unique. The purposes expansion forces you in a positive way to question the assumptions you may have about the purpose of dealing with the situation that you want to fix. Expanding the purposes of your problem into larger purposes ensures that you are trying to achieve the right purpose. There is nothing worse than developing what some might consider a great solution for something that should not exist at all (recall the die stamping operation case).

One of the most common uniqueness mistakes that people and organizations make is to consciously (or unconsciously) predetermine the level of change they expect to make in solving a problem in advance of fully understanding their purposes. Based on history and various assumptions, they decide beforehand what they think the solution will encompass and what changes will need to be made. These preconceived notions then control their effort to solve the problem. By predetermining the level of change, the techniques, and even the budget to be applied to the problem, you will likely wind up with the wrong solution or a continuation of the problem down the road.

The president and several executives of a manufacturing company employing six hundred were concerned about numerous problems that the company was having, including deteriorating product quality, late deliveries, high costs, and overtime. They met regularly for nearly eight months going over all the data they had collected to find a solution, assuming their purpose was "to figure out how to do things better." Based on the data and their assumptions, they concluded that the solution was to build a new state-of-the-art facility that would double their capacity and allow them to get control of their production, improve their deliveries, and lower their costs. The president called me to help them design the state-of-the-art factory he thought they needed.

After spending an afternoon at their facility, I requested that they set up a project team to redo the planning using SQA. Rather than accepting their predetermined purpose statement ("to do things better") and their conclusion, I began by walking them through a purposes expansion exercise. In the end, the team decided that they actually needed to focus on how to "get rid of things," a much larger level of change. By changing the purpose, the aim now became to develop management control systems to simplify and reorganize the company into more effective manufacturing processes.

This revised purpose selected from the expanded purposes led the team to create a living solution that could be accomplished within their current facility, and a new factory was not needed. Although the company could have built a top-of-the-line, fully automated, state-of-the-art factory if the initial conclusions of the executive committee had been followed, the SQA uniqueness and purposes questions allowed them to avoid wasting money for a solution they did not need.

Focusing on purposes serves another critical function relative to the uniqueness of a problem: helping you align your purposes with your values. Every problem, issue, or opportunity actually has two primary aspects: the substantive aspect and a values aspect. The substantive aspect focuses on the fundamental or basic conditions of the situation: the who, what, why, where, and how of the specific situation that may need to change. The values component reflects the desires, aspirations, and beliefs of the individual or organization. Values, desires, and aspirations are often the motivation to seek a change to a more effective living solution. Values also guide us in our decision-making process.

Incorporating values helps situate the solution creation effort into the larger context of what the organization really cares about and aspires to fulfill in its mission. Values inspire the people working on the issue to consider the importance of matching their efforts with the compelling desires of their organization. The importance of values is clearly seen if you contrast a group of people creating solutions according to values with a group of people who are working on a problem simply because they were told to fix something by their management. The latter group has no larger context from which to solve the problem. A lack of values is a formula for tactical, unfulfilling solutions. Without an understanding of the values of the organization, it is more likely than not that poor decisions will be the outcome.

We believe that the ultimate driver behind successful solution creation almost always comes down to values related to bettering the human condition. Prompted by many of the leaders we studied, we have found that solutions not grounded in bettering the human condition nearly all fall short of their full potential. In the largest context, values are the desire of humans to improve the world for themselves and others.

Betterment is, of course, a subjective term, open to interpretation among different people at different times. However, most of us would agree that there are clearly some standard definitions that would apply to the concept. One of our favorite definitions is paraphrased from Robert Nisbet (1980, pp. 3–9): Most current value systems reflect a belief in the values of the past, the worth of economic and technological growth, the scientific and scholarly knowledge that comes from reason, and the intrinsic importance and ineffaceable worth of life on this earth.

In short, in any solution creation effort you are doing, as you expand your purposes and choose a specific focus purpose or purposes to achieve, it is useful to consider one or more, if not all, of these four fundamental values:

- Greater effectiveness
- Higher quality of life and community

- Enhanced human dignity, equality, and liberty
- Individual betterment

Articulating and incorporating these values into your solution efforts will assuredly lead to better living solutions. In fact, since values and purposes are fundamentally linked, you will often find that the best solutions for change are based on identifying some type of short-fall that exists between your values and the way your purposes are being achieved. Expanding your purposes will bring to the light this deficiency or mismatch of purposes and values by causing you to begin addressing larger and larger levels of purposes until you get to the heart of the values embedded in it.

SQA Foundation Question 2: What Is Purposeful Information for the Purposes Phase?

The information foundation question serves the role of guiding you to the right level of information collection. Thinking about your purposes is a good defense against the "analysis-first" and "technology-first" traps of reductionism.

The successful people we studied avoid excessive and needless data collection, as well as the analytical subdivision modeling that typically occurs at the start of conventional approaches to problem solving. They do not believe in launching a vast effort to collect information about a problem area before they talk about and uncover what they truly want to accomplish. They devote more time on global planning (purposes) than do ineffective solution creators and relatively less time on local planning (studying causes). In fact, the successful solution creators we studied avoid the conventional urge to start by collecting data and analyzing the situation. They make sure they have identified the most important purposes first so they do not waste money by throwing costly technology (robots, office automation, and so on) or program time and effort before the purposes have been thoroughly thought out.

In our consulting work, we frequently see that research to discover the causes of problems or to develop short-term solutions drives most change efforts in the United States and in many other countries where we consult. When it comes to converting the vast new knowledge created in research and development departments into practical applications, however, the United States lags behind some other nations, such as Japan, where people are willing to take a longer-term view of progress and change.

The worst examples we have seen of this are companies that tend to ignore their larger purposes, focusing instead on the bottom line only, by far the most shortsighted value or goal in our view. When asked to state the purpose of their company, the corporate executives of these types of companies claim, "to make a profit." Certainly we support the idea of making a profit, so we ask such executives, "Make a profit *doing what*?" If making a profit is a company's most compelling value, they may end up making illegal and immoral decisions. Think Enron. Need we say more?

Profit is only a measure of how well the company is achieving its actual purpose, not the company's mission. It is a resource for having or doing something else. It is not an end in itself. Purpose can be discovered only by asking questions like, "What business are we in?" or "What service are we trying to provide our customers?" or "What mission or value do we want to accomplish?" Once these are discussed and the answers are unveiled in their largest context ("What's the purpose of *that* mission?"), the company's purposes in solving problems can be best understood and linked to their efforts of information collection.

SQA Question 3: What Is the Purpose of the System We Are Trying to Create?

The systems foundation question helps frame the expansion of purposes. After all, the purpose of the activity that starts a project is one of the elements of a system. Every system is part of a larger system, which is part of a larger system, which is part of a larger system, and so on. Thus, for every purpose, there is a larger purpose that the first purpose is supposed to help achieve. This second purpose is always larger than the first, and the bigger of the two is the one that has the greater range of possible solutions (creative space), and the bigger of those two opens the possibility of more solution options, and so on.

Consider the situation of a large medical clinic we worked with. This hospital had nearly twenty thousand patient charts (folders), each one containing test results, doctors' notes from patient visits, prescriptions, and other information. A number of events can trigger a request for the patient's chart, such as when a patient visits the hospital for any reason or a report is sent in from other hospitals, medical specialists, and insurance companies. On any given day, the hospital could not find or make available nearly twenty charts out of about four hundred requested—5 percent of them. The hospital then had to devote the equivalent of about 50 percent of one staff member's time to find the missing charts; meanwhile, staff in other departments as well as the doctors did not like being bothered by the unfortunate searcher.

With our facilitation, a team of people got together to work on purposes for solving this problem. They began by identifying the smallest purpose: "to locate the charts." That might be a fine purpose for solving the problem, but if the team had tried to create a solution for this purpose, the number of possibilities would have been quite small.

We therefore led the team to expand their statement of purposes by asking sequential purpose questions ("What is the purpose of the previously stated purpose?"). In the end, they developed the following ladder or hierarchy of purposes:

- To locate charts
- To have charts available (the purpose of "to locate charts")
- To keep charts ready for use (the purpose of "to have charts available")
- To retrieve patient information (the purpose of "to keep charts ready for use")
- To supply patient information (the purpose of "to retrieve patient information")
- To fill requests and store information about patients (the purpose of "to supply patient information")
- To help doctors and other medical personnel in diagnosis and giving advice (the purpose of "to fill requests and store information about patients")

Even if you are not familiar with clinical operations, you can see that each increasingly larger purpose broadens the range of potential solutions the task force has available to them. The final purpose, "to help doctors and medical personnel in diagnosis and giving advice," clearly opens up a larger creative space than "to fill requests and store information about patients," and that one opens up a larger space than "to supply patient information," and so on down the line.

By expanding their statements of purposes, the team eventually created 131 ideas for future solutions, far more than would have been possible for the smallest purpose. What is more, many solutions affected a different system of the hospital than the team believed could be involved in developing a living solution. For instance, supplying patient information affects a different system of the hospital than to help doctors and medical personnel in diagnosing and giving advice.

In the end, the team chose a solution that affected several of the hospital's systems. The details of their solution are unimportant for now; the point is that understanding purposes is critical to developing a systems perspective—seeing the interconnectedness of the solution to other systems.

Another important aspect of thinking about purposes and systems is to expose your hidden assumptions about systems. It is important, for example, to avoid thinking in terms of finding one, and only one, solution. The term *solution* too often suggests that somewhere out there is *the* answer, as if you will fix the entire system in which the problem exists once and only once.

The truth is, every system is a living, continuous, organic, dynamic object. For every purpose, the solution must be part of a living system that continues to exist over long periods of time. This is the reason that we use the term *living solution* in the SQA framework. Our term reinforces the idea that any solution must be "a change for today that has built-in seeds of continuing change." A living solution is in touch with its larger ongoing system. You can implement a living solution only when you recognize how it must fit or align with the system in which it resides, including its surrounding systems.

THE LIST, ORGANIZE, AND DECIDE STEPS

Given this background of how the three foundation questions help expand purposes, let us now walk through the LOD process wherein you will learn the process of examining and expanding your purposes through Smart Questions and actions.

The List Step

The list step in this phase teaches you to ask smart questions to elicit as many purpose statements as possible about your issue. The activity is intended to open up the minds of those involved beyond the initial problem statement to an ever-widening set of purposes. The process is akin to having a dialogue with yourself in which you try to expose any assumptions you have about your purpose and set yourself free to begin expanding your creative space. You might think of it as a type of off-site retreat where you intentionally throw people into a new context in an effort to stimulate their creativity, perspectives, and relationships. As several cases presented thus far illustrate, it is always possible to have many potential purposes for a situation that appears on the surface to be a simple situation (remember the stamping operation and locating medical charts).

The list step aims to overcome your habitual patterns of thinking. Some people are naturally more expansive in their thinking and willing to consider a broader range of possibilities than others. But as our research uncovered, only around 8 percent of the population think intuitively in this open, flexible way. In general, it is our observation that most people begin a problem-solving endeavor inside a small creative space. They tend to be narrow-minded and conservative as they think about possible purposes and solution alternatives. They are afraid to look at possible bigger purposes to be achieved, and they limit the possibilities for solutions that they would be willing to consider as viable.

Your creative space is a type of mental playground where you go to create solutions. For most people, their creative space is a small playground with patchy grass, no interesting games to play, and no other children to play with. Their playgrounds are surrounded by barriers, constraints, limitations, obstacles, and restrictions. The range of possibilities is limited.

Why this happens is complex, but the brief explanation is that most of us are socialized out of childhood's joyful creative spaces. As kids, we are naturally curious, inventive, and playful. But by adulthood, almost all of us learn that we need to be serious and cautious, that it's not proper to give in to our creative impulses, and that we must rein in our "go-for-it" spirit. We become socialized to live in small playgrounds where the risks are lower (and so are the rewards). We slowly become so accustomed to these small, uninteresting playgrounds that we cannot allow ourselves to move into a bigger playground, where we might have more fun doing large, expansive thinking and creating new possibilities.

The purpose of focusing on purposes is precisely to get you out of small playgrounds into a big creative space. You want to find a large playground full of interesting people, grassy areas, picnic tables, slides, trees, space to play games, and sand to build castles in. Take a moment to think about it: How big is your playground? How interesting and unusual are its components? Do you need to move into a larger creative space?

Asking questions about purposes is the first step toward building a larger, richer mental playground. Through your questioning, you enlarge the creative space of your thinking to tap into your younger, less rigidly socialized mind-set. With a new attitude, you will find more possibilities and can approach problems playfully—not with the tense, constrained anxiety that so often accompanies your efforts to create solutions, to take chances, and to change.

As a critical start to enlarging your creative thinking space, develop as many possible purpose statements in this list step. Avoid judging the merits of any purpose statement proposed by anyone. One of the best ways to do this is to use the three foundation questions as the basis for asking more smart questions about the purposes of the initial assignment. The box provides examples of the types of questions you might ask as you explore ways to stimulate thinking about purposes.

TECHNIQUES FOR LISTING PURPOSES. There are two general methods for asking smart questions and developing your list of purposes: a structured method using formalized meetings and documents and an informal conversational method. Which method you use depends on the type of issue, capabilities, and preferences of the facilitator or leader of your effort, as well as on the audience and the setting for your conversations. With time and experimentation, you will find ways that feel the most comfortable for you and get the results you desire. To become a skilled practitioner of SQA, you need to experiment to find what works for you because, as we have said, you are unique, with a unique background, skills, and knowledge.

Structured Method of Listing Purposes. The structured method for listing uses charts, notepads, and other written notes through either meetings with groups of people or one-on-one discussions with an SQA facilitator. The basic approach in both cases is straightforward: you keep asking the question, "What are the possible purposes that we are trying to achieve?" This approach is a form of brainstorming: you seek as many ideas about purposes rather than solutions as specified in the brainstorming literature.

If your group is stuck, you can use the sample smart questions in the box or develop your own questions to expand your conversations of purposes. Another effective technique we have found useful to

---

~~~~ **SMART QUESTIONS FOR THE PURPOSES PHASE**

List Step

Here are examples of the types of smart questions you might ask about purposes for your situation. These questions are offered to stimulate you to develop your own specific smart questions based on how the three foundation questions intersect your circumstances.

Uniqueness

- Are there purposes for our problem beyond those that we assumed we had initially?
- Since this problem is unique, what are its purposes that reflect our unique organization, customers, suppliers, potential markets, and community?
- What hidden assumptions do we have about our purposes?
- Since there is always more than one way to state a purpose, what are some alternative statements we can add to our list?
- What do others in our organization think the purposes of our situation might be?
- How can we help our organization think about an expanded set of purposes?

Purposeful Information

- What information do we need about the organization's mission to help identify some purposes of this situation?
- What needs and wants do our customers have that could become purpose statements for us?
- Who else might be asked to be involved because they may be able to ask and often answer questions about purposes for this situation and interrelated systems?
- What organizational values and beliefs suggest purposes that we should put on our list?
- Does the record of past performances in the area of concern suggest purposes to list?
- Are there organizational controls (for example, policies, procedures, or rules) that may need conversion to purpose statements for this effort?
- Would people outside the organization (suppliers, customers, citizens in general) understand the words of this purpose statement? Are we using jargon or "biz-speak"?

Continued

Continued

Systems
- What are the purposes of the system that we are creating?
- What systems are the stakeholders in this solution creation effort a part of? Are some of their purposes to be included on our list?
- Are there purposes to be added to our list based on the organizational inputs, outputs, environment, human agents, physical catalysts, and information aids?
- What are the parts of the system that we are thinking about that need to be considered to develop a creative, workable, and integrated living solution?
- What purposes might the availability of future technologies suggest for our effort?

trigger conversation and generate as many purposes as possible is to use the list of verbs shown in Table 3.1 as a talking point to inspire further ideas. Table 3.2 contains verbs to avoid when thinking about purpose. These verbs are measures and values, and they all imply a rate of change.

For example, selecting the first verb in Table 3.1, you might ask, "What purpose for our endeavor might 'to acquire' suggest? What are we trying to acquire? What do we need to acquire?" With groups, it is sometimes better to have each person go over the list of verbs silently, recording on their own paper as many purposes as they can. This solo work permits each person to contribute independently without group pressure, and it gives introverts equal footing with more extroverted group members. Then have each person, one after another, read out one of his or her purposes while the facilitator records them, without any discussion. Group members can also piggyback new ideas on anyone else's statement. Continue with the reciting out loud in a round-robin style until each person has no further possible purposes.

After you have generated a list of possible purposes using the basic purpose questioning technique or the verb table, it can be very useful to clarify that everyone has the same understanding of the purpose statements. You might ask, "Is the meaning of this purpose statement clear to everyone?" This ensures that everyone is aligned on the perspective embedded in the purpose statements. It is striking how even a simple phrase can have multiple meanings. If there is disagreement

acquire	coordinate	expand	organize	reply
adapt	copy	explain	outline	report
administer	create	express	perform	research
adopt	critique	extrapolate	plan	resolve
allow	debate	find	point	respond
analyze	define	fix	practice	restate
apply	demonstrate	frame	predict	restructure
appraise	describe	generate	prepare	review
argue	design	get	prescribe	schedule
arrange	detect	implement	present	select
assess	determine	indicate	produce	sell
be	develop	inspect	project	separate
build	diagnose	institute	promote	sequence
calculate	diagram	integrate	propose	setup
change	differentiate	interpret	provide	solve
choose	discuss	inventory	question	sort
cite	distinguish	invest	quote	specify
classify	do	investigate	rank	state
collect	document	involve	rate	structure
combine	draw	judge	read	supervise
compare	drive	keep	rearrange	tabulate
compile	educate	know	recite	teach
complete	employ	label	recognize	test
compute	enable	learn	recommend	trace
conclude	encourage	match	record	train
confront	engineer	measure	reengineer	transfer
construct	establish	modify	relate	translate
contrast	estimate	name	reorder	use
control	evaluate	operate	repeat	write
convert	examine	order	rephrase	

Table 3.1. Verbs to Stimulate Thinking About Purposes

about each statement, make any changes in wording needed or additions or deletions of some purposes. The process of clarification often results in additional new purposes being generated and added to the list.

An important side benefit of listing purposes is team building. As team members focus on expanding views of their purposes rather than on fault finding or on massive data collection, the group begins to share a deeper understanding of their values, mission, and goals. They often gain new insights into the system of the problem and their organizational system, recognizing interrelationships and dependencies that elements often have on each other. As the team builds a larger sense of its purposes, this process often empowers the reluctant or shy people to see how their own perspectives might be useful to add to

enhance	increase	minimize	simplify
generalize	lower	optimize	strengthen
improve	maximize	reduce	summarize

Table 3.2.   Verbs to Avoid When Thinking About Purposes

the list. It also forces some of the overly confident people to get a good dose of humility when they see that they have made too many assumptions in their proposals.

Conversational Methods of Listing Purposes. The structured method of listing is not always necessary or appropriate. In some cases, especially when you are working with just one person, you can use an informal, conversational method of expanding purposes. This type of purposes dialogue often becomes more like coaching, as you encourage the person to tell a story about what is important to him or her rather than the formal brainstorming process. The best way to invite people to open up and tell their story is through constructive questions such as those below:

- *"What's missing for you?"* This question is useful to ask when someone is upset and not exactly clear about what is not working. It can prompt the person to reflect on how he or she might want the particular situation to be, which can then lead to a more refined purpose statement.

- *"What goals or values are you committed to?"* This question is useful when you are coaching someone whose actions or behaviors seem out of alignment with what the person says he or she wants or desires. Because our actions flow from our deepest commitments, it is often useful to ask people you are working with to be explicit about their commitments and values. Values statements can then be turned into purpose statements.

- *"What's your personal purpose, mission, or calling?"* Asking people to discuss their personal purpose or mission often gets to the root of something deeper or more enduring than asking them about the idea of purposes in the abstract. For some people, a purpose or mission is their reason for being in the world. Others may find the word *calling* to be a similarly evocative word. In this way, the person can begin to identify many purposes that expand beyond his or her needs and might pertain to other stakeholders.

- *"What do you want to do?"* One small but significant point about asking purpose questions in all circumstances, including in the structured method, is that it can be best to form them in terms of "what," not "why." "Why did you do that?" "Why do you want that?" and "Why are you saying that is a problem?" tend to cause defensiveness and roadblocks to an expanded creative space. "Why" also tends to lead to subdivision rather than expansion responses about the issue. Asking, "What do you want to do?" can often lead the person to identify purposes.

As a general rule in the conversational approach, you know a question is a good one if it seems to expand the person's creative space. But be careful; some questions may inspire some people while turning off others, depending on the meaning that each person assigns to the words used in the question. It is therefore useful to phrase your questions in several ways until you find a style that appeals to the person being coached.

The setting for informal conversations can be a significant factor in whether the dialogue goes well. For example, once we were in a multiday workshop in a building with no open windows. We needed to have a conversation with a colleague about the possibilities of working together in the future. We left the building and took a walk on a heavily wooded nature trail that surrounded a number of office buildings. The formerly stiff conversation became relaxed and refreshing, enabling us to talk about what both of us really desired and what was currently missing. This led to a conversation about the kinds of work that we could do together that was energizing for both of us. After the walk, this colleague gave the name "Zen walk" to this conversation-inspiring technique. She felt refreshed, and we had a very productive talk and ended up working together successfully for several years.

THE IMPORTANCE OF MULTIPLE ITERATIONS ON PURPOSES. Whether you use the structured or conversational method, be sure to continue the questioning about purposes through multiple iterations. Too often, we have seen people yield quickly to a powerful urge to stop talking about purposes and move on to discussing the solution. This is especially common with managers and executives, who tend to want to act rather than talk. Good managers or leaders are decisive and action oriented, but their bias toward action can often short-circuit a productive conversation on purposes and the expansion of the creative space in which everyone needs to work. Therefore, once you ask your first question on purposes, make sure you have other follow-on questions that will take you and your group to an extended listing of as many purposes as possible. Be prepared to tell action-oriented managers that they must let the purposes-listing process follow its course to a natural completion.

In one session we had with a client, we began working on listing purposes with a committee whose task was to propose ways in which their large, multifunctioned organization could become more integrated. The project originated because various groups within the company were working in nonintegrated silos designing information systems. All the independent departments were having serious problems, including a duplication of services, lack of consistent service, lack of communication across departments, and, ultimately, greater expenses. In an effort to integrate the departments, the company was installing a computer system to support its new high-tech manufacturing plant.

Rather than having the committee develop solutions that focused on how to integrate, such as "have a daily integration meeting," or some such obvious solution, we began by asking the committee to explore just the purposes of their committee. The first purpose that they came up with was:

• To find someone to be appointed the "integration czar"

This may have been a reasonable starting point for the committee's purpose, but as in most other purpose conversations, it was too early in the process to accept this as the end result of the conversation. That would have led to too small a creative space.

We then asked them to enlarge their thinking: "What's the purpose of that?" Their next response was:

• To have the integration czar create an integration approach

Then we asked them the purpose of having an integration approach. They answered:

- To have people know when they need to work together on something

We went through several iterations like this, and the group finally started asking the question themselves and expanding their purposes spontaneously. They listed even more purposes:

- To have people working together when appropriate
- To perform the work correctly the first time
- To have people knowledgeable about one another's work
- To define points of integration clearly
- To create subsystems that work together
- To create a system that meets the needs of our organization

After discussion, the group decided that the purpose statement that targeted the right creative space for them was "to define points of integration clearly." They realized that in the past, they had discovered points of integration only after something went seriously wrong. They now understood that the company needed to be more proactive about defining points of interaction proactively before something "blew up." Eventually they created a small cross-functional team whose goals were to define the key interface points, hold weekly integration meetings, and assign a team member to manage particular interface issues.

One point to learn from this example is that people often tend to give snappy, quick answers to purpose questions, trying to move prematurely to the action phase. Be prepared to keep such people from rushing ahead, encouraging them to expand their purposes list through at least several iterations. Only you will know where to stop, but in our experience, nearly every workshop we have conducted has produced at least five to ten purpose questions wherein once a purpose has been identified, you still ask, "What is the purpose of that purpose?"

ELIMINATING CONSTRAINTS TO PURPOSES. Sometimes individuals and groups get stuck in their current problems because they perceive obstacles within their organization or believe that they are not allowed to go beyond a certain imaginary borderline. Some people simply have negative patterns of thought that lead them unconsciously to impose their own barriers on their actions. Rather than consider the possibilities of something working, they think of all the reasons that something cannot work.

Although skepticism can be useful at times, such as when you are assessing the risks of an expensive solution, it is not helpful at all during the list phase. This is precisely the time when you need to be open to new possibilities and ideas without regard to any imagined or real barriers or constraints. One way to shift out of naysaying and negativity is to ask, "If there were no constraints of any kind, what could be done here? What purposes could we be trying to achieve?" It is also useful to confront assumed barriers directly by asking, "What's the purpose of that constraint [or limitation or restriction or obstacle]?" This question often stops people in their tracks when they recognize that the assumed obstacle or barrier literally serves no purpose whatsoever.

Of course, there are always constraints, barriers, limitations, obstacles, and restrictions in life. After all, every solution is part of a larger system, and somewhere up the chain, there will be a barrier such as money, people, or other resources that are simply not available. But the advantage of staying open during the list step is that unfettered creativity opens up ways to eliminate many assumed constraints that did not truly exist.

Here is a case that exemplifies the value of remaining open, flexible, and creative. In this large project, the executives of a major hydroelectric company had to decide what actions to take when installing a new work standards program for constructing and maintaining their transmission towers. The project to develop the work standards, costing several million dollars, required a significant increase in the amount of work that each work crew would be required to do, and the workers' union had already come out against the assumed new work standards. The question for these executives was, "Should the company proceed to install the measurement program when the union said its members would strike if that were done?"

Fortunately, the executives took our advice and did not have a knee-jerk negative reaction during the purposes walkthrough we conducted with them. They could have insisted, for instance, that as management, they had the prerogative to require the new work standards, or that they could not throw away the money already invested in developing the program (the sunk-cost fallacy), or that it was their purview, not the union's, to determine the work standards. Instead, we facilitated them to be open to creating a list of purposes for installing the program, starting with the smallest purpose of "to set workload standards for construction." By the end of day, they had developed eight purposes and eventually selected two of them to focus on: to produce estimates of the construction work required and to plan the construction of towers.

Increasing their creative space in listing purposes allowed these executives to consider many new options. Ironically, one of the solutions they eventually settled on stemmed from an idea proposed by the workers themselves, who suggested they set their own workloads. The executives set up a trial period for the workers' idea, and within a year, management quietly extricated itself from the measurement program because the workers themselves were setting workloads greater than what the program would have set as the standards. In addition to the productivity improvements, they averted a strike that would have resulted in huge costs, reduced customer service, and long-term animosities with the union.

EXTERNAL PURPOSES. Do not forget to consider the results you developed in the People Involvement Phase as you work on purposes. Some individuals or organizations can be so intently focused on internal issues, such as optimizing work systems, cutting costs, and improving productivity, that they are blinded to purposes that exist outside their own turf. In such cases, it is our experience that only when we hear people begin to talk about the possible purposes of what their customers desire from their products or services that they are actually building a large enough creative space. Ultimately, if the people in the business are not considering the impacts and desires of customers with every problem-solving effort, the company is circling the drain and probably does not even know it.

To go even one step further, it is not only useful but invaluable to consider customers' customers. What do they want to get accomplished, and what do your products or services achieve toward those ends? This type of thinking begins to build a truly large creative space, opening up possibilities for major breakthroughs. Think about the alliances between airlines in their award programs, which allow travelers a broad range of choice about how they use their awards. In this case, you might make the analogy that the airlines customers'

customers are the families of their frequent travelers. What might they want from an airline's frequent traveler program? They might indeed want a broader range of choices for family vacations—far more than one airline could handle on its own. Thus was born the idea that several airlines could share frequent flyer rewards.

This type of breakthrough thinking is not likely to occur until you ask questions that examine the purposes of your customers' customers. Larger purposes are a way of inspiring creativity and innovation.

DETERMINING HOW MANY PURPOSES YOU NEED. How many purposes should you have after the list step? The answer is "as many as your group is able to develop in the time that they have." One group we worked with in the education field listed 153 possible purposes for a program they were developing for individually guided education.

But do not be concerned if you have only a few purposes, say ten or fifteen. Think of your initial list as just that. Purposes will likely be added as you clarify your thinking. If you think you do not have enough, just keep asking, "What's the purpose of that purpose?" for all statements being discussed.

A REMINDER ABOUT ASKING PURPOSE QUESTIONS. To repeat a point made before, because it is so important, "What's the purpose of that purpose?" is used throughout SQA instead of, "Why do we need that purpose?" or another "why" question. "What" questions are far more powerful in inspiring new thinking and opening up discussion to new ideas.

The Organize Step

In this step, you start to develop a larger context of the many purposes you have generated. This is accomplished through a technique that we call the purposes hierarchy, which we developed based on the leading creators of solutions who said they sought to define the biggest creative space within which they could work and to have a larger context of understanding about the solution to be developed.

The purposes hierarchy essentially sorts, categorizes, and orders the list of purposes you have already generated—and any that are added in the discussions about organizing. The hierarchy may take several forms: a single ladder listing that sorts the purposes from small to large, or several ladders for various small-scope purpose statements that lead to one large-scope ladder where the smaller ladders all coalesce at the same next bigger set of steps.

In addition to helping you to select a focus purpose (or purposes), creating the hierarchy is an important step in SQA because it identifies the larger context you need to have as you go through the remaining phases. Your larger purposes can inspire you to develop solution options in the next phases that may be only theoretically possible at the moment, but knowing them in advance can lead to breakthroughs when it comes time to design your living solution.

Creating a purposes hierarchy is best done with flexibility. As you will see, the process often engenders hearty debate and discussion among participants about how to order the purposes. Meanwhile, those discussions often cause more purposes to be added, crossed out, or inserted between others. You need to be open to making numerous changes in your hierarchy until everyone is satisfied.

The organize step in the purposes phase presents options in the form of different purpose levels in a hierarchy. More than one hierarchy may be discussed during the process, but most often one hierarchy emerges from the list ideas and those added during this step. The best way to do this is to start with the three foundation questions as the basis for asking more smart questions about how to organize the hierarchy. The box provides examples of these types of questions.

TECHNIQUES FOR ORGANIZING A PURPOSES HIERARCHY. There are two methods we use for this: logical (or structured) and intuitive. Both help to sort and order purposes from small to large relative to the creative space they provide for the people engaged in the problem-solving or design effort to evaluate the right solutions. They differ in how they are applied and the type of audience they are best suited for.

Logical Method for Organizing Purposes. This method is the easier and more efficient approach to arranging purposes in a hierarchy from small to large if you are dealing with a manageable number of people. The method uses logic to determine which purpose is greater or smaller, using what we call the "couplet test," in which you compare two purposes with each other by asking, "Which purpose has the larger scope?" or "Which purpose is the purpose of the other?"

SMART QUESTIONS FOR THE PURPOSES PHASE

Organize Step

To help the organize step, ask smart questions such as the following and others that fit your circumstances.

Uniqueness
- What unique purposes in our situation might be smaller or larger than this purpose statement?
- What unique skills or competence in our organization could help us sort purposes into small to large scope?
- What is unique about the situation or audience we are addressing that will help us determine the scope for this hierarchy? (The same purpose statement, such as "to have a historical record of warranty repairs," might be a small scope for the purposes hierarchy of one department but a large scope for another department.)

Information
- Does the purpose statement make sense to you?
- How well do others in the organization agree with our definition of this purpose statement?
- What are the pertinent types of data we may need from others in the organization to clarify the ordering of these two (or three) purposes?
- Is the purpose statement about data collection or developing information from various data sources? If so, this almost always indicates a smaller scope purpose.
- Does the purpose statement concern monitoring, controlling, or evaluating? If so, these are almost always larger scope than data collection and smaller than whatever purpose the control statement is supposed to help accomplish.
- What key values do people hold and what purposes are most closely aligned with the key values? (The key values people hold will help sort out the larger purposes.)

Systems
- What purposes does this one support or help achieve (larger purposes)?
- Which purposes of the purpose hierarchy lead to the purposes of our customers and the customers' customers?

- How will the values, qualities, and beliefs of our organization help determine the scope of this purpose statement?
- What purposes are most closely aligned with our organization's mission, vision, and values?
- Does this purpose statement reflect measures of success or purpose accomplishment, so that we can know when we have achieved our purpose, for example, to increase sales by 10 percent, reduce costs by 25 percent, or minimize warranty claims? (See the list of verbs that are measures and values in Table 3.2.) If so, it and the other purpose statements like it should be put aside for consideration later in the Purposes Phase and not be included in the hierarchy.

For example, in the case about the committee charged with finding ways to better integrate a multifunctioned company, consider the following two purposes from their list:

- To have people working together when appropriate
- To create a system that meets the needs of our organization

Given these two possibilities, you want to know which is the larger purpose. Using the couplet test, the answer becomes clear by relating one statement to the other. So for these two purposes we ask:

1. Is the purpose "having people working together when appropriate" so that we can "create a system that meets the needs of our organization"?

2. Is the purpose of "creating a system that meets the needs of our organization" so that we can "have people working together when appropriate"?

In this case, statement 1 makes more sense. The purpose of having people work together is to create a system that meets the needs of the organization. So "to create a system that meets the needs of our organization" is the larger purpose, and "to have people working together when appropriate" is the smaller one.

On occasion, it may not be obvious which purpose is larger, or a group may not agree on which purpose encompasses the other. This dilemma points out how subjective the ordering of purposes can be. Although sorting purposes may seem easy because they are framed in simple sentence fragments, keep in mind that different people see them through their own lenses and may understand them in very different ways.

When a group breaks into two camps about which purpose is larger, you may be able to resolve the conflict by asking one side to define what each statement or even each word means, especially the verb, and then ask the other side to do the same. In many cases, refining each side's definitions can lead to closure, or at least to a recognition that both groups need to define their terms better. Changing the wording so that it makes sense to everyone often helps bring about agreement on which purpose is the larger one.

Asking about meaning and defining terms can be used at any time during the purposes hierarchy phase. As you will see, these types of exchanges can be invaluable in encouraging people to have open conversations about the purposes they want to achieve rather than spending their time in fault finding, blaming, and defensiveness, which is what usually occurs when people sit down to resolve problems in the reductionist approach. We have consistently found that discussions about purposes create exceptional team harmony. And even when they create conflicts, the logjams are easier to resolve because they focus on positive topics, which are what people care about, while building collective intuition and agreement.

Coming back to the hierarchy, the couplet test is used on all pairs of purposes until you have arranged them all into a sequence, from small to large. As the hierarchy is developed, especially when you have good discussions about meanings and definitions, it is common that groups discover or invent new purpose statements to add to their list, and others that were considered sacrosanct initially are not used. All additions are treated in the same way to arrive at a final hierarchy.

In the above case, the purpose hierarchy looked like the one in Figure 3.2.

Intuitive Method of Organizing Purposes. There are times when the work generated during the list step produces an abundance of purpose statements. For example, one group we worked with developed over 150 statements to express the purposes of a school that was being created for individually guided education. Another group we were working with identified nearly 90 purposes for an inner-city economic investment partnership.

To create a system that meets the needs of our organization
↑

To create subsystems that work together
↑

To perform the work correctly the first time
↑

To have people working together when appropriate
↑

To have people know when they need to work
together on something
↑

To have people knowledgeable about other people's work
↑

To define points of integration clearly
↑

To have someone appointed to be the "integration czar"

**Figure 3.2.　A Purposes Hierarchy for Integrating a
Multifunctional Organization**

Generating a huge number of purposes is especially common when working with individuals or groups without professional or organizational backgrounds, or many people from broad-based, general public groups where there is a wide range of opinions and understandings. In such cases, the intuitive methods for building purposes may be more effective because it is too chaotic to use the couplet method with scores or hundreds of purpose statements and a large number of people.

In the intuitive method, you teach people to sort and order the purposes according to three basic categories: small, medium, and large. You tell the group that you are going to ask them to decide if each purpose is small, medium, or large in scope. A good example usually helps them quickly understand what you mean. Figure 3.3 shows a useful example that works to illustrate what we mean by these three categories.

In working with a diverse group, it is important to stress that you are not belittling the purpose statements they have created; you are not saying that their purposes are small, medium, or large. However, the group must accept that they need to make a decision about each purpose statement relative to the others: Which ones are small, medium, and large in scope? In the case of the organization charged with integration, the group clustered their list of purpose statements as shown in Figure 3.4.

To be able to travel rapidly to anywhere at any time (Large Purpose)

↑

To have transportation (Medium Purpose)

↑

To have a bicycle (Small Purpose)

Figure 3.3.   Simple Example of a Small-Medium-Large Purposes Hierarchy

Note: More than three categories can be used, especially when dealing with a very large number of purposes—for example, very small, small-medium, medium-large, very large, big, and huge.

Keep in mind that there is no fast way to force a purpose hierarchy. As with the logical method, you will likely have people disagree at first about which purpose is larger than another. However, groups coalesce in assigning a category to each purpose statement if they spend time discussing their definitions and the meanings of words they use. In addition, once a large group has agreed on a handful of purpose statements, they can often proceed quickly to assign the remaining purposes using the couplet test by comparing each new statement with a purpose they have already classified.

As with the logical method, do not be surprised to find people wanting to add new purposes or reclassify old ones as the process unfolds. The point of arranging them into a coherent whole is that it enables you or the group to select more easily which ones they want to have as their focus purpose to achieve.

Some companies tend to think of themselves as having very large purposes, such as "increase market share," "make a profit," "improve competitive position," "create shareholder value," and so on. Such supposed purpose statements are too often written from the narrow viewpoint of the company, not from the customers' or customers' customers' view. Other than wanting you to stay in existence for service and upgrades, customers do not care about your measures of success. Your hierarchy of purposes should deal at large levels with statements that your customers, users, or customers' customers want accomplished. Organizations of all types need the largest purposes of their hierarchies to be customer or client oriented if they are to get on the path to success. This focus will also help inculcate strategic thinking in most of the organization's behavior.

LARGE PURPOSES

To create a system that meets the needs of our organization

To create subsystems that work together

↑

MEDIUM PURPOSES

To eliminate rework

To have people working together when appropriate

↑

SMALL PURPOSES

To have people know when they need to work together
on something

To have people knowledgeable about other people's work

To define points of integration clearly

To have someone appointed to be the "integration czar"

**Figure 3.4.   Cluster Hierarchy for Integrating a
Multifunctional Organization**

ADDING INTERMEDIARY PURPOSES. When first building your hierarchy, do not be surprised to find that you need to insert some new purposes here and there in your ladder to prevent the incremental steps from being too large. For example, continuing the example shown in Figure 3.2, if the purpose "to have someone be appointed the 'integration czar'" had as its next bigger step "to have people working together when appropriate," most people would sense that the latter purpose was too large a jump in thinking and that one or more purposes needed to be added between them.

You can often tell that a jump is too large when people claim they cannot see a connection between two purposes when the couplet method is used. This is usually an indication that a new middle-size purpose statement or two needs to be inserted between the two. A key smart question to clarify the purposes and fill in the gaps is often, "What are some incrementally larger purposes of this smaller one that will eventually have the second one as its purpose as well?"

Overall, making a purpose hierarchy is usually a successful way to be sure you are phrasing purpose statements in the most effective way and setting up a contextual framework for creating a solution. In our many years of experience with SQA, we have never had a case where the final hierarchy used in the effort was the same as the initial one. People always recognize that their initial purpose statement restricts them to a narrow creative space, and they become willing and excited to explore larger and larger creative spaces and purposes.

The Decide Step

Once you have gotten agreement and built a coherent purpose hierarchy, the final task is to choose a single focus purpose or purposes. Asking smart questions will help determine which purpose generates the optimal creative space to accomplish the solution creation effort. In some cases, there may be more than one focus purpose, such as when the two or three purposes next to each other in a hierarchy seem to be very similar.

The focus purpose guides the thinking in the remaining SQA phases. It is what you continually refer back to as you create a future solution and a living solution. It is a metaphoric North Star that ensures you stay on course to your destination.

As we have pointed out, people commonly make the mistake of selecting too small a purpose for the task. This reduces their efforts to creating small solutions for small problems.

Choosing small purposes often happens when people believe that these are the most easily definable ones and the only ones for which they have the power to change. For instance, recall the stamping operation in a manufacturing company. When the manager in the company who knew SQA told me about the case, he pointed out that after he had the group go through the purpose list step and then organize a purpose hierarchy, they balked at picking too large a purpose as their focus purpose. They stated that they believed that upper management would not want them "messing around" with something for which they did not have responsibility. Nevertheless, the manager encouraged the group to expand their creative space by reminding them how much they complain about "the guys in product design," not ever thinking about what their designs meant in terms of manufacturing processes and by giving examples of possible solution ideas that some of their larger purposes offered.

TECHNIQUES FOR DECIDING PURPOSES. The same basic rules guiding decision making in the People Involvement Phase are also used to select the focus purpose from the purpose hierarchy. A decision of any sort has four major components:

1. The purpose of the decision (in this phase, to select the focus purpose)
2. Alternatives or options to consider for achieving that purpose
3. Criteria, factors, or considerations to use in evaluating the alternatives
4. A method for assessing the alternative options in terms of the criteria

We will discuss the criteria and methods for assessing the alternatives shortly, but we begin with how the three foundation questions provide a basis for deciding on the focus purpose. The box sets out some smart questions to ask to start selecting your focus purpose.

The decide step in the purposes phase uses the purpose hierarchy that has been created in the organize phase and decides what purpose or purposes are the most appropriate to provide a focus for the solution creation effort. The box provides examples of the types of questions that are used to decide the focus purpose.

Similar to the organizing step, there are two general approaches to selecting a focus purpose: a logical method and an intuitive method.

Logical Method of Deciding Purposes. The logical method that we most often use is to develop criteria to help us decide what ought to be the focus purpose. The criteria (or rationale or reasons, in the words of the manager discussed above) for selecting a focus purpose are related to what scope the specific organization will permit for the solution creation effort. For example, the upper management of the company with the stamping problem might be dogmatic about the scope of this project ("you guys are in manufacturing, so stick to your knitting"), in which case, their dictum would keep the group to selecting a smaller purpose. Or they could be more open to discussion about what they would let such a group propose (which, in our view, makes sense for the good of the company).

～ SMART QUESTIONS FOR THE PURPOSE PHASE

Decide Step

In the process of converging your ideas to arrive at the results sought in the Purposes Phase, it continues to be useful to ask smart questions to ensure that you get the most effective and creative focus purpose for which you will develop a solution. The foundation questions can guide you in asking these questions or others that stem from your situation.

Uniqueness
- What focus purposes arising from considering the initial issue should we seek to achieve to make sure we are working on the right issue?
- What are the unique criteria, factors, or considerations of our organization we may need to use to make a decision about the focus purpose in addition to those related to this particular situation?
- Are there unique weightings or importance factors the organization gives to these criteria?
- Does our organization use a particular format for assessing alternatives in making a decision, and is it applicable for selecting a focus purpose?
- Given the uniqueness of the people involved and the situation, what purposes seem to have the largest creative space that is accomplishable?

Purposeful Information
- What information will help us choose a focus purpose (such as organizational mission, sponsor expectations, market conditions, or customer expectations)?
- How much inaccurate and imprecise information about the criteria and assessment methods are we willing to tolerate in making a decision for this situation?
- What adjustments might we have to make in the hierarchy to make each purpose statement understandable as an alternative to consider in making the choice of a focus purpose?
- How long might we have to wait until more reasonable information will be available to answer these questions?

Systems
- Can people begin to envision what the system elements—its inputs, outputs, processes, environment, human agents, catalysts, and information aids elements—might be for each purpose level?
- What parts (elements) of the whole organizational system may need to be involved in making the selection of focus purpose?
- Are there parts of the organization's strategic plan that could affect the selection of a focus purpose?

Here are some illustrations of the criteria or rationale we have found that organizations use in making the decision about what ought to be the focus purpose. Not all of them will be used in every project, several are overlapping, and others could be useful in specific situations:

- Potential benefits of focusing on this purpose level

- Cost of a solution creation effort at this purpose level

- Probability of implementing a living solution developed at this purpose level

- Time available for developing a living solution at this purpose level

- Management desires in relation to this purpose level

- Organizational factors involved at this purpose level

- Lack of restrictions, obstacles, or barriers at this purpose level

- Future use of any future solution ideas at this purpose level

- Potential for controlling the operation of a possible living solution at this purpose level

- Impact of a due date for a recommendation at this purpose level

- Availability of resources to do a project at this purpose level

- Impact on long-term customer relationships from a living solution at this purpose level

- Eagerness of the organization to be a trendsetter with future and living solutions at this purpose level

For example, in the case of the committee charged with the integration effort that we discussed earlier, there were two key factors or criteria that they decided to use:

- The probability of a successful launch of their new manufacturing facility and computer system. The rationale for this factor was based on the company's having already invested millions of dollars in a new system. They needed the additional capacity and had to justify the expense to stockholders.

- The likelihood that the chosen purpose would permit them to overcome long-standing organizational barriers of working across functional boundaries. It was clear that the old ways of working in silos no longer was effective with new manufacturing methods and technologies.

Having decided on these two criteria, the committee began to apply them to the purpose hierarchy to select their focus purpose from among all the purposes listed. The process always begins at the largest purpose in the hierarchy with checking it against the criteria.

In this case, the group considered the largest purpose: "To create a system that meets the needs of our organization." It met the first criterion because a key part of the new manufacturing facility was the new computer system. But it did not meet the second criterion because just implementing the new system would not necessarily solve the people problem of working across boundaries. So, the first purpose met one of the criteria but not the other.

They then turned to the next largest purpose: to create subsystems that work together. It did not meet the second criterion. They then looked at the next largest purpose: to perform the work correctly the first time. It also did not address the second criterion. They then examined the next largest purpose: to have people working together when appropriate. It did meet the first and second criteria.

In the end, the group chose two focus purposes to guide their design effort:

- To create a system that meets the needs of our organization
- To have people working together when appropriate

Although the group initially considered the first purpose as not meeting both criteria, they ultimately decided to include it as a focus purpose because, in combination with the second purpose, it intuitively felt like the right approach for guiding the project's work. This demonstrates that deciding on an appropriate focus in many solution-creating efforts is more of an art than a science.

In certain complex cases, you may need to use more formal decision-making tools to ensure that all four components of the decision are thoroughly accounted for. For example, constructing a simple matrix with rows for the four criteria and columns for the different purposes from the hierarchy produces intersections where a group of people could formally evaluate how well each criterion is fulfilled for each purpose. You could mark each intersection in any way that works for you—a simple yes or no; a subjective scale using words like *poor, fair, average,* or *above average*; or a numerical ranking. A decision worksheet for a more detailed and thorough assessment of alternatives is discussed in Chapters Four and Five.

In summary, the general process of using the logical method of decision making is as follows:

1. Select the key criteria that guide the selection of the scope of a solution creation effort for your situation. Most cases will involve more than two criteria in selecting a focus purpose.

2. Determine a method for matching criteria against focus purposes: intuitive or more formal, such as the matrix described above.

3. Match the criteria against your purposes starting with the largest one to see which purpose levels fulfill the criteria most effectively.

4. Select the focus purpose. If you use a numerical method in matching criteria against purposes, do not automatically select the purpose level with the "best" total. If some other purpose levels have totals close to the best (plus or minus 5 to 10 percent), consider them as the possible focus purpose. As we noted in Chapter One, all measurements are inaccurate; further discussion about the one with the "best" score may indicate that more than one should be included in the focus purpose statement.

In general, the fewer focus purposes you end up with, the better. Having a small number allows the focus to be crisp and clear. We do not advise more than three. One is ideal.

The Intuitive Method of Deciding Purposes. The intuitive method of choosing a focus purpose from the hierarchy is simpler and faster, but it can be used only in circumstances that lend themselves to intuitive decision making. In this method, you ask the group of people involved if any of the larger purposes stands out as being the most viable focus purpose. In certain situations, the intuition of many people aligns, and you find that the entire group agrees on one clear purpose. Even if the group narrows the choices down to two or three purposes, it is likely a good indication that they have chosen the right ones. The intuitive method is particularly reliable when the group has had a lot of good discussion about the issues and purposes and everyone is confidently aligned about what each purpose means.

Another intuitive method to use is what we call the multivoting purpose selection process. Multivoting provides each participant with a number of votes that they can cast to determine which purposes they believe should be the focus. As a general rule, we give each participant one-third the number of votes as there are purposes. For example, if there are thirty total purposes in the hierarchy, we give each participant ten votes. They can then allocate their votes in any amounts for any purposes they want for the focus. They can cast their ten votes for just one purpose or spread them out over several purposes. After each person has cast his or her vote, we tally the total votes for each purpose to determine the winners. Then we talk about the apparent choices with the group to make sure that the purposes with the most votes really make sense to choose as the focus purposes or if a few key purposes sort themselves out of the pack instead.

If the group is not able to align on the focus purpose using this intuitive method, you can revert back to the logical method. It is important, however, to select a focus purpose within its context of all the larger purposes because it establishes "true north" for the solution creation efforts. In all cases, keep the purposes larger than the focus one in front of the group and yourself. In addition to reminding everyone to think about the larger context, these larger purposes will be used in the future solution and even the living solution phases.

Other Possible Techniques for Deciding. In addition to the decide techniques we have already described, there are several others we use from time to time:

- Each person gets one vote to assign to any purpose statement he or she considers the best focus.
- A top executive is asked to select the focus purpose.
- Each person ranks his or her top three choices, and then the votes are tallied.
- Each person assigns a score or value to each purpose statement reflecting the person's judgment about the likelihood of the purpose being achieved with a breakthrough or least-cost solution.
- A focus group of customers, suppliers, external experts, and strategy personnel in the company selects the focus purpose.

ENSURING THAT YOU ARE DECIDING ON THE RIGHT FOCUS PURPOSE. It is possible to choose the "wrong" focus purpose. In the heat of battle, through misunderstanding, ongoing conflicts, or an ineffective facilitator, poor decisions can be made initially.

For this reason, we suggest one additional action after the decide step in which you take the time to identify some measures that will help you evaluate how well the installed solutions are working to help you achieve your focus purpose. Unless you know those measures and can find ways to quantify them to define success, you will be forever chasing rainbows to find an elusive pot of gold. Just as certain measures originally identified the need for a solution creation effort to begin with, you now need to determine some new or modified measures to assess how well your focus purpose can be accomplished. In almost all cases, the focus purpose should be larger than the purpose that started the effort and thus is very likely to need other indicators that would show how well it is being accomplished.

Begin defining specific factors that should be measured to indicate eventually whether your purpose is being accomplished after installation of a living solution. For each focus purpose, we ask people to define specific, trackable factors that can be measured to quantify how well the focus purpose is being achieved once the living solution is installed. In addition, if it seems appropriate, we ask what their expectation level is regarding each factor, in the form of a "most challenging" number for the living solution after it is installed. (By *appropriate,* we mean situations where such expectation values would help make the case to management that the scope of the solution creation effort should be as big as the focus purpose would seem to encourage.) Possible factors to consider as a basis of determining how well the focus purposes are being achieved (or how successful is the living solution and its planned changes) can be found by asking the following questions:

- Are there any change-of-state criteria that apply, such as reduction of costs, maximizing shareholder wealth, making fewer mistakes, reducing delivery time, or producing more parts?
- What measures would be used for the factors we consider for our wish list?
- What indicators, such as controlling, budgeting, or motivating, do we care about?
- What are our aspirations?
- What factors are competitors emphasizing?
- What environmental, safety, health, and other social factors ought to be considered?
- How do we measure the contribution of this focus purpose to our larger strategic purposes?
- What do our stakeholders want?

Defining these factors can be very useful in ensuring that you select the best focus purpose. For example, in the case of the organization with the integration problem, we asked the group to develop measures for each of their two focus purposes. For the purpose, "to create a system that meets the needs of our organization," they chose two factors: (1) to have a yearly survey of key users and (2) to track the number of problem tickets that were generated by the help desk for the system. The initial level that they chose for the user satisfaction survey was 90 percent satisfaction for the first year and 95 percent for the next two years. They figured that if they could achieve 95 percent satisfaction for two years, they might be able to end the yearly surveys and feel the purpose was being very well achieved.

For the purpose, "to have people working together when appropriate," the group decided that the best factor to measure was to have a monthly meeting of the cross-functional managers to discuss and tally breakdowns in the key defined integration tasks that had been reported by their employees. They set an objective for the first year of fifty or fewer breakdowns per month. The whole manufacturing organization was approximately five thousand employees. They figured that if less than 1 percent of employees were having significant problems in a month, it was a good objective. Their goal after two years was ten or fewer breakdowns per month. They agreed that they might cancel the regular integration meeting if they had six consecutive months of fewer than ten breakdowns. They figured that they could deal with sporadic breakdowns as needed after that.

Keep in mind that because the selected focus purpose in many situations is often larger than the originally stated problem, the factors that caused you to work on the issue are often insufficient or even inappropriate for determining how well the selected focus purpose is being achieved. The alteration or addition of new factors may thus mean that it is necessary to identify new data that will need to be collected in order to get approval to go forward with the project or to know what measurements will need to be made when the living solution is installed.

For example, a hospital faced with a shortage of nurses defined its problem as improving the utilization of nurses (the factor to be measured). The level of this measure it selected to justify the start of a solution creation effort to achieve its assumed purpose of "to use current nurses on staff" was a 15 percent improvement. But after working with us to redevelop their focus purpose, which became "to provide nursing services to patients," several other factors became as important to them, such as response time to patient calls, on-time delivery of medications, rate of secondary infections, and number of patient complaints.

A few of these factors did not even have available data collection methods set up with which to base the evaluation of possible solution options. The hospital had to set up (with SQA) new data collection methods to assess the current level of these factors even while the design effort went forward. However, the solution that was recommended and installed achieved significant improvements in all the measures, including a 48 percent increase in nurse utilization.

Nevertheless, because any measurement is only a representation of reality, it is important to consider nondata factors to round out your assessment of success with any given living solution. For example, many companies resort to using customer satisfaction as a factor to measure how well their purposes are being achieved, and so they do customer surveys to collect data that they think will validate the expected level. However, we have found that data from customer surveys are often far from sufficient, even if the response rate is high. In-person discussions with a number of customers can often provide far greater insights about future needs or purposes and help you keep your hierarchy of purposes up to date.

KEEPING A FOCUS ON PURPOSES FROM THE TRENCHES

It is easy to think about purposes when you have a trained facilitator to help select a focus purpose or when you are isolated from the hectic environment and constant interruptions of the modern businessperson, teacher, politician, or parent. In reality, this is seldom the case. For many people, focusing on and discussing purposes must be done in the heat of battle, when they are pressed for time and creative space. Many organizations are also loathe to reexamine purposes when they have already committed millions of dollars and missed deadlines on the way to the finish line of a project that they were formerly certain was the right solution.

However, we suggest that it is always worthwhile, if not absolutely necessary, to examine purposes, even when you are in the trenches. In fact, it is when you are most absorbed in fighting fires or in an adversarial position that you need to come back to exploring your purposes. Without a focus on purposes, you can easily end up spending a day looking busy and working hard but accomplishing results with little or no significance. A focus on purposes is a focus on results. Only then can you work on what is most important and what will feel the most satisfying to you personally. Being clear about your purpose (mission, function, need, intent) also gives you the freedom to seek large-scale change and to make smart decisions quickly.

I worked with one client from an organization whose departments were essentially at war with one another. They were struggling with a tight deadline in order to finish a project, and they were already six months behind. They all wanted to do the right thing to get the project back on track, but they could not seem to break out of the cycle of constant conflict between departments.

I suggested that they take an hour or two and talk about the purposes of what they were trying to achieve. I held an impromptu mini-workshop on purposes, when we brought to the surface some of the reasons people harbored for behaving antagonistically toward one another. Through the course of these discussions, people realized that they were far more aligned about their purposes and what they were trying to accomplish than they had assumed. The sharing that occurred during this impromptu meeting created far more under- standing between the parties, and a new generosity took root about how they needed to accept one another's ideas. This established a firmer foundation for their work relationships and opened up avenues for dialogue that had been previously unavailable.

You do not need to have an all-out war in your organization to explore (or reexplore) your purposes. Even silent conflicts and resent- ments usually mean that it is time to refocus on your purposes and use at least the list and organize steps. For example, in Harvard University ethnographer Leslie A. Perlow's book *When You Say Yes But Mean No: How Silencing Conflict Wrecks Relationships and Companies . . . and What You Can Do About It* (2003), she cites a case where engineers spent many hours each week putting an elaborate report together for the weekly meeting with their boss. Because the company's prevailing culture was to accommodate management's requests, the engineers remained silent even though they had told the boss that the report was a waste of time. The irony was that the boss considered the meeting a waste of time, but he felt the engineers might think he was not inter- ested in what they were doing if he called off the meetings.

This is an example of a silent problem where using smart questions with a focus on purposes would have benefited everyone. Both the boss and the engineers could have come together to ask, "What's the purpose of the meeting?" and the ensuing dialogue and expansion of purposes would have provided them with the knowledge to cancel the meetings, find alternative ways to make them more productive, or achieve any newly defined purposes. The boss could have equally helped the situation if he had asked the purposes questions when the engineers told him the reports and meetings were a waste of time.

Whenever you are in the heat of battle, keep in mind the difference between your focus purpose and all the other factors by which you define success. We have many executives who hire us to consult on a problem and when we ask them about their purposes, they answer something like, "to make a 15 percent yearly profit." This is not a pur- pose statement that can lead to solving problems and creating living solutions. Making profits is a factor that measures accomplishment. It is not a purpose. Executives who focus on profit need to return to understanding their organization's purpose. What do they want to *accomplish* for which the 15 percent would indicate the successful implementation of a living solution? This question is also a reminder that everyone involved in an organization—workers, suppliers, and customers—will sense a disrespectful, exploitative, and manipulative relationship with the organization if its mission is defined solely as "to make a profit."

WHEN YOU DON'T HAVE A COACH

What do you do if you don't happen to have an SQA coach to help you focus on your purposes in the heat of the battle? To use a golfing metaphor, let us suggest that you tap into what we call "a daily swing thought." In golf, a swing thought is a single idea that you keep in mind during every swing. Good golf instructors realize that it is counterproductive for duffers to think about too many rules when they are learning how to swing a golf club. They therefore suggest limiting thinking to just one appropriate swing thought that keeps the focus on one major technique that will make a difference in the drive.

As this metaphor suggests, swing thoughts can be very useful in the heat of the battle when you are reflecting on the purposes of your problems. You keep your mind focused on one key purpose throughout the day. For example, while I was coaching a colleague about a personal problem, he developed the swing thought that what he needed was to "have peace." Another colleague created the swing thought "to find a place where I can make a difference." This thought helped her avoid getting sucked into the conflicts and problems that arose in her company throughout the day so she could stay focused on the major issues of importance to her project.

HIGHLIGHTS OF THE PURPOSES PHASE

- Purposes must frame your solution creation efforts. It is critical that you begin with the right purposes that give you a large enough creative space or mental playground to do problem solving or design.

- A thorough and meaningful consideration of purposes helps you articulate the assumptions hidden in your thinking and refocuses you on your values.

• The process of defining and refining your purposes begins with an understanding of the three foundation questions in terms of how they affect your purposes and the specific smart questions you ask in your situation.

• You follow the smart question steps of list, organize, and decide.

• In the list step, you generate as many possible purposes as you can, using either structured or intuitive methods to generate them.

• You organize the possible purposes into a hierarchy, from smallest purposes to largest purposes, using either the couplet method that compares pairs of purposes or simple categories such as small, medium, and large by which the people involved decide the scope of each purpose. A hierarchy should be expanded to relate your purposes to those the customer—client, patient, student, constituency—and the customer's customer seek to achieve.

• You select one or perhaps two focus purposes that become the North Star, along with the context of its larger purposes, to guide the next phases.

• You choose a few key factors to measure how well those purposes are to be achieved in a living solution.

• These factors may require you to rethink your focus purpose or choose a new one. This reinforces the iterative and back-and-forth nature within the LOD steps and among the four PPFL phases we discussed in Chapter One.

• Keeping your purposes in mind even in the heat of your daily battles is crucial. Whether the problem or issue at hand has created blatant antagonism or silent resentments among the people or departments involved, reviewing purposes helps direct everyone's focus on what really matters. Reviewing purposes using SQA prevents people from engaging in territorial conflicts, petty rivalries, and limited thinking and negativity.

CHAPTER FOUR

SQA Phase 3

Creating an Ideal Future Solution

*Do not go where the path may lead, go instead where there
is no path and leave a trail.*

—Ralph Waldo Emerson

*A common mistake that people make when trying to design
something completely foolproof is to underestimate the
ingenuity of complete fools.*

—Douglas Adams

T he purposes phase of SQA helped you define what
you want to achieve within a larger context of purposes. Now the
question is *how* to achieve that purpose in terms of what solution and
system to create and implement. That's what the future solution phase
helps you begin figuring out (along with the living solution phase that
follows in the next chapter).

A future solution is a vision or scenario of an ideal solution that
achieves the focus purpose you would like to see implemented at some
point in the future if and when the conditions were ideal. It sets up a
target solution that you will attempt to stay close to implementing in
the living solution phase. In other words, the future solution is a sort
of ideal model for the living solution you will be trying to install to
meet your initial milestones. It provides the map to guide the solution creation effort. It ensures that you do not get lost and end up with
an implemented solution that is not what you and your organization
really need.

In practical terms, a future solution is framed by four components:

1. A creative, forward-thinking plan for how to achieve your focus purpose

2. A sense of details—enough to define the elements of the future solution

3. Information to collect and research to do regarding any preparations that might need to be made

4. A time frame for implementing the solution in whatever period of time you designate

The concept of a future solution represents a major departure from the reductionist problem-solving paradigm, which has no such step. Because most people were educated to use the reductionist approach, it is absolutely crucial to understand the purposes and values gained with future solutions.

THE COMPONENTS OF A FUTURE SOLUTION

The following brief review of the four components of a future solution will provide more insight into the definition of a future solution.

A Creative, Forward-Thinking Framework for Achieving Your Purposes

A future solution is a forward-thinking solution—and we mean that literally. It refers to a level of solution that cannot be installed now because it is so forward thinking. Perhaps the technology is not available yet, the conditions are not yet right, you do not know how all of the system components would work, or other systems must be changed first. Whatever the reasons, the solution is so far ahead of the game that it simply cannot take place now.

We once worked with a hospital that wanted to develop a medication administration system. Rather than just think about a small fix to the hospital's problems with medication administration, the team developed a forward-thinking vision that foresaw the automated delivery of medicines to patients, providing just the right dose at the right time to the right patient's bedside, with automated monitoring of the patient taking the medicine. Although this vision was not yet implementable, it provided the framework for what eventually became a living solution and for what the medication administration system would become once the hospital remodels or builds a new hospital.

Another way to think of a future solution is that it represents what your competitor is going to come up with after you have developed your solution. In whatever competitive world you operate—whether personal, organizational, or societal—a future solution is what you create when you go back to the drawing board when your competitors have bested you.

A Sense of Details

The Purposes Phase has already expanded your creative thinking space by helping you reframe how you view the issue. Now the future solution helps you flesh out those ideas. However, the future solution framework must be more than a superficial concept or set of words. In terms of the hospital case, for example, you cannot just say that you want an automated medication administration system. You need to begin thinking about the details of how it might operate.

In fact, "How would it work?" becomes an often-repeated question as you explore every part of your future solution until most people in your organization can see the specific framework you have in mind. The automated system of medication administration, for instance, might be detailed as follows: "The pharmacist places the prescribed medicine in a bin for the patient, where a computerized program has a robot arm pick up one dose and place it in a chute going to the patient's tray; electronic sensors on the tray and the patient's throat would detect if the medicine were taken; and a report would then be prepared for the nurse to provide monitoring."

It is only when you talk in terms of this type of detail that others can understand what the system might look like and then ask themselves how regarding any parts of the system that are their responsibility. Clearly, the details are still futuristic and speculative at this time, but they should provide at least a cohesive, if still blue-sky, scenario of what that idea is.

Information to Collect and Research to Do Regarding Preparations

The object of developing a vision, framework, and details for how each idea of the future solution would work is to learn more about the type of information you may need to collect and the further investigations you may need to perform to obtain the greatest benefit from your solution. Getting this information allows you to help fashion your own future rather than waiting for the future to happen to you. In addition, since there is no way to predict what the future may bring, gathering information about your potential future solution provides you with a much better preparation for that uncertain future than collecting data about the past history of a problem. As we stated earlier, you want to become an expert in the solution rather than in the problem. This attitude is what leads to breakthroughs.

A Time Frame

Every situation that gets you started to create a solution has a rough expected time frame for completion. Every project our colleagues and we have worked on has at least a due date for installing a living solution, which largely predefines a time frame for the future solution. However, remember that all you need at this time is a rough approximation; you can be flexible here, allowing for further iterations that might change or expand the focus purpose you selected or the details of your future solution. Or as you create your future solution, you may find it so appealing that you are willing to live with a shorter or longer time frame than you initially expected.

THE VALUE OF A FUTURE SOLUTION

You may be wondering what purposes are served with a future solution. Why bother thinking about creating a solution that is not immediately doable and targets options at some future time? The answer is that there are two very good reasons for thinking about future solutions:

• They require you to think about what an ideal solution would be.

• They require you to anticipate the future.

Let's explore these two issues in greater depth.

Thinking About Ideal Solutions

Most problem-solving techniques dismiss, underemphasize, or disregard the concept of creating ideal solutions. Many leaders and organizations believe that ideal solutions are not achievable, so there is no reason to waste time, effort, and money thinking about and planning them. This attitude is visible in such reactions as, "Well, the ideal solution for our company is to automate more processes, but that would be too expensive," or "Our customers like things the way they are now," or "Our system works fine now, so why try to improve it?"

So why think about ideal solutions? What can be gained by spending time developing an ideal solution? Actually, there are numerous benefits to creating ideal solutions. They help you and others involved in the project in a number of ways to:

- Enlarge your creative space, to create a bigger vision of what you want
- Elevate your thinking beyond obvious first answers that come immediately to mind when you are problem solving
- Consider or reconsider if there are any larger purposes to your problem
- Question assumed barriers and constraints without considering their actual validity or recognizing your capability to go around them
- Develop a framework for what you need to do to put yourself in the ideal position where you would actually like to be
- Build early momentum to do increasingly creative work such as pursuing a significant R&D project or sketching out how a new system might work
- Provide a better road map to the team creating the solution
- Think systematically about what it will take to implement your solution

Figure 4.1 illustrates how thinking about ideal solutions can prove useful. Looking at this figure, imagine that your focus purpose is "to fulfill a customer order." Assume that the measure of purpose accomplishment in this case is the time taken from receipt to shipment of

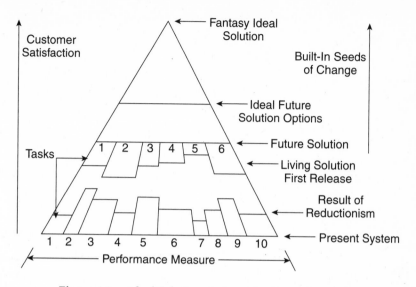

Figure 4.1.   Ideal Solution Concept for Focus Purposes

the order. Now, using this graphic, let the distance between the legs of the triangle represent the time it takes to arrive at fulfilling an order. The line at the bottom end of the triangle represents the current time for achieving the purpose.

Now assume that the problem was presented to you specifically as, "Can we reduce the time taken by 25 percent?" In conventional thinking, one usually approaches time reduction problems like this by first examining the individual tasks or segments of the process to determine if and where time can be saved. For example, you might go over the data about the first task of the existing way of fulfilling the order that you collected and ask how the task can be done faster, then determine how much time it would save here. The horizontal line at the top of the vertical bar above the first task represents the new time that changing the first task would take, and you would then note the percentage of total time saved by that component. You would then ask the same questions about the other individual tasks in the order fulfillment operation until you could find ways to shave time off as many of them as possible so that the total is around 25 percent. You almost always stop seeking any additional time saving because "we solved the problem" and "we gave the boss what he wanted."

In contrast, here's what happens when you think in terms of SQA and future solutions. Assume you have already worked through the People Involvement and Purposes phases to determine the focus purpose and the measures of purpose accomplishment. But do you automatically adopt the originally stated goal of 25 percent time reduction? No. This is actually too small an improvement when considered from a future solution perspective.

This is where thinking in terms of a future solution comes in. In a future solution, you could theoretically conceive of a 100 percent reduction in time. Look again at the triangle in Figure 4.1, and notice that the triangle comes to an apex. The apex is the point at which fulfilling a customer's request in zero time is located. Of course, zero time is absurd; you cannot fulfill a customer's request in zero time. Hence, this solution represents a fantasy future solution because it is impossible to achieve.

Nevertheless, there is value in thinking about a fantasy future solution. Rather than trying to scrounge for ways to shave small amounts of time off each individual task in the customer service operation, you use the 100 percent as a guide and thus begin to seek creative ways that might completely alter how the whole operation works, perhaps resulting in a savings of 35 percent or 50 percent or 80 percent of the time.

Look again at Figure 4.1. The second line below the apex is what we have labeled the future solution. This solution does take time to accomplish, but it reflects the potential 30, 50, or 80 percent reduction in time we just alluded to. You might say that this is as ideal as it can get, given the available technology, capital expenditure amounts, or time frame available for achieving the focus purpose selected. (The horizontal lines below the future solution line is the living solution, as you will learn about in the next chapter. As the figure shows, the living solution is not usually the same as the future solution because the latter is an ideal, largely unattainable goal. But what Figure 4.1 indicates is that the living solution aims to get as close to the future solution as possible.)

We have inspired many clients to think about future solutions. I was once asked by the president of a large hospital whose board of directors was quite unhappy with the way the hospital was performing. He wanted me to help them develop a "productivity improvement" program, and his original goal was to reduce overall costs by

15 percent, an amount he considered an enviable goal in the hospital industry. Part of his rationale was that he believed that a productivity improvement program had a better chance of being accepted by hospital personnel than would something labeled a cost reduction program.

I began by asking if he would be happy if the hospital reduced costs by 100 percent, an infinite increase in productivity. After he stopped laughing (and hinting he would throw me out of his office), I asked, "What would be the impact on your organization of a 15 percent cost reduction, even though it would be disguised as a productivity improvement program?" He thought a moment and essentially gave the answer: much resistance and unhappiness throughout the organization.

We then used SQA with a team he assembled to work on the issue, but in terms that he had previously told them about: "setting up a productivity program." In the purposes phase, the team wound up selecting as a focus purpose "to provide patient care services and to have patients return to self-sufficiency in the community." In addition, the team selected the following measures of purpose accomplishment: hospital-based infection rate (ideal level of zero), increase in productivity levels based on industry-wide standards (ideal level sought, 200 percent), and attaining the highest market share in the respective communities (ideally as close to 40 percent as possible). As a result of expanding their creative thinking space and thinking ideally, the team developed an interesting future solution in which the medical charts and all supplies (medicines, linens, therapeutic devices, and all of the others) for each patient would be located in a secure locker in that patient's room, thus freeing up time for nurses to spend with patients instead of running around gathering all the needed paraphernalia. The installed living solution did not involve the degree of remodeling that the future solution would have required, but it served as a guide for developing more effective ways of using the existing closet and storage spaces, changing the location of patient charts, using the staff's skills more effectively, and setting up computerized information systems.

In effect, this future solution inspired the entire hospital to install a living solution that achieved goals far greater than the 15 percent cost reduction that the president had imagined. And this was formerly considered a poorly performing hospital.

Anticipating the Future

The second reason for developing a future solution is that it forces you to think about and plan for the future. Just as any solution for an issue exists within a framework of complex interrelations among people and other systems, it also exists in a framework of time. It is not an isolated dead-end event but a segment on a continuum that is always subject to change and improvement.

Thinking in terms of future solutions is thus critical to how you develop and shape the solution you install today. Asking what is possible or likely to happen down the road keeps your decisions today linked to what might be possible in the future. By mentally putting yourself at a point in the future when you might have to work on this problem again, you save yourself a lot of headaches by considering that future time now. The insight you gain improves your immediate solution and helps you incorporate future adaptations into your current solution efforts.

Imagine, for example, a street intersection noted for causing a rash of accidents. The obvious solution is to install a traffic signal. Although this may seem like a reasonable solution, it may not be the best one if you were thinking about what the future could bring to this intersection. For instance, a better future solution would consider what might happen to this intersection a few years from now. Perhaps the traffic patterns may increase so much that a traffic circle or a clover-leaf intersection would be a better future solution than a light. Or perhaps you may foresee the need to build alternative routes around the intersection because the city plan calls for some new condominiums to be built nearby. Or perhaps you may recognize that a significant improvement would be to offer greater public transportation to ease congestion in the city. Recognizing that you will be faced with traffic growth, thinking about these types of future solutions becomes key to avoid precluding many other good possibilities.

Similarly, a plan to modernize a factory that produces a certain type of paint would be deficient without questioning whether five or ten years hence, there will still be a market for that type of paint and what the technology might be then for manufacturing it. Think about the issues of lead as an additive in paint. The answers to these questions are instrumental in deciding whether the plant could be designed with built-in adaptability for whatever comes next in the paint industry, or perhaps as a bare-bones structure that might be convertible to something entirely else, such as a bakery should the market for paint appear to be diminishing.

Given that all solutions have implications for the future, it is important to recognize that no matter how perfect they may seem today, they are merely transitional steps to a different future. Understanding this is a key to breakthroughs. Time, people, policies, and new purposes inevitably alter all original purposes, so every solution must be formed with the probability of change built in.

THINKING HOLISTICALLY ABOUT A FUTURE SOLUTION

As in the other SQA phases, the three foundation questions guide the development of crafting the outcome of this phase: a future solution. These three questions provide extensive stimuli to raise your "Smart Questions IQ" during the LOD process of this phase, helping you get a better handle on what types of smart questions you need to ask yourself.

SQA Foundation Question 1: How Does My Unique Situation Help Create a Future Solution?

The uniqueness foundation question is a constant reminder that the future solution must be based on—and take advantage of—the uniqueness of your situation, particularly in regard to the systems affected—even those outside your organization. Respecting the uniqueness factor requires perseverance to reject quick cookie-cutter answers or solutions borrowed from other organizations, no matter how successful they may seem in other contexts. Although borrowed solutions can often appear to offer cost savings, faster results, and easily implementable actions, they invariably fail to create a truly unique scenario that fits your situation.

Let us clarify also that the latest rage or craze among management techniques does not count as an ideal solution. We have seen it happen many times when a manager proclaims the latest theory du jour (Total Quality Management, reengineering, Six Sigma, lean manufacturing, and the others) as the "ideal" solution and then rushes to adopt it, imposing the structures defined by the trend's promoters. But accepting the latest craze, no matter how much you adapt it, is not the same as creating your own future solution based on your situation, and the results typically prove it. In fact, we get a lot of consulting assignments from companies that have adopted a "canned" program, only to discover it does not work for them. Typically, they suffer from analysis paralysis from all the data, significant resistance to the program from employees, costs of implementing the program's structure far exceed what the promoters projected—or all of the above.

It is far better to fashion your own unique ideal image of a future solution, given what your system, product, or organization needs to look like in the future. This is what the leading creators of solutions invariably seek to build: a clear vision of the system or solution they want to install for achieving *their* focus purpose. This is not to say that various elements of canned programs are not worthwhile from time to time, but they should not be the starting point for crafting a future solution.

For example, the board of directors of a $1.5 billion company with nearly 250 profit center business units wanted to install a Total Quality Management (TQM) program in all units to solve numerous problems they were having, including losing out on many new contracts in competitive bidding, higher production costs, and increased warranty costs due to the poor quality of their products. The board invited representatives of four leading versions of TQM to give presentations to its members and executives so they could choose one TQM program to install. I was invited as a fifth speaker to help them make that choice.

During my appearance, I presented SQA and suggested they could use it to help them make the final decision. When we went through the phases of SQA, though, the board surprisingly changed their mind, developing their own future and living solutions that were much different from any of the standard TQM programs. Although they borrowed a few ideas from some of the TQM programs, they largely created a unique outcome, which they called a "business enhancement program," that fit their complex company. Their customized program proposed many new methods for each unit to follow, including such actions as involving customers in finding solutions, customer service training for all employees, productivity improvement projects, and teaching strategic planning using SQA to many employees.

SQA Foundation Question 2: What Information Do We Need for Our Future Solution?

The second foundation question serves as a reminder that the process of developing a future solution pushes data collection toward a future orientation. This differs extensively from reductionist thinking in that the future solution requires you to obtain information and knowledge about a wide range of topics more focused on the future than on the present. This means you need to pay attention to expanding the definition and realm of purposeful information collection as you develop alternatives in the list and organize steps. Of course, this requires a level of scenario planning and questioning of a very different nature from reductionist thinking.

One powerful outcome of this orientation toward purposeful information for the future is that you often end up using data and knowledge to stimulate more new ideas and conceptions of ideal target solutions. A "virtuous" spiral results, in which the data and information you collect lead people to imagine more new ideas, which then require other mind-expanding data. This means that you need to tolerate an iterative approach to data collection as you research new information for each new future solution idea generated, but the payoffs can be amazing in developing new alternatives.

An outstanding example of this virtuous spiral was the project involving nurse utilization in the thirty-three hospitals of the Greater Milwaukee Hospital Council. We partially discussed this case earlier, where we mentioned that after SQA, the administration ended up involving people from the many disciplines and services represented in their hospitals, and during the purposes expansion phase, they expanded their creative space, selecting as a focus purpose "to provide nursing services for patients" rather than simply "to have nurses work efficiently." This small change in the focus purpose to achieve led the team to create a dramatic future solution, including a completely new layout of a nursing ward, a different administrative structure, the elimination of the standard nursing stations, the installation of small consulting rooms, and a facilitator's role with physicians and family members.

The hospital implemented a living solution that contained many, but not all, of the elements of the ideal future solution. However, the results of a pilot testing of the living solution showed that the nurses' utilization (time spent directly on giving nursing services) increased a whopping 48 percent, much higher than the usual 5 to 10 percent improvement from conventional nursing utilization studies, and the nurses were delighted with the solution they helped develop. Furthermore, the implemented living solution identified more purposeful information to collect that led the hospitals to even more changes to the new system that slowly moved them closer to the future solution.

SQA Foundation Question 3: What System Description Shows How Our Future Solution Would Work?

The system foundation question intersects with the future solution phase in important ways. In the beginning of the chapter, we pointed out that one of the components of the future solution is details. The need to specify the details of system elements therefore requires you to ask questions about a whole range of factors to consider in determining how the prospective future solution might work and how it fits into related systems.

One of the surprising ironies here is that having a group begin to develop some details about a future solution makes the solution come alive and feel real, even though it is not immediately implementable. This is why we suggested earlier that one benefit of developing a future solution is that it builds momentum toward your living solution.

I was working with one group of people who were defining a future solution for how to teach classes about a new method of developing software. The group really got into the process of describing their future solution, imagining that they had the capabilities of crew members on *Star Trek*. This fantasy led them to create several futuristic concepts, such as a class in which students could talk and ask questions of a very intelligent computer, which would then not only answer their questions but would start to build software automatically based on their questions.

After about an hour of describing how this ideal process could work and how effective it would be, the group got very excited about the possibilities for their project (and had quite a bit of fun along the way). The outcome was that the group expanded their creative space and began to consider options for educating software developers that were far beyond traditional classroom education, which has been only marginally successful in the past. Eventually the group developed a living solution of interactive CDs, a Web site repository of samples of software development techniques, and a vibrant on-line community of practitioners to support the development process.

We will discuss how to add this type of detail and excitement to a future solution when we review the LOD steps.

Regularities versus Irregularities of the System

One important concept about systems thinking relative to future solutions is that a future solution needs to be designed to focus on regularities rather than irregularities. Regularities are the usual, most often expected, or most significant eventualities that occur in the domain of the issue. They are the factors over which, in almost all cases, you have little or no immediate control or capability to change. In contrast, irregularities are the factors that are the exceptions to the rule. You want to prepare a future solution for the regularities of your system, not the irregularities.

For example, in a critical care facility, regularities would be heart and stroke emergency room patients since they are the most critical inputs; irregularities would be patients with all other conditions. In a brewery, a regularity would be a customer over twenty-one years of age, and an irregularity might be a class of high school biology students studying fermentation. For a car dealership, a regularity is that you would expect potential buyers to have a driver's license, and an irregularity might be a fifteen year old who has a driving learner's permit and wealthy parents who are already picking out a new car for her.

Reductionist thinkers usually try to shape solutions that work for all foreseeable contingencies, regardless of whether they are regular and irregular. That is, everyone and everything is supposed to fit into one system without making distinctions between what you would normally expect to happen and what would be the exceptions.

Unfortunately, this approach contains many downsides. First, it is virtually impossible to conceive of all irregularities that may develop in any particular situation, and the unanticipated ones are always the ones that cause trouble. Second, it tends to devote inordinate amounts of attention to the irregularities. This leads to misshapen answers for dealing with the usual events, often causing those who are "regular" to spend extra time and incur greater costs forced by the one-answer-fits-all—for example, in completing an application form. Third, it tends to narrow rather than broaden the creative space and field of possibilities as you develop solutions. Finally, many good ideas are discarded because they do not encompass all the regularities and irregularities. We have seen a variety of instances where people go into a reductionist thinking mode and negate an idea by saying something like, "That won't work because customer A expects our parts to have characteristic X [an irregularity that is not the most common]."

In contrast, developing a future solution for just the regularity conditions is much more likely to lead to an ideal solution. This may seem ridiculously obvious. Yet it is amazing how the irregularities of a situation confound people seeking solutions to problems. Think about how many customer service operations are handled at airline counters, banks, and post offices. In too many instances, people who need only simple transactions wait in lines for long periods of time, while one person conducts a highly unusual request at the counter that takes twenty minutes for the clerk to handle. This occurs because many transaction lines are structured to handle every request rather than simply the standard ones, with atypical requests being handled separately. The result is inefficient handling of most of the traffic (and we highly recommend that the U.S. Post Office examine this situation).

Recently, many airlines have installed self-service computerized check-in terminals that deal precisely with this issue of regularities. Passengers who have nothing unusual (no "irregularities") with their ticket can quickly check in using the self-service option. We have used it many times and find that it's slick and fast, just what a "regular" customer wants.

In general, a smart future solution should be designed to work under the most commonly expected and usual conditions. Once that has been determined, the living solution phase can explore ways to minimally modify the future solution to deal with the irregular conditions or to develop a separate process that does not bog down the primary system used for regular events. In other words, developing a future solution means that you assume for now that the regularities occur 100 percent of the time, providing the opportunity to be much more creative for fewer conditions than when you try to develop a solution that encompasses all possible conditions and exceptions.

Consider the following solutions we helped find for some clients.

The design of a medication administration system in a hospital began with a consideration of only the regular, most frequently occurring, or most important situations (for example, three times per day, once every four hours), as if they occurred 100 percent of the time. Once this future solution was determined, an advanced living solution system was designed to include many irregular situations, such as medicines to be administered on patient request and when certain patient conditions arose. The implemented living solution retained most of the ideas developed for the regular conditions, with adjustments for irregular conditions.

In the second solution, a department store adopted a future solution conveyer system for receiving merchandise in cardboard boxes (90 percent of the received merchandise arrives in cardboard boxes) and then created during the living solution phase a separate receiving process that substituted for roughly 15 percent of the conveyor system front-end process to handle the other 10 percent irregularities, such as wooden crates and plastic containers not suitable for the regular part of the conveyor system. (The irregular system allowed for merchandise to be put into tote bins, which were then placed on the conveyor for the rest of the processing.)

Recognizing this distinction between regularities and irregularities leads to multifaceted solutions and breakthroughs encompassing several alternatives that can be ideal for various conditions. Weaving the threads of multiple purposes, multiple needs, and multiple solutions into an effective recommendation is the challenge of the future and living solutions process.

The Benefits of Future Solution Thinking

Asking the three foundation questions about developing a future solution introduces numerous significant advantages to the process of creating solutions. We have identified more than a dozen benefits that can be gained by thinking about future solutions in the terms we have described. Consider the following.

- *The future solution process encourages lines of questioning that lead to alternative ideal solutions.* Conventional approaches favor selecting the first idea that works, but SQA encourages you to ask probing questions that lead to not one but many solution ideas for the future. Decision makers who are open to alternatives are more likely to find a breakthrough idea that makes a difference. Sometimes the better alternative becomes a key to organizational survival. Remaining open for as long as possible to various alternatives greatly enhances your chances of arriving at a potentially ideal future solution system. This requires tolerance of ambiguity, a characteristic shared by the leading creators of solutions.

- *The future solution process helps you target clear time frames on implementing the living solution.* Asking questions like, "What solution do you think would be needed the next time we work on this problem in a year or five years from now?" often helps to stimulate insights about what actions to take now. Even if the ideal long-term solution cannot be implemented immediately, you develop a greater sense of what elements might be usable today. And because these elements may also be used in a longer-term solution, they can often serve better than the quick-fixes so prevalent in conventional approaches.

- *The future solution process imposes a future orientation that permits you to start fresh.* Thinking in terms of a future solution can often prompt you to think as if you were starting all over again. A future solution frees the mind of the past and unshackles your imagination. In reductionist thinking, the fresh start approach is usually unsuccessfully attempted to be used only after you are filled with information about the present, even when a product or service is being planned for the first time. But this need not be the case. Thinking about a complete fresh start can stimulate new ideas in any solution-creating effort, such as we saw in the nurse utilization case discussed earlier.

- *Thinking of the future implications of today's change by imagining an ideal target solution toward which to strive improves significantly both the quality and quantity of breakthrough solutions that can be implemented today.* If you are building a house, you must work within your current budget. But if you have your dream house in mind and take a future solution approach, you can build it in stages.

- *The trade-offs and compromises inherent in virtually every solution are made in a forward-looking rather than backward-looking mode.* If you imagine an ideal manufacturing system but cannot implement it now because of capital or personnel constraints, you can develop interim solutions that will at least take you closer to your ideal. These types of compromises are often more innovative and efficient than letting presumed constraints limit your idea generation to short-term patches that do not add forward movement to grander visions for change.

- *Your recommendations for change contain provisions for continuing improvement.* Components that are used in the future solution can be designed with the built-in ability to adapt and change for the living solution. Components that are not part of the ideal solution can be designed to be phased out or adapted to unrelated purposes, as in the paint manufacturing that is redone with an eye toward conversion to a bakery in a later year.

- *You maximize the likelihood of developing creative and innovative solutions by setting aside presumed human, physical, informational, and financial constraints that limit your vision.* If you let alternative ideal solutions blossom in your mind, often you can find ways to overcome the constraints with an immediate innovative solution or with ideas that can be put into place over time.

- *Human resistance to change gives way to acceptance and even anticipation of change.* After designing a future solution, people are taken less by surprise because they now understand how the changes can fit into the grand scheme of things in the organization or in their lives.

- *You gain invaluable lead time for making changes in the future.* With a good sense of where you are headed and the built-in flexibility to cope with the unexpected, you can plan phased-in solutions that take you ever closer to your ideal.

- *Your solutions are easier to implement.* Having a clear image of where you are going facilitates the many minute decisions you may have to make as your project develops.

- *Creative solutions become easier.* A good future solution concept that people like dissolves the "don't rock the boat" attitude that blocks the generation of innovative ideas.

- *You can leap beyond the competition, not just catch up with them.* Reductionist thinking would have you copy what your successful competitor is doing, as in best-practices benchmarking. Future solution thinking has the potential to put you beyond where your competition is, so you can surpass their performance.

- *Your recommendations for change are likely to involve more channels developed from many options.* There is much to be gained by imagining many potential future solutions. Redesigning schools to lower the dropout rate, for example, would surely involve more than lowering the class size. The complexity of the situation and its web of interrelated problems call for a multifaceted solution with components dealing with class size, teacher training, psychological support, parental involvement, crime prevention, supplemental funding, and others. The alternative solutions developed to achieve your vision of the ideal school become the various facets of the ultimate future solution.

- *A creative environment prevails.* Defensiveness and conflict over systems and allocation of resources subside as people move cooperatively toward a common vision for the future. An expanded, continually changing sense of betterment engenders openness to many alternatives. "How can we make this idea work?" is much more positive and mind opening than "This can't work" or "We tried that before." Assuming a long-range perspective makes people more tolerant of ambiguity and the possibility that one or more parts of a problem may have no solution. People become more willing to consider every idea, acknowledging the possibility that any idea may have some merit. These attitudes maximize the likelihood of developing creative, innovative solutions. The future solution process creates excitement for the group and makes the future seem more real.

• *You avoid getting bogged down in myriad circumstances that surround any real situation by initially developing a solution that deals with only the regularity conditions.* Developing a creative, workable solution for ideal conditions eventually leads to the installation of a multichanneled, pluralistic solution that handles regularities and normal conditions. These conditions might be the situation or factors that occur most frequently or are the most critical. Then systems to handle irregularities or exceptions to the rule can be developed later.

• *You avoid wasted time in data collection regarding the past.* Developing future solution options raises many specific questions that need to be answered before a recommendation is fully developed. These questions will guide your data collection so you can avoid wasteful, shotgun, get-all-the-facts research used in reductionist problem solving.

THE LIST, ORGANIZE, AND DECIDE STEPS

Now that you understand the purpose and framework of a future solution, let's review how you create one through the list, organize, and decide steps. As an overview, the process is as follows. First, the list step invites you to tap into various "bisociation" creativity techniques to stimulate your thinking and help generate a variety of ideas for how to achieve your focus purpose. Next, the organize step sorts your raw ideas into major alternatives to consider as the future solution. Finally, the decide step involves some type of formal decision-making procedures to select what will become the direction of your continuing change.

As with the other phases, we need to emphasize that this process is iterative. You may need to cycle through the future solution LOD steps multiple times, or even occasionally go back and revise your focus purpose or ask other people to get involved in order to maximize creative thinking. This is not to suggest that the LOD process is never-ending, but that to be an effective creator of solutions, you must be willing to revise and refine your ideas and visions as new information and ideas are created while performing the process itself. In all situations, you have a time line to which you are trying to adhere, so while you can never have perfect information, completing the four SQA phases is not an endless journey; decisions still need to be made in a timely fashion.

The List Step

As the first step in developing a future solution, this is where you attempt to create a very large number of ideas. Because the future cannot be predicted, the best anticipatory tool you have at your disposal is the freedom to create a wide variety of possible future solutions. There is never a single perfect solution, so it is far wiser to create many possible ideas without prejudging which ones will work or rejecting solutions based on subjective measures.

The first focus in the list step is on asking questions that encourage the formation of ideas rather than trying to move quickly toward creating just one solution immediately.

Asking smart list questions will help you develop many conceivable future solution ideas. Throughout this process, everyone involved in creating ideas needs to keep an open mind that is oriented to the focus purpose and its larger context of purposes. Our studies of successful creators of solutions show that although each may have some preferred tools and techniques to inspire creativity in themselves and others, there is one universal guideline they all follow: *be open to any and all new ideas.* This mind-set is required to nurture other people's ability to think creatively and abstractly and to focus their efforts on purposes. Everyone must be willing to accept and tolerate a certain level of ambiguity that results when you deal with a wide variety of possibilities, because listing means that you seek out as many ideas as possible—even ideas that may seem at odds with each other or negate other ideas.

As in the other phases, there are structured and unstructured methods to listing. Before we discuss the specifics of each method of listing, however, it is important to review a number of generic tools and techniques that are often used in the creativity field to enhance the thinking process.

INSPIRING CREATIVE THINKING AND IDEAS. Creativity is still largely a mystery in terms of the precise nature of the process by which people learn to generate new ideas. However, one theory that is widely accepted about where creativity develops and how it operates is based on the concept of bisociation. This theory suggests that all ideas and breakthroughs are born in the brain when two thoughts, two models, or two statements are mentally forced to intersect.

For example, you can mentally force the mind to consider the intersecting of your focus purpose and a stimulus word by asking the question, "How could our focus purpose be achieved ideally by means of, for example, a *ladder* [or any other random word chosen from the dictionary]?" This forced intersection stimulates the mind toward the development of new ideas. Indeed, the question can be asked many times over of different people, and you will receive different answers. The question can also be asked many times over using different bisociation words in place of *ladder.* Any bisociation word can prompt people to connect ideas: *brick, lion, zebra, toaster, spaceship,* and so on.

No one knows just how the brain does this, but the bisociation theory has become the foundation of many specific creativity techniques used to stimulate people to invent new ideas. There are dozens of techniques that tap into the power of bisociation to help people force connections in their minds that inspire ideas. A few of these creativity techniques are as follows:

- *Analogy and metaphor.* In this technique, you seek out new ideas by asking people to think about their purpose in terms of a metaphor or analogy. The goal of this forced thinking is to juxtapose or bisociate the focus purpose with the analogy or metaphor as the basis for generating a new connection. For example, you might ask, "How would our system act ideally if it worked like the systems in *Star Trek* [or in a ten-speed bike or a spider web, for example]?" Some creativity experts try to force connections by visiting and wandering through a park, a museum, or a store or reading poetry, art books, sports articles, plays, or fashion magazines to see if any analogies arise that can lead to new ideas. Whatever you do, the goal is to expose your mind to other words and ideas that might spark a connection.

- *Comparison.* This technique uses ideas and solutions from completely different fields to spark creative ideas for your purpose. It works by selecting a field in which the purposes may be similar, and then you apply them to your system. "How could our purpose of registering voters be achieved ideally if we could use the type of system used by UPS to keep track of its shipped packages?"

- *Principles.* Almost every content area has a set of principles that describe desirable and ideal conditions or solutions for different components of the system. For instance, in designing a kitchen, you need to consider the floor plan, layout, structure, accident prevention, clean-up, and other uses of the kitchen. In this creativity technique, you use the principles of some other system to juxtapose with your system. For example, you might use the principles behind designing a kitchen to see how they intersect with your purpose. This could generate questions such as, "What would the floor plan of your new kitchen need to look like?" "What would clean-up need to be like?" "What type of counter space would we need?"

- *Free association.* Free association is based on the bisociation idea that any thought, object, or vision that occurs can intersect with another thought or purpose as the germ of a new idea. Free association is often done loosely, by simply thinking freely about many ideas using words drawn at random from a dictionary or by drawing shapes on paper that start a chain of associations in your mind. Fantasizing about "perfect" answers is also a good way to free-associate, such as dreaming about a solution that takes zero time, or has zero costs, or satisfies customers 100 percent of the time. You can also tap into the official projections and forecasts of well-known futurists to stimulate an intersection of a futuristic idea with your purpose. For example, how can the forecast decline in birthrates in Europe cause purpose X to be achieved ideally? Or how would a system work if we lived on the space station or the moon or Mars?

- *Technology and science-fiction inspiration.* This technique involves using future technologies and even science-fiction ideas to intersect with your purpose. Play the role of a science-fiction writer assigned to write about how to achieve your purpose. What if biotechnology could change the molecular structure of the material you are dealing with? What if you could slip a computer chip into your product? How would it behave? What if you could freeze the material for ten years?

- *Imagery.* This creativity technique uses one of the measures of purpose accomplishment you selected in the Purposes Phase to envision what the solution might look like if that measure or factor were completely achieved. What might an intersection of roads look like if your measure of purpose accomplishment were zero traffic accidents? What system of handling sales orders would use 100 percent of each resource (workers, paper, computer time, and so on)? Then do the same individually with the other measures. The solutions you envision and the measures themselves stimulate ideas about how that ideal future might be reached.

- *Scenario writing.* This technique develops a story or narrative about a future event or thing. Think of the process as developing a good story that you can tell others to illustrate your ideas. This technique can be used at three levels: to describe the future when an ideal solution is in place, to describe a future solution in place, and to describe the actions required to realize the second scenario. The technology fiction tool can also help with this technique.

- *Pretend.* Useful for personal or family problems, this creativity tool combines scenario, imagery, free association, and technology fiction. How would you achieve your purpose if you won a lottery that provides you with a one-year release from all obligations and allowed you to go anywhere? How would you achieve your community purpose if you were given free advertising on area television channels?

- *Historical or biographical case.* The historical method is based on thinking of a past event that had an unusual or outstanding result and letting that case intersect with your focus purpose to generate new ideas. The biographical method suggests you think about a particularly bright and effective person whose personal characteristics you know and understand, and then ask yourself, "What kind of outstanding solution would he or she develop to achieve this purpose?

- *Worst-case scenario.* This method puts to use any negative ideas or constraints that you have thought of. Rather than letting them appear as barriers to a solution, you make a conscious effort to develop these worst-case scenarios to help identify obstacles or problems that might arise after the new system is in use. You then think through how to do deal with these discrepancies and barriers, fantasizing how you could eliminate them. The worst-case scenario stimulates the question, "How can an ideal system be developed to do away with these constraints or negative results?" "What if the unthinkable happened and we could eliminate them?"

• *Supplemental aids.* Many of the above techniques can be augmented by the use of visual aids. For example, you can use flash cards, posters, or CDs with artwork to inspire ideas and juxtapose images with your purposes.

Many other creativity techniques exist, and you can certainly create your own as well. The important thing is to avoid the temptation of the reductionist approach where you first analyze and subdivide the problem into its component parts and then try to explain away any ideas that do not seem to work. Maintain your focus on purposes and solutions, keep an open mind, and generate as many innovative solutions as you can for the purposes you have selected. The basic concept these techniques engender in SQA is to get you to do what leading creators of solutions and creative people in all fields do: look at achieving the focus purposes in as many different ways as possible.

ASKING QUESTIONS TO INSPIRE CREATIVITY. Notice that most of the creativity techniques use a questioning approach, usually beginning with the words, "What if . . . ?" or "How can we . . . ?" A questioning approach is vital to the creative process because it opens the door for the brain to wonder and expand its creative space. The goal of creativity questions is to give the mind freedom to seek out blue-sky ideas, that is, thoughts that have no grounding in reality at the present moment. As Albert Einstein said, "Imagination is more important than knowledge." Your task is to tap into the deliberate and forced use of idea-generating stimulators to enlarge the scope of possible solutions. For example, review the following questions and notice how expansive they invite your mind to become:

• How can we ideally achieve our focus purpose by means of doing something that is impossible today?

• How can we ideally achieve our focus purpose by means of completely disruptive products, services, technologies, or organizations of the future?

- How can we ideally achieve our focus purpose by means of the analogy of a telephone system (or a computer chip, DNA double helix, can opener, fuel cells, or something else)?

- How can we ideally achieve our focus purpose to create value for everyone by means of linking our processes to the processes of our suppliers, other businesses, and customers?

- How can we ideally achieve our focus purpose by means of a Rube Goldberg contraption or a "reverse salient," that is, considering smaller purposes in the hierarchy one at a time?

- How can we ideally achieve our focus purpose by means of using a concept from available databases of technology developments, patents, research results, and so on?

- How can we ideally achieve our focus purpose by means of creating products or services for needs that our customers do not express or that new customer groups may want?

- How can we ideally achieve our focus purpose by means of a metaphor, such as planting a vegetable garden, planning a vacation, or having a picnic?

- How can we ideally achieve our focus purpose by means of a zebra, mechanic, yacht, rubbish, comb (or any other randomly selected word from the dictionary)?

- How can we ideally achieve our focus purpose by means of what the flash card says? (Flash cards, each with a word or phrase or picture or drawing or cartoon, are shown as stimulators.)

- How can we achieve our focus purpose by having ideal inputs (or outputs, processes, environment, human enablers, physical enablers, and information enablers)?

- How can we ideally achieve our focus purpose by finding new uses for or combinations of our current products or services or for our operating process steps?

- How would an ideal solution for achieving the focus purpose smell (look, sound, feel, taste)?

- What if we used a robot (jet engine, camera, watch, scanner, car, or any other technology) to achieve ideally the focus and larger purpose. How would it work?

- How could we ideally achieve our focus purpose by means of what is currently considered the best practice in similar or unrelated types of organizations?

An example of the valuable impact of thinking ideally concerned a city hospital that was physically divided into two sites four miles apart. A team of people from both sites and representing several functional services was working on the issue of how to allocate millions of dollars in capital improvement funds between the two sites. Over the course of one and a half years, the team had not been able to reach a decision, despite having spent nearly $300,000 to have an architect draw up seven master plans based on different splits of the money. As you might imagine, being a diverse group of people, the reductionist approach to analyzing their situation led the individuals, subconsciously if not consciously, to seek to "protect" their current positions and garner "their fair share" of the available funds.

When a new facilitator was hired to use SQA, the team decided, *in a day and a half,* first on the purposes that the hospital as a whole needed to achieve, rather than just what each site was accomplishing, and second on a future solution that represented the very ideal idea to consolidate the hospital into one site and convert the second site into a retirement home that would be a new line of business and revenue stream. (In the living solution phase, the team translated this ideal to an implementable and continuing change action plan along these lines.)

STRUCTURED METHODS FOR LISTING. One of the best structured methods for generating ideas is forming a task force or group of people to work with the creativity techniques together. Groups have a built-in advantage in that the members help to expand each other's creative ideas. Just as in a brainstorming session, one person's suggestion often ends up acting as a bisociation trigger for another person, inspiring yet another new idea. This creates a cycle of creativity and usually results in a large number of ideas being developed.

One caveat about groups, however: the leader and the members must agree to clear rules about the process, especially ensuring that members are not afraid of being ridiculed for presenting outlandish ideas. People need to believe that the group honors mutual trust, encouragement, and openness. Everyone must make the commitment to support the search for expansively creative thinking, which is the key to the group's solution creation potential. The team can set its own ground rules and choose any creativity techniques they prefer. The administration of creativity teams commonly includes the following types of procedures:

- Criticism is prohibited when ideas are being generated; only in the organize and decide steps can judgment and assessment be used.

- Freewheeling thought is encouraged, no matter how crazy the ideas may seem. Group members must feel they are allowed to say even the wildest things without fear of ridicule or censorship.

- A group leader to lead the discussion can be someone who is not a stakeholder.

- All ideas are recorded so that each receives consideration.

- Questions are used to stimulate or motivate creativity.

Several additional techniques can help establish a creativity-friendly environment, such as putting idea boards or easels in the meeting and break rooms to encourage the written notation of ideas, inviting speakers to visit the group to present creativity techniques, regularly having "exchange your problem" days when someone else can work on the issue, hanging motivational posters on the walls to encourage creative thinking, sponsoring field trips for team members to museums and other places for inspiration, and having "blue-sky" days where everyone is invited to think about the problem or project.

One of the most effective ways to use each individual's unique creativity potential as well as to get the benefits of piggybacking ideas in a group is to use the following procedure. Have each person silently record whatever ideas occur to them as the leader presents various creativity stimulators (bisociation words). After ten to twenty stimulators are presented, each person reads aloud one idea, which is recorded on an easel sheet (or each person uses a computer to record ideas, and then each person one at a time transfers one idea to the computer projector and reads it aloud).

The procedure is repeated round robin until everyone has presented all his or her ideas. As each idea is read, everyone else can piggyback ideas to his or her own list if the announced idea stimulates yet another idea. When no other ideas are being offered, each idea on the list is read aloud, and the group is asked if the ideas are understandable. As they are being explained and discussed, the major question to keep asking is, "How could this idea be made to work?" This is done to keep the attitudes positive (to keep out the negativity of "that won't work" and "we tried that before and it didn't work") and to encourage further piggybacking.

CONVERSATIONAL AND INTUITIVE METHODS OF LISTING. In some cases, particularly when working with a small number of people, it may be more effective to do the list step using less formal methods of developing possible future solution ideas. This can be conducted more like a simple conversational method, wherein you help create ideas.

The most powerful technique we use here is storytelling. When we use this technique, we invite the person to tell us stories about how he or she imagines the future solution. Good questions can inspire individual storytelling just as they do in a group environment. As a general rule, a question is a good one if it is evocative for people being coached and if it leads them to a larger creative space. Some questions that are particularly useful when coaching someone to create stories include these:

- How do you envision a way in the future to achieve your focus purpose?
- How do you want your world (and our organization) to look in the future?
- How would your world work if you could invent the future?
- How would your ideal organization operate?
- How would you try to achieve your focus purpose if you started all over again?
- How can you encompass activities you enjoy into an ideal system for achieving your focus purpose?
- Where do you want to be in three years?

HOW MANY IDEAS ARE ENOUGH? At the beginning of the chapter, we noted that the main objective of the Future Solution Phase is to create as many ideal ideas as possible. You may be wondering how many are enough and when to stop.

Perhaps the best answer to this question is that you can never have too many ideas about the future. All ideas may be useful—now or later on, no matter how offbeat or weird they may seem. A recent case illustrates this. A large company had me facilitate a one-and-a-half-day strategic planning retreat for its nine top executives. Of the forty-five purpose statements that emerged, it seemed to me that there were many solution ideas listed but not many real purpose or mission statements. In the statement clarification part of the phase, I asked the group to decide what each statement represented: a real purpose, a solution idea, or a measure of accomplishment. Only twelve were purposes, twenty-six were solution ideas, and seven were measures. After further work clarifying this confusion, only five of the original purpose statements wound up in the hierarchy of seventeen. But among those early solutions, many were included in the future solution list step, and the others were declared to be potentially useful for other parts of the organization, so they were forwarded to other departments.

This is not to say that you can go on forever with ideas. One crucial element to the success of SQA is that it links the focus purpose with the "how" question: How can this solution ideally work eventually? The emphasis on "how" ensures that you will eventually arrive at a living solution that contains implementable results, actual changes, and real products and services. Although this practical orientation may eliminate some ideas unrelated to all the purposes to be achieved, it is still quite typical that you will receive many ideas.

So perhaps the best answer to how many is enough is to say that it helps to have large numbers of ideas, but not so many that they become overwhelming to the group. More is almost always better, and ideas will almost always be added (and some deleted) even if you think this step is completed. A sufficient and not overwhelming number of ideas can be very subjective, though. In one project concerning how to better manage and control missing files in an insurance company, the group developed 131 ideas, which they did not consider too many. In a project regarding the design of a knowledge management system, the group created nineteen future solution ideas and judged this "more than we can handle." The group and outside reviewers (including the approval person or group and professionals in the field) must be the determiner how many to develop.

The three foundation questions also provide the basis for asking more smart questions about the developing future solution ideas. The

SMART QUESTIONS FOR THE FUTURE SOLUTION

List Step

In addition to the questions generated using the creativity techniques discussed, continue asking yourself the three foundation questions to keep on track while developing the future solution. Here are some sample questions to consider.

Uniqueness

- What are some ideal future solution ideas for our unique situation?

Purposeful Information

- What sources of information can we tap to stimulate creativity in developing ideal future solution ideas?
- What future solution ideas would a group of employees provide in a survey asking how they would envision achieving the purposes if we started all over?

Systems

- What ideal inputs (less as well as more costly) for achieving the focus purpose might our future solution have?
- What ideal outputs (less as well as more costly) to achieve our purposes do we want our system to have?
- What are some ideal processes we might use to produce the outputs?
- What ideal environment conditions would be needed within which a future solution should operate?
- What ideal human agent characteristics would be needed for operating a future solution?
- What ideal physical catalyst ideas would be needed for operating a future solution?
- What are the values of the system—the goals, motivating beliefs, quality perspectives, global desires, ethics, and moral matters—we want?
- What are the measures we need to maintain our system and determine how successful it is: criteria, merit, and worth factors, and objectives of how much, when, rates, and performance specifications?

box provides examples of the types of other questions you might ask as you explore ways to stimulate thinking about ideas for ideal future solutions to achieve the focus purposes.

The Organize Step

The organize step is where you begin to put some order into the usual mass of solution ideas developed during the list step. Often, some ideas conflict with others, some are possible components of several possible future solution alternatives, and the rest are usually snippets of ideas that might be useful to combine with other alternatives. This step helps you sort them all out and develop three to five major alternatives that are substantial enough to consider as candidates for the single ideal future solution that will be determined in the decide step.

Developing multiple options to examine is a critical part of what Ohio State management professor Paul Nutt states is necessary to long-term success. In his book, *Why Decisions Fail: Avoiding the Blunders and Traps That Lead to Debacles* (2002), he emphasizes the importance of continuing to develop options even when one appears acceptable.

The ideas proposed in the list step are usually one of three possible types:

- A plausible major future alternative (MA) that you eventually want to consider as your future solution (the idea as stated contains most of the basic skeleton for it)
- A possible component (C) that could be incorporated in more than one major alternative
- A detail (D) that may or may not be useful in creating your future solution or may have value in other projects of yours and others

The purpose of sorting ideas into the three categories is to be able to recognize which ideas come from that larger creative space and are candidates to be developed into future solution ideas. These are the MAs, whereas components and details are best to use as part of other larger major alternatives.

The challenge, of course, is to determine which ideas are MAs, Cs, or Ds. We suggest a simple but effective methodology to help you decide which category your ideas fall into. Begin by asking the following questions about each idea recorded during the list step:

- Is the idea a potential self-contained means of achieving the focus purpose?
- Is the idea describable in system terms (inputs, outputs, operating steps) to ensure workability?
- Is the idea more than a "flag and apple pie" statement? These types of statements—such as "automate it," "train people better," "stop the waste," and "increase market share"—are so bland that no one would ever object to them; they lack the full throttle of creativity you seek. Good creative statements need to be more than this.
- Is the idea more than just a component or detail that could be incorporated into other major alternatives?

If you can answer yes to three of these four questions, you should consider the idea as a major alternative by the end of the organize step. If you or your group decides that it is not an MA, do not throw out the idea; it can become a component or detail in another alternative or used in another project. Always keep in mind that if an idea feels like "just" a component or a detail, it may contain the seeds to be combined with other ideas or expanded into a major alternative.

STRUCTURED METHODS OF ORGANIZING. The organize step can be accomplished using a structured approach in which you ask each person to independently classify each idea as MA, C, or D. Alternatively, if you have a facilitator, he or she could call out the first idea and ask the whole group to vote on an assignment of MA, C, or D and then record the result. Determining the classification of each idea is up to the group, but in general you need at least a certain level of consensus. If there is still disagreement after a few minutes of discussion as to whether an idea is, say, an MA or C, it is best to move on and mark it as a combination MA/C (or C/D) and then proceed with the rest of the ideas. By the time you are done with all ideas, the group may be able to come back to those undecided ones and make a final determination.

It helps to use various tools, such as flowcharts, activity networks, operator charts, organization charts, dynamic flow and feedback loop models, and layout diagrams, to show how the idea might work. For example, you might draw flowcharts, activity networks, and relationship networks in order to describe the systematic workings of an idea, or you can draw operator charts to show the human agents in the system, or layout diagrams to show the physical enablers and environment elements. New tools are continually being proposed.

For complex ideas, you can draw a rough system description to describe how it would work. The word *rough* is used because the purpose of doing any detailing of an idea here is to have enough information for selecting a future solution as a viable alternative in the decide step. The questions to ask are based on the systems questions noted above. Many more system details will be added in the living solution phase.

Another benefit of thinking about ideas from a systems perspective is that the questions help you consider the total customer-consumer experience as part of the output element. Customer total experience, for example, from the initial exposure to the product or service through contact, purchase, use, and disposal, is more likely to be considered by the system framework of thinking.

CONVERSATIONAL AND INTUITIVE METHODS OF ORGANIZING. The same techniques discussed above can also be used in a conversational approach to organizing ideas and selecting MAs. If you are a facilitator, have participants examine which ideas seem larger, more encompassing, and more interesting. This discussion will often separate the wheat from the chaff, helping organize the ideas into those that can become major alternatives.

Another conversational technique is to use the storytelling approach, asking the person to continue telling a story about how he or she sees the solution unfolding. Many people can tell an informal story about an alternative but have difficulty explaining the details in a formal, structured approach. The essence of a story or scenario for purposes of organizing major alternatives is to describe roughly how an idea would work and what its consequences would be. The story should describe a picture or image of the unique ideal forward-looking aspects of the idea and try to identify what additional information may be needed if the idea is selected as the solution for the future. Once the story has been told, go through the listed ideas and see if you can now sort out the major alternatives, components, and details based on the story.

AVOIDING NEGATIVITY AND FALSE BARRIERS. It often occurs during the organize step that people review the list of alternatives and proclaim many of them impossible to do. They may protest about the irregularities, saying things like, "We can't do that because 10 percent of the time sometimes we need X, Y, or Z . . ." or they may point out some barrier, constraint, limitation, obstacle, or restriction that they claim interferes with the alternative.

Negativity promptly kills creativity and nascent ideas. If you find people making such negative statements, the best way to deal with them is to reposition their statements in the context of the regularity concept. For example, assume you are working on how to incorporate electronic invoicing into your system and someone proposes a solution that works for 90 percent of the customers. To the person who points out that the idea does not work for the other 10 percent, remind them that it is better to create a special solution to deal with the irregularities.

Of course, you may engender a conversation on what is regular versus irregular, but you can then clarify that issue if it has not been done yet. Or ask about expanding the purposes of dealing with that irregularity and what would be a future solution for achieving the purposes of that irregularity. For example, you might ask what the purposes are of providing service to the 10 percent of customers who cannot do electronic invoicing. You may find that your purposes might include keeping them as customers, while working to get them to move to electronic invoicing at some time in the future. Or you could propose an outsourcing service for them to use. This is a larger creative space than saying simply, "The electronic invoicing solution just won't work."

The three foundation questions again serve as another way to ask more smart questions about how to organize the future solution ideas. The box provides examples of these types of questions.

THE OUTCOME OF THE ORGANIZE STEP. No formula exists to figure out how many major alternatives you might want from the ideas you developed and sorted in the list and organize steps, but our experience is that 15 to 25 percent of the original list will become major alternatives. In terms of hard numbers, by the end of this step, we recommend that you aim to have from two to five major alternatives for a future solution. Each review you perform of an idea is an opportunity to raise questions about it, modify it into an MA, or use it to generate more ideas.

SMART QUESTIONS FOR THE FUTURE SOLUTION

Organize Step

As you do the Organize step, whether structured or conversational, be sure to continue asking Smart Questions in order to check your progress and ensure that you are not neglecting issues. Here are examples of the types of Smart Questions you might ask at this stage.

Uniqueness
- What are the ideal major alternatives that we should consider before selecting one of them?
- What are the specific terms and language our people use to discuss the solution?
- How do our organization's cultural norms fit with that idea?

Purposeful Information
- Does this information about future solutions make sense to you (adequately tell the story)?
- What questions that need information to be collected are raised for you in the process of dividing ideas into major alternatives, components, or details?
- What other perspectives about the future solution idea should we consider beyond the information we have?
- What is the reliability of the sources of our information as we try to project the working of a possible major alternative?
- What possible major alternative scenarios could explain the data we have collected about the future?
- What does your experience tell you about the data we have collected about the future?
- Would discussions with others help round out or tell a story about how an MA might work?

Systems
- What other creative ideas can we get by expanding each system element (inputs, outputs, processes, human agents, physical agents) in this solution idea?
- How can we organize the future solution ideas into a set of holistic ideas that make sense to us and our stakeholders?
- What are the key connections between the various future solution ideas?
- How can we build in favorable user experience with the MA's outputs?

The final outcome of the organize step is to create a brief statement for each major alternative and a short systems description of roughly how it would work under ideal and regularity conditions. The description can take many forms, but the more detail you can add, the better, because this description is the best way to ascertain how each MA would work and to minimize unintended consequences or unexpected outcomes.

Keep in mind that you may later need to add more details when you get to the decide step to help clarify each alternative before selecting the best future solution. For example, each system element may need more insight into how it will operate, or an input element may need more details about the values and beliefs you want associated with the inputs or some measures or methods of control or interfaces with other elements and systems. An output element might need more details about its values and beliefs, measures, control, and interfaces. These same characteristics can raise questions as needed to add details about the other elements.

The Decide Step

Now that there are several major alternatives to consider as possibilities, the goal of the decide step is to identify a single preferred future solution for achieving the focus purpose. However, keep in mind that although you will select just one alternative as the future solution, the others may still represent options to reconsider during the Living Solution Phase (presented in Chapter Five) if you discover that the chosen future solution is not appropriate or if external conditions and contingencies change enough to invalidate this choice.

So how do you select a future solution for regularity conditions? In our view, the primary criterion is how well the major alternatives meet the measures of purpose accomplishment (MPA) you defined in the Purposes Phase. You therefore need to determine what information is necessary about each of the major alternatives to enable you to assess its benefits and consequences in terms of those MPAs. That information is primarily related to how the future solution MA would work. In other words, you want to make an assessment about the kind of results the future solution would achieve. Will it help you achieve your focus purpose as well as get the "best" levels of the MPAs?

Consider only these two MAs for the department store illustration: (A) the conveyor with automatic opening of the box and preprinting of the tags and (B) have vendors put on the tags. Again, to keep this example simple, consider the MPAs to be (1) cost per merchandise item in getting tags on each item, and (2) time taken between arrival of merchandise and placement of items on the selling floor. Given this, enough detail for each of the MAs needs to be available to give the team a way of estimating its cost and total process time. Depending on the extensiveness of the project and the arena where the eventual living solution will be installed, the MA with the least cost and total process time will most likely be selected as the future solution.

This does not mean that you should not also take into account any other factors or measures that you might have for each potential future solution. For example, you might want to consider associated risk, environmental friendliness, ease of use, convenience to user, simplicity of implementation, the ethics related to the alternative, demographics of population age groups, number of skilled people being trained, equal rights for disabled workers, and so on.

In other words, such other factors that are identified here might be considered as likely additional MPAs. However determining how to quantify what each alternative does in relation to these possible MPAs is very difficult and is the reason they are almost always treated as subjective factors, as noted above. Some of these additional MPAs, such as associated risk, environmental friendliness and sustainability, ethics of using an MA, or convenience to user, may need to be extensively explored to determine their impact on selecting an MA as the future solution.

STRUCTURED METHODS OF DECIDING. The most formal method of deciding requires the use of some type of decision worksheet. We have devised one of our own, the Smart Questions Decision Worksheet, shown in Exhibit 4.1. This worksheet can serve as a guide for asking the necessary questions and on which to record the responses in a straightforward structured method. We introduce it here because in many cases, selecting a future solution is a strategic decision.

The scope and complexity of the alternatives you are evaluating will determine how extensively you decide to use the Smart Questions Decision Worksheet. It is a convenient form to fill out and use in any

PROJECT_____

Who Involved in Making Decision_____ Date_____

PURPOSE		A B	A = Rating of alternative

PURPOSE
- ☐ Select people to involve
- ☐ Select focus purpose(s)
- ☐ Select measures of purpose accomplishment
- ☐ Select major solution alternatives
- ☐ Select future solution target
- ☐ Select _____
- ☐ Select _____

A B   A = Rating of alternative
        B = Risk, probability of occurrence
C   C = A x B x Weighting

Scale used for rating (A)
- ☐   5 (excellent), 4 (very good), 3 (good), 2 (fair), 1 (poor), 0 (not acceptable)
- ☐   100 points to be divided up among alternatives, with higher amounts for preference
- ☐ _____

WEIGHTING
- ☐ 1 = Least important; 1.5 = 1 1/2 times as important as 1; 3 = 3 times as important as 1
- ☐ Divide 100 points among factors, with higher amounts for greater weighting
- ☐ 5 (absolutely needed), 4 (very important), 3 (important), 2 (worthwhile), 1 (desirable)
- ☐ _____

Risk or probability of occurrence (B)
- ☐   0 to 1 (ex. 0.25, 0.75) probability, with higher probability value = very likely occurrence
- ☐   1 to 0 (ex. 0.90, 0.10) risk, with higher number = less risk
- ☐ _____

COST = Investment : expected life + annual operating cost

Factors/Consideration/Criteria	WT.	Alternative					
		A	B	C	D	E	F
1.							
2.							
3.							
4.							
5.							
6.							
7.							
8.							
9.							
10.							
TOTAL OF MULTIPLIED VALUES							

Alternatives:
A_____   D_____
B_____   E_____
C_____   F_____

Exhibit 4.1.   Smart Questions Decision Worksheet

decision-making process, and it also serves as a clear record for everyone of what factors the final decision involves. It is especially useful for situations that will require significant change, such as introducing a new product, service, or market; making a major change in a corporate system such as accounts receivable; designing a new strategic plan; or purchasing and installing new equipment. (In such situations, documentation in addition to the worksheet is likely to be necessary to support the entries on it.) The worksheet helps you think about questions such as these:

- What scale best represents each measure of purposes accomplishment?
- How much of the measures can be achieved by this alternative?
- How important is this measure relative to the other measures?
- How much do we know about how the alternative might work in the future?
- Should we make a physical prototype or pilot facility or set up a computer simulation of the performances of the two (or three) alternatives that look promising?
- What impact would a change in external factors have on the workability of this alternative?
- How can we measure the impact of the alternative on the rest of the organization?
- Would a thorough risk probability assessment help in evaluating alternatives to reduce the likelihood of unintended consequences and even unanticipated outcomes?

Keep in mind that the worksheet contains nothing about a key question in doing your evaluation: How will each alternative work? That information comes from the LOD steps, where you need to think about each major alternative as a system. You need to make sure you understand enough about the inputs, outputs, process, human enablers, physical enablers, information enablers, and the environment in which the proposed system lives to give yourself some assurance that the major alternative is a viable potential solution in the future. In other words, can you tell a story about each major alternative that provides a vision of the future state it would produce?

Many methods are available for ranking alternatives, such as rating scales for each MPA using 0 to 100; yes or no; five points from "completely accomplishes" to "does not accomplish it at all"; and estimates of weight, dimensions, and costs. You may also need to weight the importance of various factors, in which case you sometimes need to do multiple assessments as the weightings are adjusted to reflect different trade-offs and uncertainties, such as those indicated regarding the likelihood that particular conditions might occur, the risks to assets, and complexity of implementation. We will explain how to use the worksheet in the following paragraphs.

The Smart Questions Decision Worksheet contains all of these considerations in a format that facilitates a reasonable choice from among alternatives. The worksheet also provides a good indication of when you may need more detailed and technical evaluation tools. We will not cover these situations here, but there are many references to techniques, such as multiattribute utility, social utility, information gap decision theory, and multiple criteria decision analysis, almost all of which are embodied in their related software packages. One of the reasons we do not discuss the many techniques capable of being done by software is that they do not allow for the human perspective we consider critical when using the Smart Questions Decision Worksheet. Most decision-making software does not produce better decisions; it simply helps keep track of the answers and may assist in making decisions more quickly or with easy computational models.

Using the Smart Questions Decision Worksheet. We demonstrate how the worksheet works by using the department store project to select a receiving system (with conveyor belts) for regularity conditions as discussed earlier in this chapter:

- Top line. List here the people involved in making the selection. In this case, the people were members of the project team. In more complex projects, you might also involve the deputies of the president or CEO, buying executive, or chief financial officer.

- "Purpose" box. Check which purpose the worksheet is serving. In the example case, the purpose of the decision in this phase is to select a future solution.

- "Factor/Consideration/Criteria" box. List on these blank lines the measures of purpose accomplishment. In this case, they include the tagging cost per merchandise item, the time taken to process a shipment of merchandise from receiving to placement on sales floor, improper tagging error rate, and amount of merchandise damaged, plus other factors that bear on the decision. They could include in the example case the cost of making the changes, the impact of changes on union contract provisions, the likelihood of simple modifications to incorporate irregularities, technical skills available, ethical considerations, and social consciousness.

- "Alternatives" list. Give names to the major alternatives identified in the organize step. In the case of the department store, option A was the conveyor-based alternative, a signal sent from receiving to tag control to get preprinted tags ready, a dedicated elevator to bring merchandise to the conveyor on the marking room floor, boxes automatically opened at the bottom that will serve as a pallet, the top automatically removed and placed on another conveyor, and tags placed on merchandise. Option B was to have vendors put on preprinted tags sent to them with the purchase order. Option C was to have vendors add price to their tags. And option D was to eliminate tags and use vendors' bar code as price and inventory control information. These labels (A, B, C, D) correspond to the columns on the right.

- "Weighting" box. This box lists the possible methods of weighting your factors. Check off which weighting method you will use. There is also a blank line to add a different weighting method.

- "WT" column. If desired, use this column to show the weighting number you select to indicate the importance of each of the factors/considerations/criteria. In the case of the department store, we selected the first weighting method from the Weighting box: the scale of 1 to 5. In the case of the department store, tagging cost per merchandise item gets a 3 (meaning three times as important as the factor with weight = 1); the time taken to process a shipment is weighted 5; the improper tagging error rate is weighted 2; the amount of merchandise damaged is weighted 1; the cost of making the changes is weighted 2; the impact of changes on union contract provisions is weighted 2; and the technical skills available is weighted 1.

- "Alternatives" boxes. Record the scores for each factor. Notice that there are three cells at the intersection of each alternative and each factor. The use of these cells is explained in the upper-right-hand box. Notice that cell A is used for the general rating of each alternative. Cell B is used for more complex situations where risk and probability of occurrence of certain events are important. Cell C is for recording the result of multiplying the weighting in cell A by the value in cell B (or just multiplying cell

A by the weighting if just weighting is involved). If it's a simple situation, use cell C to enter the rating for each alternative. In the case of the department store, using the first scale in the upper-right-hand box, alternative A was rated 4 on factor 1 (entered in cell A at the intersection of alternative A and factor 1) with 12 entered in cell C (weighting of three times the rating of 4). Alternative B was rated 3 (cell A) on factor 1 with 15 entered in cell C (weighting of five times the rating of 3); and so on through all the alternatives and factors.

• "Total of Multiplied Values" line. This line is the total of the C cells for each alternative. This is the *bottom line,* so to speak, where you can see which alternative had the highest score.

Normally, the alternative with the highest total score wins. However, do not automatically select the alternative with the largest total. If there is a difference in score between several alternatives of less than around 5 percent, remember that all entries in the calculations have been subjectively determined. You may need to have additional group discussion to uncover changes that everyone may believe ought to be made to the weightings, ratings or measures, assessment numbers, and perhaps the way some of the options might work.

We hope you recognize that using the Smart Questions Decision Worksheet as well as doing the Organize Step almost always requires collecting or generating information. There are likely to be assumptions and questions about the workability of and evaluation details concerning each idea and certainly the major alternatives. Obtaining this information about possible future solutions should be done to provide greater assurance of making a good decision. Such information continues to illustrate what SQA means by purposeful information collection and the spotlight on developing a solution-oriented rather than problem-based mindset.

Also remember that selecting the alternative with the highest total will still involve subjective judgments (trade-offs in most cases) and "feelings." The "feelings" factor could be dangerous because it may be a way, as Nutt (2002) notes, of "misusing evaluations" for personal and political benefit. We have no way of avoiding such misuse except to remind you to be sure to review the three foundation smart decide questions in the box in the terms outlined in the Smart Questions Decision Worksheet.

An important benefit of the Smart Questions Decision Worksheet is the way it can help you avoid the "technological imperative," by which we mean the tendency to focus on the technology as your solution rather than considering the factors that will make a solution work.

Conversational and Intuitive Methods of Deciding. Many groups resort to using an intuitive method to make their final selection of a future solution. Not surprisingly, groups can often make this decision quickly as soon as they recognize that they can always return to the future solution phase and reevaluate their choice, keeping other major alternatives open as options as well.

WHAT TO DO WITH ALTERNATIVES NOT USED. Many of the alternatives that were labeled components or details, as well as the "losing" major alternatives, may well be considered at a later time as useful in other departments of your organization or as a backup to the selected option in case it does not work as planned. Those that are potentially valuable for the living solution that you will soon be developing could be saved in a "parking lot" to reconsider as you develop the living solution phase. Think of a parking lot as a place of holding ideas that may be usable in the future. Some ideas may be useful for future design efforts even though they are not immediately useful. (If you have prepared fairly detailed system descriptions for each alternative, the elements of the description could also be a useful way to store ideas in a knowledge management database. Someone looking for product ideas, for example, could search for entries in the output elements of those in the database.)

Finally, remember that all the ideas and the future solution itself are an invaluable learning experience for the people involved as well as for the whole organization. This is a great approach for building a learning organization—one that is able to learn and adapt as conditions change.

DEFINING A FUTURE SOLUTION IN THE HEAT OF BATTLE

It may seem easy to organize and decide on a future solution when you are in a workshop with a trained facilitator, isolated from your usual hectic environment of voice mail, e-mail, and the constant interruptions of the modern businessperson, teacher, or parent. But

—₩— **SMART QUESTIONS FOR THE FUTURE SOLUTION**

Decide

The process of deciding also requires that you continue to review your situation and ask appropriate smart questions as needed. Such decision questions might include the following.

Uniqueness
- How does or should our uniqueness affect the workability of each alternative?
- What benefits, if any, would we get by using a small part (such as a software package) of an available solution rather than a unique one?
- What unique relevant factors (such as regularity) should we consider as we decide on a future solution?
- How can we decide on a future solution for regularity conditions in a way that recognizes our organization's unique ways of making decisions?

Information
- With how much judgmental, inaccurate, and imprecise information are we willing to make a decision about this situation?
- How long might we have to wait until more reasonable information is available (for example, for probability factors, risk tolerance, or costs)?
- What are the pertinent types of data the Smart Questions Decision Worksheet identifies as necessary to collect, and how do we get it without messing up the collection and use of the data?
- What additional information do we need to collect in order to feel comfortable with making a decision about the future solution for regularity conditions?

Systems
- What details about each system element are needed to specify how the alternative will work so that we can make a sound decision?
- Are there values, measures, and controls that could be specified for each element that would make an alternative more understandable, so that we could make a sound decision?
- What interfaces with other systems may need to be factored more thoroughly in our alternatives to make them work better and affect the evaluation we make of each of them, so that we could make a sound decision?

can this be done in the heat of battle, when you do not have enough time, energy, or focus to evaluate a long-term future solution for achieving your purposes?

We would suggest that the answer is yes. Not only is it possible, but we think it is usually necessary. Although there may be rare situations of extreme urgency when a quick decision trumps thinking about an ideal future solution, it is worth the time in most cases to create a future solution. In fact, the best time to have a future solution to achieve your purposes is when you are absorbed in firefighting or in an adversarial position. Without the direction of such a target, you can end up wasting time and stalling productive change because of what you do on the spur of the moment. Having a future solution, even though its time horizon may be shortened from three years to a matter of weeks or days because of the battle, is a focus on results—on what is important.

Here is an example. We were facilitating a manufacturing company's strategic planning activities. The executives had done very well in developing their focus purpose. They were starting to come up with ideas about the ideal way of reorganizing the company and producing its products and services when two different government-owned manufacturing facilities, located in opposite sections of the city, were put up for sale. The company had already decided that a new manufacturing facility was needed in order to expand its product line according to its strategic plan, but they had not designed such a plant yet. The executives were therefore delighted to hear that the other manufacturing facilities had become available. They discussed various pros and cons of each facility, such as its location in relation to where employees lived, cost per square foot, maintenance history, utility of the current transportation arrangements in the city, and ease or difficulty of installing the current manufacturing system.

The executive group told us about the opportunity and said they were leaning toward facility A because it was the best bargain based on cost per square foot purchase price, costs of grounds and building upkeep, and other considerations. Given that they were talking about moving the current manufacturing system to this new facility, we asked, "What future solution would that lead to?" and "How would the new product line be incorporated?" We spent several hours listing some ideal solutions to answer those questions, quickly reviewing them to determine possible workability, and estimating the impact of the ideas on achieving the company's long-term mission and vision.

Not surprisingly, the final outcome from discussing the future solution was a decision to purchase facility B. The executives examined the configuration of the two buildings (A was U-shaped and B was rectangular) and realized that facility B had much greater flexibility than A, allowing them more adaptability to change their products and to use state-of-the-art manufacturing equipment, while having only a 5 percent higher purchase cost basis.

BENEFITS OF THE FUTURE SOLUTION PHASE

People may wish they could create ideal solutions, but they too often lack the tools to do so. We have therefore expanded the Future Solution Phase of the leading creators of solutions to incorporate holistic thinking and LOD questions as a way of showing you how to continue to use your creative thinking within an overall process that brings many stakeholders to the task and makes sure the right purposes are being fulfilled through the best "ideal" solution. We are confident that this process brings long-term benefits into any solution creation effort. Following are some of the benefits of this phase:

- Having a future solution improves the results you can get today because you can make decisions about what will more likely lead to the desired future.

- Trade-offs and compromises needed for selecting a future solution are made in a forward-looking mode, especially helpful in accepting the sunk-cost concept, that is, not letting the amount of money already spent on doing something stop you from walking away from that expenditure.

- What you do today is done within a framework of continual improvement and adaptability.

- So-called resistance to change gives way to acceptance and even anticipation of change because of the future orientation and involvement in shaping the future.

- Valuable lead time is gained for future changes because you know where you are headed.

- You can leap beyond competition, not just catch up.

- Contingency or backup alternatives are already available.

- A creative environment is far more likely to exist when discussions deal with determining the future solution.

- Creating solutions with purposes and ideal aims helps to establish an atmosphere of fun.

- You do not let current knowledge limit your thinking.

HIGHLIGHTS OF THE FUTURE SOLUTION PHASE

- The future solution represents the ideal solution you would like to have. It is a motivating goal for where you would like to be and how you would like to resolve the issue or problem ideally. However, it may be a solution that cannot be implemented now because of any number of reasons, such as the technology not being available, a lack of funding, training that is still required, or additional human resources needed.

- An important value of developing a future solution is that it helps you expand the possibilities for your solution in several ways. First, it demands, because of the effort to think ideally, that decision makers view a situation from various perspectives, putting aside any social, political, cultural, or environmental barriers. Second, it challenges the propensity to avoid risk. Third, it encourages the generation and growth of innovative ideas by maintaining an openness to using a wide variety of tools, techniques, and modes of expression to discover it.

- A variety of creativity tools can be used to develop future solution ideas. These tools are most often based on the bisociation concept of creativity in which you attempt to force a new connection between your focus purpose and a word or phrase in order to stimulate a new idea.

- In the list step of this phase, you aim to develop many alternative ideas from which a future solution can be selected.

- In the organize step, you aim to categorize the ideas generated in the list step into one of three categories: major alternatives, components, and details. Some of the ideas for components and details may be combined into a major alternative. As this sorting into categories is going on, assumptions and questions about workability of ideas provide insight into what purposeful information needs to be collected. In general, you aim to have several major alternatives as you enter the decide step.

- In the decide step, you focus on which future solution best meets your needs, considering the regularity concept. You aim to find a solution that meets the largest majority of situations rather than the smaller irregularities.

- All future solution options not selected can and should be recorded and kept as contingencies in the event that the living solution does not work, as well as to be potentially useful to other departments in your organization or for other efforts.

CHAPTER FIVE

SQA Phase 4

Building a Living Solution for Today and Tomorrow

It is a bad plan that admits of no modification.

—*Publius Syrus*

This phase translates the work of the People Involvement, Purposes, and Future Solution phases into a recommended change that can be implemented in an immediate time frame, as well as a plan for additional projected changes to come.

We intentionally call it a "living" solution to emphasize that solutions seldom perform perfectly when first installed and that additional stages of change need to be continuously planned in order to come as close as possible to the future solution.

How does the living solution differ from the future solution? First, recall that the future solution is an ideal solution; it is a prediction of what you would like to build at some point down the road. But since so many predictions do not happen and your future solution is an ideal solution anyway, it is usually impossible to reach its lofty goals immediately. What if the R&D needed does not prove fruitful, customer acceptance is poor, supplier commitments for changes are not met, an outside disruptive technology appears to change the competitive environment, there are changes in internal systems, or the company is sold?

Second, the future solution may be built around regularity conditions. A living solution needs to incorporate methods to handle the irregularities while departing as little as possible from the future solution. It is even possible that in attempting to incorporate ways to handle the irregularities, the future solution may need to be changed or modified.

Third, the information you gathered in the organize and decide steps of the Future Solution Phase may be shown to be faulty or lacking in content. In addition to the possible impact of the new information on the Living Solution Phase, such different information may cause you to return to selecting a different future solution. These considerations show the iterative nature of the SQA. At each phase you move forward, but you refine your design all along the process.

Such possibilities are the reason that you have a living solution. Whereas a future solution represents an ideal toward which you want to work, a living solution starts with what can be accomplished now based on and building toward what you want as the future solution. The solution needs to be detailed, actionable, and installable now. It needs to specify who is involved, what actions will occur, and what the intended result will look like, feel like, and be like.

In practical terms, the living solution has three features:

Feature A—a detailed description of recommended changes now that come as close as possible to the future solution

Feature B—a plan for what successive stages of change and improvement have been decided on and a time frame for when they will occur in order to move the installed solution further toward the future solution

Feature C—an installation plan to begin work on the first stages of change

These three features are highly interrelated. In developing them, you need to think about all of them simultaneously because the decisions you make on one may influence the outcome of another. There is always a certain amount of give and take in the manner in which you finalize the three features.

The design of the medical center at a large midwestern state university illustrates how the three components are highly interwoven. In this project, the task force had determined that their ideal future solution would best be built around what the medical center should look like in twenty-five years, based on the demographic trends of the state, the medical center's declared purposes, and two important considerations that they could not predict: the invention of new medical equipment and new diseases.

These considerations thus required that the design of the medical center contain a great deal of built-in flexibility that would allow them to change the configuration of the interior spaces over time. The task force designed a futuristic center, composed of four equal-sized building modules connected at the corners of each building, forming a connecting set of diamond shapes. Each building had its own core utilities in the center, and all interior walls and partitions were movable and reconfigurable.

The rough time frame for building called for constructing one module now, having the second module built approximately six years later, the third module in twelve to fourteen years, and the fourth module in around twenty years, thus finalizing the fully envisioned future solution on time in the twenty-five year time frame. An architectural plan was drawn up for the first module. In addition, the future plans included having the medical center establish a new planning committee about seventeen to nineteen years down the road to redo the SQA exercise in order to develop the next medical center future solution.

This example shows how features A and B were largely accomplished first. It should be noted that building the medical center in stages also reflected a lack of funding in the state for all the modules to be built at once. In addition, the stages were predicated on certain future conditions occurring.

Finally, the actual installation plan (feature C) was accomplished in several steps: (1) setting up a time frame for presenting the whole future and living solution package for approval to the medical faculty, university administrators, and legislators; (2) getting building cost estimates (partially started during the development of the architectural plans); (3) sending the plans out for bids; (4) selecting a contractor; (5) developing construction time lines, partial payment amounts and schedules, and dates for contractors and subcontractors to work; (6) setting up regular inspection and performance controls; and finally (7) groundbreaking ceremonies.

In addition, everyone recognized that changes still might occur to the features if, say, the proposed construction materials were not available or the project fell behind schedule or the city implemented new construction codes, traffic, and so on. However, in these cases, the goal was to keep all such changes as close as possible to the guiding future solution.

Whether your problem involves creating a solution for something as complex as building a medical center or you are focused on a smaller system, the need to develop the three living solution features is the same. Regardless of the size of the project, all three planning activities are essentially required.

THE CHALLENGES OF CREATING A LIVING SOLUTION

In the Living Solution Phase, reality sets in. Whereas the sky was the limit for future solution planning, creating the living solution requires that you identify and face any barriers, constraints, limitations, obstacles, restrictions, and irregularities that you did not get rid of in the Future Solution Phase. Creating the ideal future solution allowed you to fantasize and accept hypothetical conditions—for example:

- Technology that is not yet available
- Skills that are lacking or need to be developed over a long time frame
- Changes in attitudes and organizational cultures from the various players in the pending change
- Important irregularities not yet handled
- Required resources that are not yet allocated
- Unexpected outcomes or unanticipated risky consequences
- Skepticism from key decision makers

While these conditions were mainly waved away while creating the blue-sky future solution (as we told you to do), you now need to figure out what can be accomplished within the actual conditions.

Nevertheless, you still want to make your living solution come as close as possible to your future solution. You must find ways to minimize the influence of any possible impediments through the efforts you will make in this phase.

Creating the three features of a living solution takes a great deal of time. One reason is that this phase often requires that several events or tasks occur before you are ready to implement the immediate change, such as these:

- Preparing proposals to get the resources for development and follow-up of parts of the future solution
- Forming a project team
- Addressing various aspects of your organization's approval process
- Purchasing equipment
- Preparing and implementing formal organizational change activities
- Setting up a transition plan from "here to there"
- Training and coaching personnel
- Monitoring outcomes of the changes

As a result, this phase is the most time-consuming one, and it challenges you to continuously ask a wide range of smart questions about many aspects of the project. But the *total* time needed for the whole solution creation effort is usually less than the time it takes for comparable planning activities done with conventional approaches. The work done in the three previous SQA phases has prepared you to create the living solution without nearly as much backtracking as occurs with reductionism. In addition, the SQA process has helped you create a mind-set for creative progress and success, resulting in the right solutions. It's like the difference between travel across country without an accurate map (reductionism) and having an accurate and detailed map and plan (SQA).

When my wife and I used smart questions to remodel our kitchen, we spent a great deal of time selecting our focus purposes and designing our future solution. But we were able to detail the living solution in a short amount of time that surprised the professionals we were working with because of the preparation we had done in the Purposes and the Future Solution Phases.

HOLISTIC THINKING ABOUT THE LIVING SOLUTION

Creating a living solution can be done only within a holistic mind-set because you need to deal with the present moment as well as the future simultaneously. To some extent, in fact, you need to think backward from your future plan of successive stages to the present moment of what can actually be installed today.

It is useful to start this phase with an approximation, as was done in the medical center case, of the goals and timing of the change to be made before the future solution is planned to be installed, and then of the change before the next to last, and then of any additional changes between that one and now. This mental challenge usually sets up ideas that pull you into the future and thus requires extensive reflection using the three foundation questions as you come to grips with the uniqueness of your situation, the amount and type of purposeful information you will need, and the relevant system descriptions.

SQA Foundation Question 1: How Is the Living Solution Unique?

The living solution is a powerful reminder that every situation is unique. Its three features force you to recognize that what you install now and plan to implement later can be applicable only to you and your circumstances. This is why it is virtually impossible even to try to copy the solution someone else adopted, again illustrating why uniqueness questions are so critical.

Furthermore, you need to keep in mind that the living solution literally takes over and becomes the new unique situation that replaces the old uniqueness. That is, after a change, your organization is in some sense a new organization.

The medical center project illustrates the importance of uniqueness thinking in determining all aspects of a complex living solution. In this situation, the hospital had to take into account the unique economy and revenue projections of the state, its demographics and disease rates, its interrelationship with the state government system, the interactions of this medical center with others in the state, future advances in medicine and technology, and many other issues. These unique factors influenced what information had to be collected and what system the final hospital plans would take to satisfy their needs now and in the future.

SQA Foundation Question 2: What Information Do We Need to Develop the Living Solution?

In a way, this is an easy question to answer: the information needed is identified by the unanswered issues that arose while developing the future solution, particularly in regard to the key question, "How will it work?" When you ask this question about each component of the living solution based on your plans for getting to the future solution, you automatically identify the data and information you will need to collect. However, this question becomes even more paramount as you go about developing the living solution because you must now answer it concretely and without hesitation about every aspect of the change you are creating.

Another major type of information you will need to collect is related to any irregularities that were set aside in the Future Solution Phase that must now be incorporated into the living solution. Not only do you need to think about how the regularities will work, but you also now need to ask, "How can we find something to work for handling the irregularities while staying as close as possible to how the living solution works for the regularity?" This also means that you need to plan for any necessary arrangements that the irregularities will add to the costs, time frame, or measures of purpose accomplishment compared to the projections you made in the future solution for the regularities.

In the department store case presented in Chapter Four, the store had merchandise arriving in wooden and plastic containers as well as merchandise arriving in standard cardboard boxes. This required the store to ask during the Living Solution Phase, "How do we deal with the 10 percent of the merchandise arriving in wooden and plastic containers? What system do we need to accommodate these irregularities?"

As a result, the store had to devote time and energy during the LOD steps of the Living Solution Phase to develop a parallel system for handling the irregular shipments. (As you recall from Chapter Four, they designed a parallel system for a portion of their receiving department, in which the irregular wooden crates and plastic containers were sent on regular, not dedicated, elevators to a special area set aside near the "regular system" cardboard box area. After the irregular containers were opened, their merchandise was put into specially purchased tote bins and then placed on a conveyor belt to join the regular system.)

An important caveat to note here is that as the number of unanswered questions about how it will work goes up or as the time and costs of getting the answers increase, the more likely it is that your living solution will not be as close to the future solution as desired. This is only logical, because if you had the information right now, there would be no reason to put off installing the future solution exactly as developed.

In addition, the gap between your questions and answers will make a difference in your ability to determine the timing of future changes in feature B of the living solution. For example, in the department store example, the company was able to query vendors that shipped merchandise in wooden crates or plastic containers to find out when they might be converting to cardboard boxes. Narrowing this gap in information helped them set up several future milestones in which they were able to plan for successive phases of changes in their conveyor system that took them much closer to their future solution.

SQA Foundation Question 3: What Are the System Specifications of a Living Solution?

We have been examining the concept of systems, but it is finally in this phase when you need to focus on creating and implementing the solution in the form of a coherent system, not as isolated parts. Because every solution is a system, now is the time to begin asking, "How will it work?" for each system element: How will the inputs work for this solution? How will the outputs work? How will the operating systems work? and so on. In effect, the living solution must be thought of in terms of a fully functioning, systematic, whole operational system.

Systems thinking is an important paradigm shift from reductionist thinking, where detailing a solution is usually completed by repeating a question such as, "Have we thought of everything?" In this phase, the system framework provides quite specific questions about individual items as parts within a whole system, as well as systems connected to other systems. Your mind must begin seeing the spider webs of connections between everything. This is a big leap in thinking ability, increasing mental horsepower dramatically. This is how you become empowered individuals and organizations.

The most constructive way we have found to think systematically in creating solutions is using a system matrix. A matrix is nothing more than a checkerboard made up of rows and columns. Using a matrix to create the living solution system ensures that you have identified all critical components of the system. The components of the matrix (each of the cells) act as stimuli for asking the questions you must be sure of answering in order to have assurances that the system will work.

We use a 6-by-8 matrix, shown in Exhibit 5.1, though you can fashion your own or modify this one according to the nature and complexity of your problem. In our matrix, the rows represent the elements of the system as discussed in Chapter One, and the columns represent dimensions, attributes, or characteristics of those elements.

Here is a description of what each cell in the matrix contains. We begin with the elements:

- *Purposes:* The missions, aims, needs, primary concerns, and functions of what is to be accomplished (the what). Your thinking here reflects the focus purposes of what you intend the living solution to achieve.

Fundamental	Values	Measures	Control	Interface	Future
Purposes					
Inputs					
Outputs					
Operating Steps					
Environment					
Human Enablers					
Physical Enablers					
Information Enablers					

Exhibit 5.1.   The System Matrix

- *Inputs:* The people, things, and information to be worked on, made, or processed into outputs (the who and what). Your thinking here reflects who or what will be changed or modified by the solution.

- *Outputs:* The solution products, services, and responses that achieve the purposes, desired and undesired consequences, and outcomes (the who, what, and where). Your thinking here is also in terms, as appropriate, of customer and market types, categories or brands of outcomes, and forms of relationships sought (such as alliances, franchises, licensing, or acquisitions).

- *Operating steps:* The operating steps for changing inputs into outputs, such as the flow, layout, unit operations, and dynamic interactions of process steps (the how, where, who, and when). Your thinking here reflects the action steps or work activities or tasks that are required to operate the system, turning the inputs into outputs.

- *Environment:* The physical and organizational environment, including the organizational policies, politics, structures, roles, cultural setting, beliefs, and assumptions. Your thinking here reflects the social, organizational, and political, as well as physical (such as a clean room) environments needed for the effective implementation and operation of the solution.

- *Human enablers (or agents):* The personnel and their skills, responsibilities, level of participation, and other attributes (who, when, where, and how). Your thinking here reflects who will do the work in the operating steps that enable the solution and processes to be installed, operated, and maintained.

- *Physical enablers (or catalysts):* The equipment and facilities (how, where, when). Your thinking here reflects the physical things or technologies that will enable the solution and processes to operate.

- *Information enablers (or aids):* Books, instructions, training manuals, Web sites, and so forth (where, how). Your thinking here reflects the information that will enable the solution and processes and other enablers to operate and be maintained.

The columns in the matrix contain the dimensions:

- *Fundamental:* The physical, substantial, structural, or real characteristics of each element in the rows. This is the basic description of, or the story about, the system, as we described a system in Chapter One and illustrated briefly in Chapter Four on the Future Solution Phase.

- *Values:* The ethics, morals, values, motivating beliefs, global desires, quality, and sustainability expectations of each element. Values reflect your thinking on how the system element incorporates the identified values of your organization and other organizations that may be affected.

- *Measures:* The criteria by which you assess the performance of each element in the rows. It reflects your thinking on how you will decide on the success of the solution when it is in operation in meeting your objectives and performance specifications in the fundamental and values dimensions. The measures of purpose accomplishment are the base of what many of the specifics will be in this dimension.

- *Controls:* How to set up feedback loops to evaluate and modify the elements or system as it operates. It reflects your thinking on how you will make sure the fundamental, values, and measures dimensions stay on track and get you the results you want.

- *Interfaces:* The relations and dynamics of all elements in regard to other systems or elements. It reflects your thinking on who and what in this and other systems are affected by and can influence the successful operation of the fundamental, values, measures, and control dimensions of the element.

- *Future:* The planned changes and research needed for each dimension over time, in most cases determined from the future solution. It reflects your thinking on how you see the future changing the system.

A NOTE ON THE SYSTEM MATRIX. This system matrix is a different definition of a system than you will find in other professions. In those, outputs are often assumed to be the purpose of the system, whereas this system framework shows that purposes are not the same as the outputs.

For instance, consider the book you are holding. In some traditional definitions of systems, "to produce books" is considered the output. But this answer misses the value of considering the larger purposes of a book, such as conveying information about its subject, developing skills in readers, and gaining knowledge. These other purposes are stimuli for questions that could well generate other living solutions than books. A system that considered these other purposes might end up deciding that the best living solution for them is not a book but a CD, a Web site, a radio show, a mentoring relationship, or a training video.

In addition, many other systems combine the human, physical, and informational enablers into a single input, whereas they are separated here because this provides a better basis for asking smart questions. A human enabler, for example, needs many unique specifications in a living solution that differ from the solution's specifications of a customer. Lumping the enablers together as a single input almost always leads to assuming that "all enablers are the same." Such generalities often ignore critical factors about enablers that can be vital in crafting the details of your living solution.

An important point regarding the use of this system matrix is to recognize that developing a living solution often requires developing many parts to a solution. Thus, a complete living solution may have several systems that need to be considered. For example, in the medical facility discussed here, we may consider the physical structure as a system, the organizational change effort as a system, and the information technology as a system. Each of these is required to build the complete living solution, and so they should be separately developed with SQA using their own systems matrix.

USING THE MATRIX AS A QUESTION MATRIX. The matrix is first and foremost a reference tool by which you ask questions to develop the detailed plans for features A and B in your living solution. We therefore fondly call the matrix a question matrix, although the answers you generate eventually flesh out the matrix cells and turn it into a descriptive systems matrix that allows you to build features A, B, and C.

The matrix is thus a way of organizing the various questions you need to ask for each cell or intersection of elements and dimensions of the matrix. You started to answer some of these questions about the elements in the Future Solution Phase when you were developing the major alternatives and asking how the alternative might work. The living solution requires detailed specifications of how it *will* work now. Here is a breakdown of how the matrix serves to remind you of questions as a stimulus to consider all possible complexities of a system.

A question matrix can be developed to any level of detail to help you in using SQA in your unique organization. For example, one question for each of the forty-eight cells in the system matrix is a minimum number. We developed a question matrix for one organization that has three to six questions per cell.

Elements. All question matrices stem from the intersection among the following basic questions for the elements and those for the dimensions in the next section:

- *What purposes should the system serve?* The purposes cells of the matrix develop questions to help you confirm what the system should be accomplishing. Back in Phase 2, you began to establish the hierarchy of purposes and selected a focus purpose or purposes for the project or change effort as a whole. In using the matrix now, you can double-check the information from Phase 2 and use it to assess if the other elements of your systems all work to support that focus purpose.

- *What inputs should the system have?* What people, things, and information do you need to have worked on, processed, or changed? And what must you start with that will be included in any solution you come up with? Are there people who are worked on or changed by the process (for example, patients in a hospital or customers in a store)? Do you need specific information to start working on or converting to make your solution work? Some physical items to ask about could be required amounts of steel, powdered plastic, money, a floppy disk, or a sales order form. Information could be a bank account balance, the location of an executive, knowledge content for a course, or production statistics.

  Every system usually requires several types of inputs. A manufacturing system, for instance, might need information about the steel, such as the width and strength, as well as the metal itself. A hospital needs patients and the accompanying information inputs, such as previous test results and medical records.

- *What outputs that achieve our purposes do we want the system to have?* What types of physical items, information, people, and services do you want as the desired outputs or outcomes of your system? What are some possible undesired outputs or consequences of your system, such as pollution, dislocation of workers, scrap, or waste?

Outputs can also be properties such as performance, proprietary, or physical and chemical characteristics of the output when actually being used. What sort of handling characteristics do you want the product to have (such as in an automobile, where handling characteristics are part of the output of your manufacturing process)? What should be the customer's or user's total experience of, introduction to, ownership of, and communication with your product or service? What are the intangible outcomes of brand identification, matching or anticipating customer and market trends, and reliability?

You need to determine these desired outputs so you can anticipate the net gains in value that come from the living solution and be prepared to deal with the undesirable side effects as part of the system specifications.

- *What are the processes and operating steps we will use to create the outputs?* What are the necessary steps to convert the inputs into the outputs? How should input flow to output? What are the unit operations or identifiable changes in the inputs as they are transformed into outputs? How do you lay out your work area to make these transitions move smoothly from one to the other? Such steps include precedence order or sequence of tasks, movement, storage, meeting, decision, or control.

Are there parallel channels for processing different inputs? Are there points at which such parallel channels interrelate? In what fashion do they come together? Do they merge or intersect? Does one take over and the other stop? How do the steps affect the whole network?

- *What environment do we need to create within which the whole system will operate?* An environment is the psychological, political, cultural, legal, physical, or economic factors that you want factored into a living solution. No human is an island, and no answer or solution takes place in a vacuum. You need to address this aspect directly through direct questions, or your solutions will not work. For example, what is the corporate culture, management style, organizational ecology, and organizational climate (rewards, activities, symbols, policies, and others) that you want or need to create at your workplace to enable the living solution to be successful?

Some of the sociological factors to ask about include the state of technology in the organization, the company culture and history of change that form the background of the current attitudes of the managerial and supervisory personnel, the morale and reality of its workers, the operating controls and rules for personnel, and the social interaction and communications of the people involved. Furthermore, the smart questions you ask should be framed in terms of determining what aspects of the environment to specify to facilitate the operation of the solution.

These factors concerning the environment include more than those of the local workplace. They include the culture of the geographical and national area in which your workplace is located. Ask questions about any such particular cultural or historical issues by country or geography that may affect solutions to your problem. Are there any psychological, political, legal, or economic issues that should be factored into the living solution? Could any of these factors be better specified to help achieve a more effective, creative living solution?

While we were doing a workshop with a group of leaders in Belgium who came from a number of different countries and cultures such as Germany, England, France, Denmark, Belgium, and Holland, it was important that we spend a significant amount of time at lunch each day. This allowed the participants a chance to talk with each other in a relaxed, casual atmosphere where a good deal of learning and team building occurred. If you were to look at the lunch from an outsider's perspective, it would have appeared as if everyone was wasting a lot of time. We could have eaten lunch in the meeting room while we continued to work, but that was not the right thing to do given the environment and the diversity of the participants, where lunches are perceived to offer important socializing time to develop trustworthy relationships before business can be conducted.

Also, be sure to ask about physical environmental factors. Would climatic factors such as temperature, humidity, noise, dirt, light, or colors of machines and walls play a role in an effective solution? Are accessibility, spatial aspects, shapes, and relationships issues of design of the physical facilities and equipment? What resources are to be used in the system that could be made available on a naturally sustainable basis rather than on continuing depletion of resources? Could any of these factors be arranged to achieve better outcomes and reduce residual impact on those working in the organization?

- *Who are the human enablers we need for operating our system?* These people are not usually the same people as those who might be "inputs" or "outputs" to your solution. In a hospital, for example, these are not the patients but rather the nurses, orderlies, doctors, and others who enable the transformation of inputs (sick people) to outputs (healthy people). In some cases, there may be overlap in having individuals act as both inputs and enablers. But in general, clearly distinguishing between the two elements will help significantly in asking the right questions about the specific roles such individuals play in the system.

  Ask about the skills that human enablers or change agents need. What different types of personnel do you need to achieve the solution or to monitor controls or change input items? Must they be able to reason, perform tasks with particular dexterity, make decisions, evaluate, learn, create, or act as diligent monitors or sensors during the course of the process of changing inputs to outputs? What sort of rewards, reinforcements, and other behavior modifiers should be applied to these human enablers?

- *What sorts of physical enablers do we need within our system?* What sort of equipment and facilities will you need? What physical resources will help you in each of the steps of transforming inputs to outputs? Some common items that are often physical catalysts are machines, vehicles, chairs, computers, e-mail, Web sites, phones, teleconference facilities, filing cabinets, buildings, tools, jigs, automatic devices, paper, projectors, desks, sensors, shipping pallets, and even lighting and heating energy.

  Be sure to distinguish between what is needed to make the outputs and what is needed, for example, in the outputs (such as oil to heat the factory versus the oil in a finished automobile motor). Many items can be one thing in one context and another in a different context. For example, a chicken on an *egg* farm is a physical catalyst or enabler. A chicken on a *chicken* farm is output. A computer may be a physical enabler in an accounts payable system, an input in a computerized maintenance system, and an output in a computer manufacturing plant. Again, the definitions of the elements will help significantly in asking the right questions about the specific roles such items play in the system.

- *What sorts of information enablers do we need within the system?* What knowledge and data resources will help at each step in the process but are not part of the outputs? Do you need computer programming instructions, standard operating procedures, maintenance manuals, policy manuals, training materials, or Web sites? Do you need expert guidance, such as a media consultant or legal adviser, to embody the role of information enabler?

Dimensions. The dimensions specify what we consider to be six critical properties or attributes for each element in a living solution. You may find that your situation requires subdividing some of these or adding more. Think of this as a framework that you can modify as needed.

Here's how we use the dimensions to ask questions about each element:

- *What are the fundamental characteristics of the element (what, where, how, who)?* What are the tangible, overt, observable physical or other characteristics of the different elements of your solution? What is it? Where will it take place? How will it answer the question or solve the problem? Who will be involved? Notice that the definitions of the elements are basically related to the fundamental dimension. For example, the focus purpose from Phase 2 is the fundamental dimension of the purposes element of the system.

- *What are the values of the element—goals, motivating beliefs, quality perspectives, global desires, ethics, and moral matters—you want?* Values are something that we desire, and we use them to help make decisions—to choose what is best and most desirable. What values are associated with the different elements? What is the value of the work on this project? Values may be based on what you experience (that is, feelings, emotions, desires, passions, and sentiments). They may also be related to your goals (for example, to have fun, make a profit, enliven living spaces, eat gourmet foods, improve productivity, have a system based on naturally sustainable resources, ensure privacy of personal information, to make money). They may set ideals for living or practicing a profession such as law or medicine. They may also relate to defining and preserving (or changing) cultural and human values.

An example of a value associated with an element comes from the nurse utilization example. In that situation, one of the outputs of the nursing care utilization living solution was that patients receive the care that they need. However, the question with this particular output is, "How do you characterize the care that they receive?" In other words, "What sort of care is it that they receive?" The values that the hospital sought to operationalize were thus quality care that was also timely.

Values help you decide the best directions to take when building living solutions. They guide the development of the whole living solution, both elements and dimensions. They permeate the whole solution. Focusing on values lets you address whether to stick with your existing ones or set out to change them.

For example, your workplace might have a value that says, "Get the product out the door even if it is not perfect." You might want to ask if that is as beneficial to your company as, "We make the highest-quality, close-to-perfect products for our customers." Answering with the second value means you have to set up specifications in many elements and dimensions that move you toward the new value. The new values will guide you toward development of new solutions.

• *What are the measures we need to help determine if the fundamental and values dimensions are being maintained as the system operates?* How will you find out how the system and its elements are performing as the living solution? You need measures that help you assess how the various elements are working together as a whole solution. Measures can be monetary or nonmonetary. For example, you may have objectives relative to human enablers such as getting a 30 percent increase in training hours per employee within one year; or relative to your output element of increasing customer satisfaction and loyalty by 90 percent within two years; or contributing to corporate social responsibility as part of your environment element by increasing the number of volunteers and hours from all levels of the company by 40 percent for each of the next three years. All of these raise issues relative to what and how you measure the success of the elements of the living solution.

Keep in mind the issue of collecting only purposeful information here, remembering that there is no way to measure everything about reality and that measures can never be completely accurate and precise. As we have discussed, too much unnecessary data can get you into as much trouble as inadequate amounts. So measure carefully and just what you need to if you can.

- *What are the controls we will need to maintain our system as it operates, based on the measures?* The control dimension is critical as a way to foresee contingencies and avoid solution break-downs. The control dimension asks, "How can we ensure that our living solution works as we had intended, without glitches?" "How do we compare the measures of what is happening as the system operates to what we set up in the living solution?" "What actions might be taken if we are not getting the results from the living solution as specified?" The measures that you have defined thus become devices that can tell you when you have potential or real problems. Controls are about defining what level of the measures that you have defined and what your strategy might be for dealing with them.

  Ideally, you want to know if you have problems before they become critical. You want to avoid the "Houston, we have a problem" (*Apollo 13*) scenario where you become aware of a problem after it has reached a crisis.

  For example, the value of customer satisfaction is often measured by customer surveys (as well as by specific data about response times for inquiries, on-time deliveries, customer turnover rate, returns and rejects, and referral rate). However, the response rate on surveys is often quite low, so the survey may not be valid as a good measure, and you would want your control system to indicate this so you can switch to other ways of checking customer satisfaction, such as in-person visits and talks with many customers. In addition, you might have a strategy that if your customer satisfaction rate falls below, say, 80 percent, you will find out why and begin remedial action to fix it.

  Various techniques can help you predict and manage these random problems. If you are dealing with a sophisticated problem, such as a computer network, you will find various probabilistic approaches to deal with such issues in the fields of chaos theory and adaptive systems. However, just as measures of many of the system elements (particularly the fundamental and values dimensions) can never be complete, accurate, and precise, the control dimension will similarly be incomplete. There is always a level of gut feeling needed about how things are working. In a sense, you have to be a little like Sherlock Holmes, monitoring what is going on—both what is visible and what is not clearly visible.

For more straightforward situations—what to do at the cafeteria during lunch hour when there is a huge rush, for example—you can use common sense and advance planning rather than a complex control system. Simple questions usually suffice, such as, "What are the contingencies about which we need to think up solutions ahead of time? Do we need standby cashiers to help with the rush? How do we keep track of whether we are running out of something in time to make more?"

- *What are the interfaces with other systems or elements we will need to operate and maintain our system?* No solution exists in a vacuum, so you have to make explicit the relationships between your solution and other systems, people, networks, and conditions in the world, and even between one element and another in the same system.

  This requires you to think and ask questions about the consequences of implementing your solution. Will it change any other systems? Does it affect other areas at your work or in the world at large? If you require overtime from workers, what impact will it have on traffic in your parking lot and child care costs? All of these interfaces with other systems and issues outside the immediate sphere of your solution should be questioned here.

  In addition, the interaction of different elements of your solution should be questioned at this point. Some measures, such as costs, delays, and resource utilization, are most often considered only in terms of the particular system. Interface questions raise the issue of the effects of the solution or its technology beyond its initial implementation. For example, the costs of poor quality start with those of rework, warranties, and scrap or discarded work. How will your solution deal with the issue of quality? What are the impacts to the system to fix poor quality?

  There are often hidden aspects of solutions that you should address in this interface dimension. These include such hidden costs as unnecessary paperwork, wasted meeting times, and internal communications that ought to be the subject of a project to improve; lost revenues due to marketplace failures to meet customer needs; losses incurred by customers due to the poor quality of outputs; and losses in the socioeconomic realm that affect a community such as products that cannot be recycled, have harmful side effects, and whose production processes add to the toxicity of the environment.

You also need to formulate answers about the interface between your solution and existing systems. What sort of bridges might you need to build to connect or network your solution to other systems? What can be done to improve sustainability of resource usage by changing inputs, outputs, operating steps, environment, and physical enablers? How will your solution affect other suppliers and stakeholders? A living solution frequently involves networks of connections among internal and external organizations and people that need to be established or continued in some form. Interfaces can also include such aspects or factors in order to ensure that your solution keeps working well.

- *What is the future of the elements of our living solution system?* Most of the questions for this dimension come from the future solution. Sometimes it is also worthwhile to examine the future of the solution if it were to be pushed to its extreme top or bottom limit. What, for example, would happen if the living solution were wildly successful or depressingly ineffective?

Although the interface dimension addressed this question in the here and now, the questions that you ask about the future dimension aim to establish contingencies for your solution through time. Do relationships between elements and dimension stay the same as they are now, or do they change because of predictable changes in the future? What R&D changes or trials should be planned to occur when you have a future solution to guide you? The future dimension draws on and uses the future solution to detail what impact it would have on the elements and their dimensions.

BENEFITS OF THE SYSTEMS MATRIX. The systems matrix helps you to develop questions that lead to creative, effective, and detailed answers that eventually help define every aspect of the system. By using the matrix, you obtain a number of benefits.

- *A common language for discussing and describing problems, solution ideas, and recommendations.* The elements and dimensions provide a common language for describing the complexities of the living solution that everyone involved can agree on. As needed, it also helps stimulate the development of mutual stories, meaning a narrative of what a coherent solution might look like. Stories can often be instrumental in envisioning a solution and generating options. Because a story is supposed to be a representation of a past, present, or possible future reality, a system framework raises questions that help the narrator to consider the factors that may make the account more understandable.

- *Detailed specifications for what your living solution should look like once it is put in place.* The matrix helps you lay out the major activities and events needed to move from questions to answers, that is, from future solution to living solution and to the implementation of the approved plan. Although there are many other tools and checklists to help depict various aspects of a system, most are inadequate because they fail to interrelate all elements. In contrast, the systems matrix lets you pull all of the elements together to see how they fit into the context of all other implications and aspects of the potential solution. The importance of developing a systems matrix is that it helps you become a powerful systems thinker. As Larry Bossidy, chairman and CEO of Honeywell, and Ram Charan, a counselor to CEOs and corporate boards, state in their book *Execution: The Discipline of Getting Things Done* (2002), "If a strategy does not address the hows, it is a candidate for failure" (p. 179).

- *Crucial information on how any solution will function over time.* Too often we come up with solutions that work now but fail to take into account easily predictable changes in the future that may affect them. The matrix provides a level of protection against becoming complacent about your first installation. By forcing you to think of everything as part of a fluid, ever-changing system with dimensions and elements, you avoid trouble down the line. Continuous review of the matrix also encourages you to predict desirable future changes that might need to be made whenever there is newly available technology or information.

- *Explicit documentation of both the future and living solutions.* People often forget that a specific solution will get them only so far and then they need to take other steps. By using the systems questions in the matrix, you can clearly address what happens after your solution has served its purpose. The matrix leads you to a much more thorough speculation about the future. The future dimension of the matrix forces you to think about any possible answers to your questions with the future in mind.

- *A reduction of the odds of failure.* The matrix can greatly reduce the chances of failure due to unexpected causes. It helps surface potential pitfalls and weak points in the planning phases. The matrix can also be used as the basis for crisis management in that it helps you see what may need to be done when handling crises (think of major product crises, such as those concerning Firestone tires and the Tylenol tampering case). The system matrix provides an excellent way to minimize unintended consequences, unwanted side effects, and efforts at pushing technology for technology's sake. For example, many methods and tools that human agents use can be error provocative, and such possible sources of accidents should be avoided if possible by asking smart questions now, as well incorporating in the living solution ways of handling any crisis or accident that occurs. The law of unintended consequences—any change or policy for the future will very likely produce unexpected reactions or unanticipated consequences—will always be a real-life factor to consider, but the odds of failure are significantly reduced with a system matrix. For example, most communities have experienced significant problems with their 911 emergency call system, which is overwhelmed with calls and cannot distinguish legitimate emergencies. But many of these might have been anticipated if questions about the fundamental, values, and measures dimension had been asked when it was designed.

- *Assistance in making decisions.* Because every decision involves selecting one alternative from several at each point where a choice must be made, the details embedded in a matrix framework are often crucial. The SQA phases require many choices, and selecting the eventual recommendation is the crucial decision, requiring all the details of system workability to be available.

- *Simplification of control and correction procedures.* The matrix puts controls in the perspective of the larger system and lets you stop micromanaging while delegating decisions to the appropriate personnel. It also lets you simplify the complexity of a solution because it exposes many levels of possible interactions of the whole living solution.

- *Encouragement of continued learning.* Any organization must continue to learn in order to grow. The matrix, with its emphasis on solutions, fosters an environment of continued education and development of both systems and workers. If you want to increase the intellectual horsepower of your organization, here is a powerful tool.

A Case Study in Using the System Matrix

An example will illustrate how the system matrix helped produce questions that aided in the development of a living solution for a client of ours who was aiming to produce a knowledge management (KM) system. The following list illustrates the types of questions that the team in charge found critical to ask about the system elements as they designed the KM system:

Purposes

- What should the KM system accomplish (make knowledge accessible to all employees, provide a resource for training, use knowledge as an asset, categorize project and customer knowledge, maintain a record of value-added knowledge such as patents, licenses, research reports, customer databases, parts descriptions and catalogues, and so on)?

- What are the values of KM: generate new knowledge, leverage our knowledge base, retain tacit knowledge of those leaving the organization, transferability of knowledge? (Questions for the other dimensions follow from these.)

Inputs

- What level of information and knowledge should enter the KM system: project or work group, strategic decisions, related external knowledge, system matrix descriptions of competitors, and so on?

Outputs

- How should the KM system be organized?

- Can all outputs be described in system matrix terms to provide a whole story and easy access by anyone seeking specific element-dimension information, types of technical know-how, and so on?

- What possible unintended consequences or unanticipated occurrences should be considered and handled?

Operating Steps

- How and when will the inputs be handled to produce the outputs: gather reports and knowledge and information resources,
  prioritize them, determine the quality of the inputs, organize
  them into the output categories, enter the knowledge in the
  database, publicize availability of updates?

Environment

- What physical and organizational policies and procedures
  should we have to set up and use KM effectively: a separate
  department, organizational role definitions, top management
  commitments, internal or outsourced platform?

Human Enablers

- Who will be assigned, trained, or hired to implement the
  process: content or KM-skilled persons, capabilities as a coach or
  facilitator or consultant, full or part time?

Physical Enablers

- How will the KM data be stored and handled: computer based,
  paper records, CDs, transparencies, microfiche?
- At what physical location will the equipment be located and outputs stored?
- Are special temperature and humidity specifications necessary?

Information Enablers

- What operating instructions, maintenance manuals, and software packages are needed for all the elements?

THE LIST, ORGANIZE, AND DECIDE STEPS

You are now ready to translate the concepts of uniqueness, purposeful information, and the systems matrix into selecting your living solution. As in the other phases, moving through the LOD steps follows
the divergent and convergent thinking pattern that is necessary to create many options from which one is selected.

The explanations that follow of how to go through the LOD steps
is largely focused on creating features A and B of the living solution—

the detailed description of the solution that can be implemented today and the plans for future changes in stages. These two components go hand in hand, as your decision must take into account what can done today versus what must be postponed until a future time, based on the factors that influence your time frame, such as the state of technology, funding, and available human resources. Feature C, the actual installation plan for what will be accomplished today, will be discussed in greater detail at the end of the chapter, although you need to think at least minimally about the installation plan as you go through the LOD steps.

The List Step

The list step for creating features A and B of the living solution is similar to that for developing the future solution list: develop as many options as you can that stay as close as possible to the future solution. To produce many options, you once again tap into the creativity techniques related to bisociation. For example, you could ask, "What are the ideal ways we can think of to stay as close as possible to the inputs [outputs, process, environment, and human, physical, and information enablers] of the future solution by means of a [random word, flashcard, or whatever bisociation technique you want to use]"?

In many cases, you ask this and similar questions to determine how close you can come to a particular component or element in the future solution. For example, a future solution may have a component that involves electronic transmittal of a student's test scores to several users of the data. The cost of such a procedure, availability of financial resources, and legal privacy policies may have been some of the reasons that the component cannot be used now. So the question is, "What creative ways can we think of to stay as close as possible to that component?" In one case, the living solution component used a multipage pressure-sensitive form to have copies to distribute to users.

Handling the irregularities in the living solution is another reason that creativity is needed. In addition to developing a way to incorporate each irregularity so it stays as close as possible to the future solution, you want any costs, time, or other resources needed for the living solution, in addition to those in the future solution, to be as small as possible, as depicted in Figure 4.1. The department store case illustrates with extra space and costs what was done to handle wooden and plastic containers.

The living solution list step continues the emphasis you have learned throughout SQA on being creative in order to develop as many ideas or options as possible. Therefore, the above question can be asked about each irregularity with the many system and stimulator words identified there to indicate how it is possible to develop as many ideas as possible even in this last phase.

TECHNIQUES FOR LISTING. Overall, as with the future solution questions, you can use either a structured method or the conversational or intuitive method to begin developing list ideas that might identify possible living solution options for feature A, the detailed description of the solution.

As we explain the techniques for developing a living solution, we will follow one case study through the LOD steps: a project to plan and design a method for convincing a group of a company's employees to become outsource contractors.

Structured Method for Listing. The structured method for listing is similar to the Future Solutions Phase, in which you tap into bisociation questions in a group discussion to generate a number of ideas and options.

The three foundation questions provide a basis for asking more smart questions about developing living solution ideas. The box provides examples of the types of other questions you might ask as you explore ways to stimulate thinking about ideas that stay as close as possible to the future solution for achieving the focus purposes.

Case Study. Here is an example of how asking smart questions leads to a living solution list. This client, Outsourcing Technology Company (OTC), does a multibillion-dollar business outsourcing information technology (IT) workers to other companies. The OTC workers do the computer work in-house for a company, but OTC manages them. IT is not the only activity that OTC makes available for outsourcing; it also provides accounting, payroll, manufacturing, research and development, and marketing services.

To obtain workers and perform the service that is being outsourced, OTC usually hires many of the IT professionals who are already working at their client companies. However, getting workers to leave their company happily to work for OTC is almost always a volatile process that takes a good deal of care to manage. The problem for OTC was how to find and convince workers to become outsource contractors rather than stay employed at their companies.

~~~ SMART QUESTIONS FOR THE LIVING SOLUTION

List Step

The following sample smart questions can be asked in addition to those presented previously in the holistic thinking and system matrix sections, and all of these will surely stimulate you to consider questions unique to your situation.

Uniqueness
- What are the ideal ways we can think of to stay as close as possible to the future solution for this component that leverage our unique capabilities and environment?
- How can we develop a living solution and implementation plans that work within our surrounding environment and systems while staying as close as possible to the future solution?
- What are currently implementable ways we can think of to stay as close as possible to the future solution for this component (service, action, process, or something else) that would take care of the unique irregularity conditions in our situation?

Information
- What specific information needs to be collected about this component to help me stay as close as possible to the future solution and describe how it would work?
- What information do we need about implementation processes in our organization that would help list ideas for staying close to the future solution?
- What information should be gathered about an irregularity condition to help determine ideas to list that will keep the components as close as possible to the future solution?

Systems
- What are potential input ideas for overcoming a reason (for example, technology not available, resources not allocated, time frame too short) that would not let us adopt the future solution now?
- What are potential output ideas for our living solution?
- What are potential operating steps ideas for our living solution?
- What are potential environmental ideas for our living solution?
- What are potential human enabler ideas for our living solution?
- What are potential physical enabler ideas for our living solution?
- What are potential information enabler ideas for our living solution?

In the case of OTC, a number of major future solution alternatives had already been proposed. One was to create an expert system on the topic of outsourcing transitions. These systems are like an elaborate, interactive help menu, only they usually provide much more information to answer any question on the topic at hand.

Meanwhile, at the project team meeting for creating a living solution, I set the context and focused the team by posing the basic living solution question: What are some possible solutions that stay as close to the future solution as possible? The team members were savvy computer geeks who knew that creating a true expert system was beyond their ability to produce for all intents and purposes. As a result, it was clear that the chosen future solution, though perfectly valid, was still rather impractical to do as the living solution. Expert systems are difficult to develop because it is nearly impossible to truly imitate the power of the brain and the complex process of individuals' developing and applying knowledge in dynamic and complex situations.

So the question now was whether they could develop a living solution out of their concept of an expert system. For example, could they create some type of transitional database containing an evolving methodology of best practices, tools, and techniques that people in outsourcing transitions could search? Admittedly, a transitional database of a living and constantly evolving outsourcing methodology did not impress these computer geeks in the same way as a real expert system did, but this modification of the future solution got the group off the ground. Moreover, it continued to support their focus purpose: to have outsourcing information available to help outsourced employees feel welcomed and valued in their new company.

Having come up with this living solution idea, we then asked ourselves additional smart questions whose answers helped us develop a matrix of the outsourcing methodology elements (in terms of inputs, outputs, processes, environmental agents, human enablers, physical enablers, and information enablers). Exhibit 5.2 shows examples of the types of smart questions the OTC group members needed to ask and the answers they came up with.

Notice that some of the ideas listed in Exhibit 5.2 are generated by expanding questions from the system matrix. For instance, you need to ask about each element of the system matrix—what its purposes are and where it comes from. What are the inputs to the future solution inputs? The inputs to that? What outputs will the future solution outputs produce? What are the outputs of that? And so on.

What are other potential purposes of the living methodology system in addition to those determined with the purposes questions?
- To have an updated and evolving record of outsourcing methodology
- To enable change agents with practices and tools
- To have a state-of-the-art practice of outsourcing transitions

What are potential inputs that stay close to the future solution?
- Current outsourcing transition practices
- Change agents
- Outsourced employees
- OTC

What are potential outputs that stay close to the future solution?
- Updated methodology, practices, and tools
- Empowered change agents
- Outsourced employees who feel more valued and empowered
- More successful outsourcing business for OTC

What are potential processes or operating steps for converting the inputs to outputs that stay close to the future solution?
- Ensure the project team has all the resources needed
- Decide on an approach to creating the methodology
- Create a draft of the methodology
- Review draft with sponsors and other change agents who are affected
- Create tools and templates to support the methodology in the field
- Publish the methodology
- Train change agents in the use of the methodology
- Determine the schedule for the next revision

What are potential environmental elements that stay close to the future solution?
- Use a virtual team approach to developing the methodology since this will save on travel expenses
- Have a project team that is clear about its task, roles and responsibilities, budget, and deadlines for completing the project
- Have a methodology that breaks new ground, not simply a best practice (copying what others are doing)

Who are potential human enablers who stay close to the future solution?
- Smart Questions coach
- Sponsors of the project
- Change agents who have been outsourced and understand the experience
- Project team members

(Continued)

Exhibit 5.2. Living Solution Smart Questions and Answers in the OTC Case Study

What are potential physical enablers that stay close to the future solution?
- Computers
- Internet infrastructure
- Telecommunication equipment
- Word processing software

What are potential information enablers that stay close to the future solution?
- Social scientific research about what makes human transitions or major changes most successful
- Experience of outsourced employees
- Outsourcing best practices

Exhibit 5.2.   Living Solution Smart Questions and Answers in the OTC Case Study *(continued)*

The value of this questioning is that it helps you get to the details of the elements of the living solution. Ideas that result from such questions should be listed on an easel sheet or with any recording methods used to date.

Conversational and Intuitive Methods. In many cases, the conversational or intuitive method suffices to develop a list of living solution ideas. This is especially true when you follow along the system matrix, covering each element and dimension as you ask questions and flesh out list ideas. Each cell in the matrix prompts you to ask critical questions that can guide the conversation to describe the elements of each living solution proposed.

In a case of planning a center for software development, the group decided to use the conversational method. We summarized the living solution ideas on a large chart with seven columns. From left to right, the columns contained the attributes of the planned center (system elements and dimensions translated to the specific terms of the firm) and what state the attributes should be in at three months, six months, twelve months, eighteen months, twenty-four months, and thirty-six months. (Notice how this chart combines the development of features A and C for this project.) The last column, in effect, was a description of the future solution that the group had selected. As the specific conditions of the attributes at the various time intervals were being discussed, many ideas were listed for this step.

Sometimes a name may be given to the living solution alternatives to help an organization relate its own background to SQA. For example, a living solution for a strategic plan may call the first year of stages of successive change toward reaching the future solution a business plan for the year. The next year's stages would then be called the tentative business plan for that year.

HANDLING IRREGULARITIES IN CREATING A LIVING SOLUTION. One of the main goals of the living solution phase is to find solutions that accommodate both the irregularities and regularities of the situation. Ironically, asking questions about irregularities often leads to ways to eliminate the actual causes of the exceptions, thus facilitating the design of a much more effective and creative living solution.

To deal with the issue of irregularities, ask the following types of questions: What purpose does this irregularity serve? What do we want to accomplish with it? How could we achieve that purpose if we started over again? How would the start-over solution work in system terms? Surprisingly, you may come up with even better ideas to handle the irregularities and transform them into regularities.

For example, in the OTC case, the team determined that in general, the outsourcing methodology would normally be used over the Internet into a secure corporate Web site. However, the team noted that they still had an important irregularity 10 to 20 percent of the time when users would be at client sites and unable to access the corporate site. The team therefore listed some possible solutions:

- Have a CD version of the guide and tools available for employees who traveled regularly.
- Publish a hard copy version of the guide and tools.
- Have portions of the guide and tools that could be downloaded using modem connections.

You will see which option the team chose later as we review the organize and decide steps.

The Organize Step

Once you have developed numerous ideas for your living solution in the list step, it's time to organize them into more clearly defined options to be considered for selection in the decide step. By the end of the organize step, you should aim to have a minimum of two or more major options in preparation for the decide step. However, continue to spell out the details for each option to provide some assurance of its workability and ease of implementation.

TECHNIQUES FOR ORGANIZING. Once again, there are structured and conversational or intuitive methods for organizing.

Structured Methods of Organizing. The organize step starts with a discussion about how the listed ideas might be grouped into options. One way to do this, for complex solutions, is to repeat the procedure used in the future solution organize step: determine for each living solution idea whether it is a major alternative, component, or detail. Although we have found this useful in a few cases, for other than the most complex cases, most of the time, the organize step is done in a more cursory way.

In all cases, though, the most important part of the structured method for organizing the options for a living solution is to use the system matrix as the basis for asking questions based on the dimension cells of each element to determine how the option will work. The aim is to get enough details about each option to let you select one in the decide step. Because the living solution needs to have much more specific detail to arrive at feature A, the organize step involves many more specifics than those identified in the future solution organize step. For example, you may need to consult various databases to identify how a particular technology included in the future solution might actually work, or to explore all issued patents to determine if a technology might exist to do what the future solution would like to include. Such information gives more realistic data about each living solution option to help in the decide step

All six dimensions for all eight system elements are not always explored in detail for some projects. As a general rule, though, it can be very useful to explore all forty-eight cells if the project is large or complex. However, as the system decreases in size, scope, and complexity, a more limited exploration of the dimensions usually suffices, or more important, identifies a few focal element points that reflect the uniqueness of your system.

When the OTC team considered the system they were designing, they determined that the values dimension was particularly important and unique to their situation because one of the key issues they needed to deal with was how to help newly outsourced employees feel they were valued members of the outsourcing company. The importance of values led the team to explore the values dimension in the organize step, after which they derived statements about the values they needed to achieve, as shown in Table 5.1.

The discussion and development of the values dimension helped the project team organize their living solution concepts and further refine their ideas to capture the importance of helping new employees feel like valuable and contributing members of a new organization. In this case, it led to the development of a workshop specifically targeted to new employees to help them plan their careers in the new company and envision a future for themselves.

Other Smart Questions to Ask During the Organize Step. In addition to considering uniqueness, size, and complexity of systems, here are some other questions often asked in projects as a result of probing

Output Components	Values to Build into a Living Solution
Updated methodology	In the methodology and practices, there should be explicit instructions, sample communication events, and messages about how to communicate that the outsourced employees are valued by their new company.
Empowered change agents	Change agents who are facilitating the outsourcing process should be instructed on the importance of communicating to outsourced employees about the issue of valued employees.
Outsourced employees who feel more valued and empowered	There should be a workshop that could help the new employees participate in designing their own future within the outsourced company.
More successful outsourcing business for OTC	It is believed that outsourced employees who feel more valued will result in more successful business practices and could also result in some future marketing messages to potential clients

Table 5.1. Values Dimension of Outputs of the OTC Case

certain dimensions of the various elements, such as the value dimension of outputs. You may also find them useful in organizing your list
ideas into options:

- *How can we make our product or system user friendly?* One major
  issue we often encounter in developing a living solution relates
  to how to make the output product or system user friendly.
  Unfortunately, there is a tendency to resort to new technology as
  the panacea, and many groups frequently make technology the
  heart of a future solution. The emphasis in the late 1990s on
  technology caused many organizations to overly rely on it in
  their solutions.

  However, in our view, the recession of the new economy can be
  largely attributed to a serious lack of consideration about how
  much users effectively benefit from many technology products or
  systems. For example, huge hard drives on computers are difficult
  to back up. It has become so time-consuming and cumbersome
  to back them up reliably that many people no longer do this regularly. Those who still have floppies may be at less risk of total
  loss of data. Although the huge hard drive appeared to be a great
  future solution at that time, it left users operating in a less-than-
  friendly environment that still has not been fully solved.

  As a result, it helps to moderate your desires for technological
  user friendliness by asking such questions as these:

  - How will the solution option improve the user's productivity?
  - Does the option project simplicity?
  - Is the option user friendly and convenient?
  - Does the option pose any risks to the user?
  - If appropriate, is the option fun to use, and does it project a
    good image?

It is not possible to eliminate all use of technology, and that
would not be smart. But the organize step provides the chance to
reflect on your output elements and their dimensions to reduce
the likelihood of mistakes when you begin implementing your
living solution using technology.

- *Are we falling into the sunk-cost fallacy?* This question is especially useful because so many options fall into this trap. There is an almost universal tendency to claim that since a lot of money and time have already been spent on developing this product or system (the costs already "sunk" into the project), the organization should continue to put more money and effort into completing it. This is a favorite claim of politicians who want to commit more funding to a project that is already over budget and has not met deadlines or even come close to producing milestone results.

  Unfortunately, far too many executives in companies and government agencies make this claim. The fallacy is simple: having already expended a lot of money, the sunk cost, we do not want to lose it, even though results show it does not and may never work. However, you need to avoid the trap of throwing good money after bad. Purposes and future solution questions should always be asked about any option that proposes to continue such funding as the way to avoid the trap. Asking this question should help you avoid identifying only living solution options that require not wasting what has been already expended.

- *Are there any unintended consequences?* Every change relative to a living solution becomes part of one or more larger systems, and every system is a node on a relationship network. Nearly every solution therefore includes a possible conflict or unintended consequence caused by a "system dysfunction" between one of its elements and dimensions, such as between a physical enabler and a human enabler. No matter how much you have attempted to maximize the change, there are always things that will go wrong. This is Murphy's Law.

  As a result, the options you create and the many questions logically raised by each element and dimension cell are critical tools for probing these imponderables in the decision process. The system matrix does not always provide the information needed, but it does significantly increase the likelihood of catching many glitches that could affect the eventual installation and success of the immediate change and future changes within your living solution.

- *What future trends might require us to need new resources as we build the system?* For some projects, you may need to rethink various dimension issues relative to changes over which you have no control. For example, the environment element and its dimensions may portend significant impediments to the immediate workability of your solution or the future implementation of planned changes. These impediments may then create a need to change your plans.

  For example, a number of trends invariably affect the general environment in which many solutions occur: the aging of the population, a new baby boom that may be occurring, the growth of entrepreneurship, the rate of technological developments, greater threats of terrorism, and increasing cultural diversity. Do these or other environmental trends affect the potential viability of your living solution options? Do they suggest a need for additional resources as you continue development?

- *How much time is available for building the system?* In reviewing your projected timing to implement the living solution, especially when the time frame is long, it is critical to set up interim deadlines and milestones for subtasks. You may need to take into account that each living solution option still on the table may have different tasks and time frame needs. Each option may require different methods or modes of implementation; for example, one option may require a one-time installation, while another requires dividing the solution up into smaller installations that work slowly toward incremental success.

  Time and resources also shape one of the most important interim decisions in the organize step: whether to develop a prototype model or set up a pilot facility to test the operating steps. You may wish, for example, to do extensive computer simulations, or draw charts and flow process graphs, or do focus group studies, or in some other way validate the workability of a proposed option before moving on to the decide step.

- *Especially for complex and large-scope projects, does each option incorporate procedures that could handle a crisis should one occur?* As all of us have learned in the last couple of decades, crises can develop in many different circumstances in unexpected ways: the Tylenol tampering that caused deaths and the Bridgestone-Firestone tires–Ford Explorer cases, for example. Although the unintended consequences question may address part of this question, such consequences are usually slow to emerge. A potential crisis is best handled when you are developing living solution options by heeding the critical words from the classic definition of crisis: "A crisis occurs when the structure of a social system allows for fewer possibilities for problem solving than are necessary for the continued existence of the system; . . . when the negotiated order of a collective system does not allow a problem to be resolved" (Drazin, Glynn, and Kazanjian, 1999, p. 286).

These structures and "negotiated orders" are other ways of defining the elements and dimensions of each living solution option.

Since a living solution is something to be done in the future, there will be assumptions and conjectures about both how the recommendation will work and what the presumed conditions of internal and external systems will be. Thus, uncertainties are always a part of creating solutions. As the living solution ideas are being organized, identify within each major alternative, and possibly across all of the alternatives, which assumptions are most likely to cause positive results (better results than expected) as well as negative difficulties or even failure. Then try to develop a sequence of events that might occur to have each assumption shown to be inappropriate. This will provide some insight into where to incorporate in the alternative or all of them methods of coping with what may become a failure or a crisis. For example, avoiding the difficulty of a particular emerging technology considered to be a foundation for the workability of one or more alternatives not working may be handled by developing a version of the alternative with another technology to be developed concurrently. Developing one of the two versions would be stopped if the other one proves capable of fulfilling the expectations of the assumption.

Incorporating such contingency plans in the living solution alternatives being organized from the list ideas, even if they only identify points of uncertainty, will prove helpful in the decide step.

Conversational and Intuitive Methods of Organizing. The organize step of this phase can be done conversationally as well by using the systems matrix to ask questions about each proposed idea, as well as reviewing the six additional smart questions on pages 214–17.

If you conduct this review in an ad hoc meeting, be sure to define the agenda clearly so as to force team members to focus in depth on the living solution options. The purpose of the meeting is to clarify the living solution options, add detail to them, explore connections with other systems, and see how the various options might work. Remember that the goal is to sort the list ideas and organize them into a few clear and discrete options that you would like to consider for implementation.

If you use the conversational-intuitive approach, be sure to impose a meeting framework that will lead to complete results, in the same way that you think systematically about the solutions. Exhibit 5.3 shows a sample agenda that we have used in ad hoc conversational meetings with clients during the organize step. This example shows how a systems framework helps you conduct the meeting. You can also develop alternative agendas as a way of specifying the multiple living solution options sought in the organize step.

HOW TO KNOW IF YOU HAVE ANSWERED ENOUGH QUESTIONS. The best method to determine if you have asked enough questions in order to get sufficient details about each living solution option is to ask someone not associated with the project if the story you tell them about each option makes sense. Pay particular attention to the questions they ask because they may give you the insight about what other information you need. If there are no other questions or those that are asked are answerable with the details you already have, you are ready to move forward to the decide step.

The Decide Step

In the software business, everyone knows that the first release of every new program automatically includes bugs. It is accepted that Release 1.0 is likely to change in some aspect and that new releases and versions will be required to address any errors and to make improvements that customers want.

A similar concept needs to be applied to any solution effort. In SQA, no solution should ever be considered final or complete. Future releases and versions of the solution will always be necessary. That is the impetus for teaching you to create a living solution and not think of your installation as final.

As a result, when you arrive at the decide step of a living solution, make sure you keep in mind that you will be implementing several releases and creating feature B that spells out a plan to move you

What are the purposes of the meeting?
- To organize the listed ideas for the OTC project

What are the main outcomes you want from the meeting?
- Have major alternatives, details, and components identified for the living outsourcing methodology

What are the ground rules (environment) for this meeting?
- Record action items
- Allow everyone the chance to participate in the planning
- No sidebar conversations
- Allow the facilitator to do his or her job

Who will play what roles in the meeting (human enablers)?
- Facilitator: Mary Smith
- Scribe to take meeting notes: Roberto Castro

What will be the next steps (process, future dimension) for the team after the meeting?
- The team will decide this during the meeting and record future action items

What are the agenda items for this meeting (process or operating steps), and how much time do we allocate to them?
- Check in: 5 minutes to allow people to say what's on their mind in order to "get present"
- Agree on the purposes of the meeting: 15 minutes
- Agree on the desired outcomes for the meeting: 15 minutes
- Organize listed OTC living methodology ideas into major alternatives, components, and details: 90 minutes
- Determine next steps: 10 minutes
- Process check: How did the meeting work? Did we get the results that we were looking for? 5 minutes

---

Exhibit 5.3.   Sample Agenda for an Ad Hoc Organize Step Meeting in the OTC Case

toward the ideal future solution, giving you time and options to redesign the living solutions as needed.

As always, the decide step can be done using structured or conversational methods.

STRUCTURED METHODS. Once you or your team has enough detail about each organize solution, it is time to select which solution or solutions will actually be implemented. For this, you can use any number of software packages that contain formal methodologies in the decision-making field. You may know or have been exposed to one or more of these formal methodologies:

- Multiattribute utility models
- Cost-effectiveness analysis
- Pair comparison
- Sensitivity analysis
- Contingency analysis
- Variance analysis
- Subjective probability assessment
- Expert consensus
- Information gap decision theory
- Integrated cost uncertainty assessment
- Risk analysis and assessment

Explaining these techniques is beyond the scope of this book, but suffice it to say that most are some form or variant of the Smart Questions Decision Worksheet explained in Chapter Four. In general, many of the software packages that contain these techniques use similar methods to SQA to help you make decisions. Typically, you enter the same type of information that you have learned to prepare in using SQA, such as alternatives you are considering; criteria, factors, and measures to be considered in making the selection; and the importance (weighting) you assign to each factor. Then the software usually has you input data specific to one of the above problem-solving algorithms, following which it makes its particular calculations and recommendations.

However, in our experience, many of these packages draw blanket conclusions such as "Alternative X is best" based on claims that certain risks are lower or have been removed from that selection. Based on the hundreds of projects we have worked on and our years of experience, however, our advice is not to trust decisions from software packages alone. Bargaining and negotiating the trade-offs that are usually needed to select and implement a holistic living solution, especially one containing uncertainty, probabilities of occurrence, risk, and values and ethics issues, are usual for most decisions. This is the case even where extensive models and software have been developed for a particular area, such as with risk assessment techniques for decisions in finance, engineering, insurance, safety of products or human activities at work and in the home, and economics.

For the purposes of this book, we highly recommend that you use the Smart Questions Decision Worksheet to conclude the decide step if you are using a formal approach. The worksheet is generally adequate for most issues and many, if not all, complex ones. The explanation we gave in Chapter Four on how to use the worksheet is equally valid for the decide step of a living solution, with the caveat that your decision for this phase needs far more detail, supporting measures, and thoroughness than during the Future Solution Phase.

CONVERSATIONAL AND INTUITIVE METHODS. The decide step can be accomplished using a more informal conversational or intuitive approach along with the Smart Questions Decision Worksheet. The conversational approach is usually very effective when a team has been working together over the course of the entire SQA process and demonstrates that it can function with a single mind-set. The conversational approach can also be used as a supplement to the formal structured approach as a verification of the final decision.

The OTC team used both the formal structured approach and the conversational approach because they believed that there was still an element of the decision to be made intuitively based on the team's informal conversations on a day-to-day basis. Through these conversations, the technical experts advised that the Web-based outsourcing guide with hyperlinks and downloadable tools was too complicated to do within their budget and time constraints.

As a result of these intuitive assessments, the project team decided that the most workable solution was to create the outsourcing guide and tools using standard office software readily available to all team members and consultants in the field. They projected, however, that the output from the office software could eventually become the basis for a Web-based version later. They also decided that the guide and tools would be available for download on the Internet and that a CD version of the guide and tools would be created and distributed to meet the irregularity conditions of consultants at client sites without Internet access.

COPING WITH POLITICAL AND SOCIAL FACTORS AROUND YOUR FINAL CHOICE

It is likely that over the course of your work with SQA, you may have occasionally touched on various political or social factors that could influence your choice of solution, but you likely put them aside (as we recommended) during the future solution phase so you could create an ideal solution devoid of such considerations. However, at this time, it is likely that you can no longer sidestep these factors in the decide step. You must now decide how to implement solution ideas that may be adverse to some people. You will therefore need to ask hard questions:

- Which alternative provides a unique and valuable strategy that other options cannot match?
- Would we be better off just tinkering with what we have rather than embarking on a different path?
- Does our management team have a shared appreciation of where the future solution is leading?
- Do we know if the plan balances its direction with particular high-business-impact areas?
- How do we know we have the skill sets necessary to move ahead with this alternative?
- What are the ethical and social issues that we should be considering about each alternative?
- Are there interpersonal, ethical, moral, and social issues that might interfere with choosing this solution?
- If we select this alternative as our living solution, what is the likelihood that R&D will be able to accomplish the needed developments to let us move toward the future solution?
- Will the costs and time needed for implementing this option make it very difficult to obtain the expected benefits of the solution?
- Will we be able to acquire the money to install the solution even if the benefits of it far exceed the costs?

• Will the risk tolerance of our management and R&D
  departments play a role?

Coping with these kinds of questions at this point requires that you
ask once again about the purpose of the issue behind the question, then
what the purpose of that issue is, and so on. For example, if your R&D
department seems to have an issue about moving forward with the new
aspects of a product, you might find yourself asking some critical questions about what the purpose of R&D is relative to the solution design.

In many situations, you may indeed find that the supposed issue
that appears to block your solution disappears or becomes irrelevant
when compared to other necessary purposes. But if the issue is worth
considering, be sure to add it to the list of criteria that the living solution must fulfill. However, in the long run, be clear about the measures
of purpose accomplishment, and make those your key decision factors.

In the OTC outsourcing case, the sponsors of the project were clear
about three criteria that they needed to pay attention to in selecting
their solution. First, they required a short time frame because the company was expanding rapidly, with new outsourcing deals coming in
on a regular basis, providing them with a great urgency to get a solution in place. In fact, the sponsors specifically desired a four-month
time frame in which to create and implement a solution. Second, there
was a fixed budget for the project even before the solution was even
defined. Finally, the solution had to support the focus purpose of the
project: to help newly outsourced employees feel welcomed and valued as productive team members. Therefore, the solution or solutions
that could best meet these three requirements would clearly be the
one that would be selected.

In short, selecting the solution that will become your first release
will in many cases require that formal standards of expected performance be set up for each of the stages in moving toward the future
solution. You will need to establish values, measures, and control
dimensions at these stages that make advances sought in the future
solution. Setting up such expectations will also need to include your
installation planning activities, where you account for various changes,
schedules, and accomplishments within a specific time frame and budget. Such installation decisions may in some cases be a function of the
cost-time trade-off considerations in selecting which option becomes
your first release.

THE INSTALLATION PLAN

At the beginning of the chapter, we indicated that the third feature of the living solution was an installation plan covering the steps that would need to be done to implement the first-stage change.

For clarity, we need to distinguish here between *implementation* and *installation*. An implementation plan, in terms of SQA, begins immediately in Phase 1 with people involvement and continues throughout the SQA phases. To be truly effective, the holistic implementation plan must be designed as the solution is being designed. For example, getting a change effectively installed usually involves many tasks that should be considered during all the activities that occur in the People Involvement, Purposes, and Future Solution phases, and certainly no later than in the Living Solution Phase:

- Getting a champion and others involved for the recommended change and its future solution
- Preparing a proposal to get financing, transitioning, or phasing in the plan
- Ordering equipment, tools, and facilities
- Arranging for construction if needed
- Training
- Monitoring of initial use of the solution
- Normalizing or optimizing the solution while in operation

Presentations about the project status may be needed at various points in the whole project as well as during installation.

Because of this, SQA considers implementation as beginning immediately in the People Involvement Phase. If you recall, the Smart Questions People Involvement Worksheet (Exhibit 2.1) helps to identify critical people (contributors, affected people, decision makers) to involve with the subsequent purposes, future solution, and living solution questions.

In contrast, we are talking in this chapter about installation planning, a specific stage of implementation. Installation planning can be considered the result of the living solution decision. Unfortunately, one of the key mistakes that unsuccessful project managers of change efforts make is to neglect planning how a project's change recommendation will be installed until the very end, assuming that they cannot know how they will implement something until it has been fully designed. This is usually too late.

Thinking about the installation plan thus must be done nearly simultaneously as you develop features A and B of the living solution. To create the installation plan, you need to ask the same types of questions as the entire SQA process has covered, such as:

- Who should be involved in developing the installation plan?
- What purposes should the installation plan accomplish?
- What would be an ideal future solution for achieving the focus purposes of the installation plan?
- How close can the living solution come to the future solution for achieving the focus purposes of the installation plan?
- What are the details of the installation plan system (inputs, outputs, process or set of steps required, environment, human enablers, physical enablers, and information enablers)?

Thinking about installation as a system itself is a powerful corrective for a common mistake of thinking that *installation* is simply a synonym for getting approvals, buying equipment, putting equipment in place, training, monitoring, or correcting errors. Each of these requires a solution or system that can be created with the same smart questions. This also continues SQA's focus on bringing creativity to all aspects of creating solutions.

In the OTC case, developing the installation plan took on as much importance and seriousness as the decisions regarding selecting and designing features A and B had taken. The teams' plan revolved largely around employing a large number of change agents who had backgrounds in outsourcing projects and could participate in the process of designing and writing the outsourcing guide and tools. The selection of these individuals accomplished two key objectives: the guide was richer and more complete because these agents brought firsthand experience to the design task, and the change agents themselves became more educated in the process and committed to using the guide even before it was complete. In fact, the change agents who were involved in developing the materials became coaches for other change agents who were either not involved in the process or new to the outsourcing process.

Many installation plans include training programs, but even these can be better designed by using SQA. For example, one project we worked on required a new service order system that affected the work of sixteen thousand people out of forty thousand employees. Involving all sixteen thousand in the solution creation effort is almost impossible. The sixteen thousand people were spread out over many company locations in five states. First and foremost, the People Involvement Phase tried to get as many people as possible involved. We invited representatives from all the company's geographical locations and functional activities to join the project task force; each representative was also required to report to and get further input from their constituencies about the options being considered in each SQA phase prior to the decide step in each one. The concept that buy-in works best when people are involved was carried throughout the project.

As a result, the training system for the sixteen thousand people was much different from the standard training approach: "Here is what the change is, and this is how you are now going to do your work within it." To achieve the focus purposes of getting the commitment of all employees to accept the change and to prepare everyone to operate the system, the SQA-designed training exposed to everyone the following information:

- The reasons the service order system was redesigned
- Who the project team members were and how and why they were chosen
- The focus and larger purposes selected for the service orders
- The measures of purpose accomplishment and why they were adopted
- The options considered for a future solution and an explanation of how a final one was selected
- An explanation of the living solution and why it was selected
- Details about each person's role in operating the living solution system
- Practice with the methods, with frequent referrals to purposes, future solution, and measures of purpose accomplishment to explain why certain activities were prescribed

In addition, all employees were asked to submit their own ideas about any of the options described in the review of the SQA process: purposes, future solution, and living solution.

In the end, the project team estimated that this training program development took around 5 percent more time than conventional training would have required, but the very favorable responses of the trainees at the end of their sessions more than paid for the extra time. There was a strong buy-in to the changes, as well as a general acceptance of what everyone's role was and how any problems that might arise during the switch-over were to be resolved. The responses also indicated that the trainees had a greater sense of what the project team called strategic thinking about the whole company. Involvement, even at this late stage in this rudimentary form, is the best change agent.

EVALUATING YOUR LIVING SOLUTION AND NEXT RELEASES

In evaluating a living solution, we recognize that any solution created today will require changes over time and may always need to be improved. But we live and work among complex systems that do not lend themselves to easy prediction. We seldom know every consequence or impact of implementing a new system or solution.

The process of defining next releases for a living solution is therefore a process of creating a road map, feature B of the living solution, that will take you to your destination—your ideal future solution. As you go through the installation process and gain experience using the new system, you eventually get feedback with which to evaluate what is working well and what is not.

We advocate both a quantitative and qualitative approach to evaluating this feedback using the measures and controls you set up in the system matrix for Feature A as quantitative indicators of progress. Also, recall the seven-column representation of the several stages of the software development center change in terms of system attributes, working backward from the future solution to the living solution of today. What you expected to do at, say, the three-month stage can be used as a qualitative way of determining how you are progressing and what you may need to include in the next release.

You may also wonder when you should begin working on the installation plan for any next releases. That depends on your system. However, keep in mind that because your future solution contained a particular time frame, as time goes on, what you once considered the future needs to be revised sometime before the end of that time frame, since there is an even later future time period ahead of you.

In working with our clients, we suggest that at a certain time, the client begin anew the entire effort to go through SQA to determine a new future solution. The timing of this varies with each solution. For example, we might suggest that it be done in the second year of a three-year time frame. We call this a "sunset review," borrowing a term from the government: the solution is revisited near the end of its designated life existence to determine if it should continue to remain in effect.

Even if one of the releases eventually leads to abandoning the whole solution concept, it is important to treat it as a learning experience rather than a mistake. The group should be open from having worked with SQA to going back and assessing how the whole solution creation process can be improved for future efforts.

For example, in the case of OTC, it was clear after six months that the solution was working well. However, post-installation evaluations suggested that newly outsourced employees wanted more communication with their new leadership team. A number of communication events were already built into the practice guide, but the newly outsourced employees wanted even more. Furthermore, the company found that more coaches were being required to support an ever-increasing pipeline of business. As a result, the company hired and trained more change agents to support the outsourcing efforts. The newly hired change agents also became part of the expanding communication network. OTC simply needed more communication events and more human communicators of the outsourcing methodology.

GETTING RESULTS IN THE HEAT OF BATTLE

The key to staying results-focused in the heat of battle is to review the systems matrix frequently, so you can be continually reminded to ask smart questions about the system elements. By making the system matrix second nature to your thinking, you will remember to ask smart questions even during the barrage of activities that you likely face during the course of a regular day. The system matrix will remind you to ask questions like, "What parts of the system are we not considering but should explore?" and "Have we fully assessed our purposes, outputs and inputs, the environment, and the enablers—people, physical, and information?" These questions about the system elements will help you to become a more powerful systems thinker.

In addition, whenever you are in the heat of the battle, remember always to revisit the three foundation questions. In focusing on these, you will see that nearly any issue can be understood and dealt with in the light of one of these questions (or the corollary questions they foster you to ask). The foundation questions instill a certain degree of wisdom in recognizing even the rare issue that may not have been adequately addressed in your living solution, as well as help you respond to ideas and suggestions from others about the issue while preparing you to ask the three smart questions about it: "What is unique about this issue?" "What purposeful information do we really need to know about it?" "What system is this issue part of?"

HIGHLIGHTS OF THE LIVING SOLUTION PHASE

- The living solution differs from the future solution. Whereas the latter is an ideal solution that represents where you want to be at some time in the future, the living solution represents what you can do and what you can plan for now.

- The living solution contains three features: a detailed description of recommended changes now that come as close as possible to the future solution, a plan for successive stages of change and improvement and a time frame for when they will occur in order to move the installed solution toward the future solution, and an installation plan to begin work on the first stages of change.

- The best way to develop the living solution is to use a system matrix to ensure that you can describe all the elements and dimensions of your solution in as much detail as possible to answer the question, "How does it work?"

- The living solution LOD process is similar to that used for the future solution, except that you need a greater level of detail and assurance that you have accounted for every aspect of the system matrix. The list step can tap once again into the creativity bisociation techniques to generate ideas, or you can use a conversational approach. The organize step is best done by reviewing the system matrix to ensure that each option generated during the list step is workable and implementable. The decide step can be done by using the Smart Questions Decision Worksheet, aided as needed by using decision-making software.

CHAPTER SIX

The Power of SQA

Two Case Studies

Success is never final.

—Winston Churchill

The best way to understand SQA fully is to see it in action in real-life cases. This chapter is devoted to walking through two actual situations where SQA was used to create solutions. As we go examine these cases, we will demonstrate how this holistic process can be consciously used to create solutions in many types of situations. We also provide comments, set out in italic type, to highlight important decisions and turning points in the situation that demonstrate the value of SQA or to emphasize where the organization made critical mistakes that affected the outcome.

We want to stress that although these cases will help you learn about smart questions, you will need some experience using SQA with your own issues for it to become truly meaningful to you. You will no doubt occasionally wonder about the reasoning that led to certain actions within SQA as you read these cases, and our answer in advance is that experience as practitioners led us to do what we did. Therefore, be patient with yourself and the process. SQA is a relatively simple paradigm to learn. Getting success with it in complex situations, however, will take some time to master.

Changing your usual paradigm about how to plan, design, improve, develop, and create solutions and systems is much harder work than trying to change the operating system you have on your computer. This paradigm shift is likely to be baffling as you start to use it. But keep thinking in the holistic SQA way as you approach solution creation, and the paradigm will definitely replace your current reductionist view (assuming you are indeed part of the 92 percent of folks who currently think that way). Remember too that we are also continually learning from our practice and research about ever better methods and techniques developed because we too face difficult situations where the standard SQA concepts need tweaking to produce the desired results. We will continue to seek ways to simplify the process.

If you happen to be part of the 8 percent of the population who intuitively think this way, learning the structure of the SQA paradigm will help you explain to others and teach them just what and why you ask the questions and do the things you do (and help your relationship with others much more than saying, "Can't you see this is the way to go about planning?" or "Don't you understand this is a bigger picture to work on?").

We hope you will notice in these cases that the SQA holistic PPFL process is a form of project management or road mapping for small as well large complex planning, design, development, and solution creation efforts. In addition, the second case illustrates how SQA is used iteratively even for one of the SQA phases of the big project PPFL process.

THE LOADING DOCK CASE

Organizations often tackle problems using a reductionist approach that leads them down the road toward the wrong solution. These kinds of cases were noted in previous chapters, but here is one reported in "complete detail" so you can get a sense of the real-time thinking and excitement that SQA can create in a group task force, as well as the significant, positive results that SQA can generate.

Pop quiz: What is the reason we put "complete detail" in quotation marks? Our reason is given below.

Background

This company is a very large national provider of semiperishable products. One warehouse out of the company's twenty-four national warehouses was experiencing high costs, excessive overtime, poor delivery records, and diminished product quality at its loading dock. The manager of warehouses and the supervisor of this warehouse noted that their weekly performance reports in comparison to the other warehouses were showing these problems existed. When the trend continued for three months, they decided to assign an engineer to determine how to solve these problems.

Eliot, the engineer given the assignment, was asked to answer the question, "How can we solve the problems on the loading dock?" Eliot asked the manager and supervisor about the data they had indicating there were problems and started on the project the next week. He went to the loading dock (with spaces for sixteen trucks at a time) and occasionally asked workers about the pile-up of cases. He also inspected the area where cases were often damaged to figure out how the process of checking and moving the cases caused damage.

Eliot then went to work collecting data about flows, costs, damage, and errors in cases loaded. After a couple of weeks of getting data, making models of all of it, and locating most of the causes of the problems (for example, misplaced order documents, double and sometimes triple handling of cartons, and absenteeism), he thought about how to solve the problems. Having attended a week-long workshop on automating warehousing and truck and railroad loading a couple of months earlier, Eliot had been contemplating the idea that the problems could be eliminated by automating the loading dock all the while he was collecting and analyzing data. This became the main solution he worked on.

After detailing the solution and getting cost information over the next few weeks about the equipment needed, he compared the costs for how the loading dock now operated versus the new way it might operate under automation. He was pleasantly surprised when he analyzed that the $60,000 cost of installing the automation would be paid back in eight months from the savings in operating costs. The proposal he prepared made him very proud of and excited about the changes. He submitted the recommendation to the supervisor, who was also delighted with it. As the two of them discussed the dramatic improvement, they decided the change ought to be made at all twenty-four warehouses.

Proposing the automation change represented a collective cost for all twenty-four warehouses of $1.5 million. This meant that the proposal had to be submitted to higher levels in the organization for approval, since the local warehouse supervisor could approve only the $60,000 expenditure. So the proposal was sent to the manager of warehouses, who approved it, and sent it to the director of distribution, who also approved it. The director of distribution then prepared a report on the company's loading docks for Paul, the vice president for general operations.

Notice how Eliot's thinking approach followed the conventional reductionism. All the others who had to approve the proposal did the same, looking only at the analysis data and the costs in the report to check the calculations and reviewing the recommendation for workability. Eliot and the others never asked questions about the purposes that really needed to be accomplished. They also never asked any of the holistic thinking questions about the uniqueness aspects that each of the other warehouses may have had, since they served different customers, had a different product mix, and were at various distances to their customers. All this purposeful information was lacking about the warehouses, as was a systems view of the proposed changes.

The vice president for general operations, Paul, glanced at the report quickly but decided to ask Cliff, one of his staff assistants, to review it and provide him with an assessment of its merits. "Look this over and let me know in about a week if I should approve it."

Notice that Paul did not involve any other people; no loading dock workers or operations personnel were invited to participate in the review.

Cliff read through the report, and his initial reaction was that the proposal looked good. It solved the problem (as defined) by proposing automated loading docks for all the warehouses whose costs would have a payback period of eight months. The report seemed complete, with various flowcharts, statistical analyses of time delays, accounting evaluation of excessive costs and overtime, studies of the damage to the quality of the product due to overcrowding on the loading dock, and so forth.

Before reading more, think about how almost all such reviews you have participated in or seen performed before have been conducted. What is the likelihood that you, in Cliff's position, after verifying a few calculations and cost estimates, would have told your boss that the proposal was okay to approve?

Phase 1: People Involvement

Cliff had attended an SQA workshop a year and a half earlier, and so had been using the new paradigm in his own work since that time. (*His good track record is probably the reason Paul asked him to handle this review.*) As impressed as he was with the quality of the report, he now always approached his assignments by reviewing any recommended results according to SQA.

Cliff's first step was therefore to talk a few colleagues, Bob, Terry and George, into helping him with the assignment. He felt he should have also involved or talked to others, such as other warehouse and loading dock supervisors at other company warehouses, but the one-week deadline led him to start at least with these three people who worked in other departments of the company and had firsthand knowledge of the loading docks and distribution patterns. Unfortunately, during Cliff's initial discussions with Bob and George, their first questions related to the adequacy of the data in the report and whether Cliff had considered collecting more data about the problem to correct the omissions.

Our answer to the pop quiz above is that you can never get complete data or information about any reality, as Chapter One pointed out. Similarly, there is no way Cliff and the others could ever get all the data about the loading dock problems.

However, Cliff prevailed in getting Bob's and George's cooperation along with Terry's to continue the review in this way. The group set up a formal meeting as their first step in evaluating the proposal. Because of the short amount of time Cliff had available, he only briefly mentioned the kinds of topics that the Smart Questions People Involvement Worksheet (Exhibit 2.1) addressed and the possibility that others might need to get involved in the next couple of days.

Phase 2: Purposes

Because the three others had not been previously exposed to SQA, Cliff launched the first meeting by stating, "Let's start by asking about the purposes of the loading dock, the place where the initial problem was identified. Think about the purposes of the loading dock in as many ways as you can. I'll record your statements on the easel."

Notice that Cliff recognized the importance of using an easel in the meeting so everyone could see all the options and ideas espoused. An easel (or whiteboard or computer display of individual inputs) is a valuable ingredient in any type of group meeting. The key is to make assumptions visible and conscious. It is hard to skip over them when they are set out in black and white. Also note he encouraged consideration of broad perspectives.

As the group began stating possible loading dock purposes, Cliff put their random statements on the easel's chart paper. The participants listed a number of purposes:

- To fill orders
- To supply dealers
- To load trucks
- To have customers use our products
- To consolidate shipments to dealers
- To make company products available for sale
- To deliver products to dealers
- To transport products to dealers
- To provide service about our products
- To sell company products

With this, Cliff stated: "Now let's organize these and other purposes we think of as we go along from small to large scope. We start by asking about what the smallest-scope purpose is. Then we will continue to ask, 'What's the purpose of that purpose?' for each of the successively larger purposes until we have included the purposes of our customers and our customers' customers. So the first thing to do is determine what the smallest-scope purpose is. Let's do that by asking which of the first two purposes on our list is smaller. That is, is 'to fill orders' smaller or larger in scope than 'to supply dealers'? Another way to ask the question is, Is the purpose of 'to fill orders' 'to supply dealers' or is the purpose of 'to supply dealers' 'to fill orders'? If you pick the former, that makes 'to fill orders' the smaller scope, and if you pick the other statement, that makes 'to supply dealers' smaller."

All three participants quickly selected "to fill orders" as smaller; Cliff then asked the same comparison questions about "to fill orders" and "to load trucks." The latter was selected and then compared with the same comparison questions to the next purpose statement on the list. "To load trucks" was picked again, and then compared to the next purpose. After "to load trucks" was picked again, Terry commented: "Cliff, looking at the rest of the purposes on the list leads me to suggest that 'to load trucks' is the smallest one of all the rest." The others agreed, and "to load trucks" became their smallest purpose.

Cliff wrote that purpose on a new easel sheet, and then continued asking questions that could help the group establish a purposes hierarchy:

CLIFF: Now what's the purpose of loading trucks?

TERRY: What about "to deliver products?"

As Cliff was about finished writing that as the purpose of "to load trucks," George commented: "But it seems there is a more direct yet larger purpose of loading trucks. What about 'to consolidate shipments?'"

When the group agreed "to consolidate shipments" was the purpose of "to load trucks," Cliff inserted it on the easel sheet between the two he had already written down. He also reminded the others that they could add purpose statements that were not initially listed. This questioning and probing led to organizing a purposes hierarchy as shown in Exhibit 6.1.

Notice that the group both categorized the purposes and filled in the purpose statements to avoid a "big jump" or gap of purposes between any two that they may have written down for the hierarchy. Note also that not all purpose statements on the initial listing appear in the hierarchy and even purposes that were not on the initial listing are incorporated in the hierarchy. The reason for this is that the question asked about each purpose put in the initial hierarchy organizing step is, "What's the purpose of that?" not "What purpose on our initial listing is the purpose of that?"

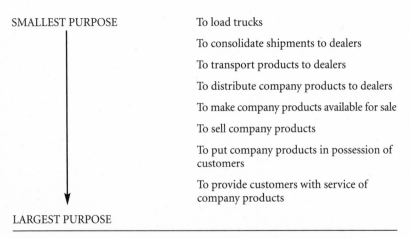

SMALLEST PURPOSE

To load trucks

To consolidate shipments to dealers

To transport products to dealers

To distribute company products to dealers

To make company products available for sale

To sell company products

To put company products in possession of customers

To provide customers with service of company products

LARGEST PURPOSE

Exhibit 6.1.   Purpose Hierarchy for Loading Dock Case

Cliff next stated: "Now we need to start with our biggest purpose and ask if we should try to develop a solution to achieve it or move to the next smaller one to determine if it should be our focus. In other words, what purpose should be the focus of our efforts to develop what the solution ought to be, considering the time and resources we have available to come up with an answer to Paul's question, and what are the broad capabilities and responsibilities of those of us in this group?"

The group looked at the largest purpose first, "to provide customers with service of company products," and decided that it was "too big" for them to work on. They lacked the time and resources to accomplish this purpose. So they asked the question about the next smaller purpose, and then again and again for the next smaller purposes, and they decided each was also "too big." But when they reached the purpose of "to distribute company products to dealers," they decided it was what needed to be accomplished.

They were determining the right problem to work on!

Cliff pointed out, "Given this focus purpose, let's develop what factors we should measure to determine how well it is accomplished. They will almost certainly be different than those used for evaluating only loading dock solutions."

BOB: Speed of delivery to dealer.

GEORGE: Cost of operating the whole distribution system.

CLIFF: Dealer satisfaction.

These were selected as the factors to measure for determining the focus purpose accomplishment. Incidentally, amid the generally exciting setting, as they contemplated the potential innovative solutions they could envision as the purpose hierarchy expanded their creative thinking space, several solution ideas were proposed as possibilities even as the purposes were discussed during the organizing of the purpose hierarchy.

Notice that the group was acting quite methodically, but they were jumping the gun on a solution and making assumptions about how best to fulfill the purposes they had identified. This is a tendency that needs to be minimized, if not avoided, but it happens often. Cliff did not discard any solution ideas. He recorded them on another easel sheet labeled "possible solution ideas." He quickly went back to the question of measurement factors and then used that solution idea sheet as part of the list step for the future solution and living solution phases.

Phase 3: Future Solution

Cliff built on this enthusiasm and now wanted to increase the number of possible future solution options. Because of his time limitation, the group brainstormed some ideas instead of using some of the formal structured creative bisociation techniques that we discussed in Chapter Four and that Cliff had learned in his workshop. The group listed several ideal options; after all were listed, they categorized them as major alternatives (MA), components (C), or details (D):

1. Move mini-manufacturing facilities to sites of big customers (C)
2. Produce all products at each factory to eliminate consolidation needs that required so many warehouses (MA/C)
3. Ship directly from the factory to the customer based on electronic ordering from the customer (MA)
4. Set up an alliance with noncompetitive companies that ship products to almost all the same dealers to combine distribution systems (MA)
5. Get extra trailers at each location to use as "warehouses" to store minimum-size quantities of each product for certain customers so the products would not have to be placed in the warehouse and then moved again when an order was being filled (D)

The group was excited to have several future solution options rather than just one. They recognized that all the options were more forward thinking and creative than the initial solution of automating the loading docks. They reviewed the five and assigned a major alternative, component, or detail designation to each, as shown above. They perceived that the major alternatives could lead the company into new areas and could be trend-setting options. Because of the time limitations, they only roughed out some details based on the systems questions for how the three options listed as major alternatives might work. The question now was which one to select. Which one would become the guide for developing the actual recommendation?

After much discussion in terms of the factors that measure purpose accomplishment, the group decided that option 4 would be a good future solution idea in a longer time frame than they had available to consider. It was put aside for later consideration. Similarly, option 2 was set aside because the board of directors and manufacturing would have to be involved in deciding if it was a good strategic future solution to serve as the guide for now.

They decided option 3 (to ship directly from their factories to customers based on electronic ordering) was a good ideal future solution for two years from now. It was clearly blue sky, in that the company did not yet have electronic ordering. More important, though, their future solution had a significant corollary: the company could literally sell the twenty-four warehouses because they would not be needed given that products would now be shipped directly to customers. However, it was clear to the group that this solution could be difficult to persuade others in the company to follow. As one member, Terry, told Cliff, "The VP may really toss you out if you tell him that! We better go over that system to make sure it can work and that huge savings and much better customer service will occur."

Notice that the group was not afraid to develop and select an ideal future solution, despite several limitations and constraints, including the fact that the company did not currently have an operating model based on direct shipment or the technology installed for electronic ordering in mass quantities. However, they also recognized that option 3 would be a significant operating change for the company, and so their next task was to make sure they had the right information to support how well it could work.

Phase 4: Living Solution

Cliff and the rest of the group began exploring the implications of option 3. The team believed that this option made the most sense for the company to reduce its costs and solve the initial loading dock problem. Cliff posed the following question to the group: "How can we understand this option to determine what modifications, if any, would make the system workable and yet stay as close as possible to this ideal?"

The group set out to define in detail how option 3 would be implemented and what changes it would require to start installation as soon as possible. Several ideas were listed, such as rearranging some manufacturing activities to give each one a greater variety of products to ship immediately and setting up a couple of warehouses to handle the irregularity of shipping to small dealers.

Using a systems matrix for detailing the ideas, they decided to recommend as the living solution that twenty of the warehouses be sold now. That would leave the company four warehouses, which would be used to consolidate small orders of products shipped primarily to low-volume customers. The group sketched out their recommendation, including such factors as training current employees for new positions; arranging for possible early retirements; developing the details of the interrelationships that would be required among the remaining four warehouses, the factories, and the shippers; and reassigning personnel. They suggested steps the company might take in the future to move the distribution system toward their ideal future solution of electronic ordering and direct shipments to nearly all customers, as well as toward their other projected future solution options embodied in options 2 and 4.

Notice that the group expended significant effort to systematically understand how option 3 might be implemented and how it affected many areas of the company. They provided a detailed installation plan, attempting to account for the repercussions or interfaces in systems matrix terminology that the new distribution method would have on the company, especially in terms of employee assignments, reporting relationships, retraining needs, and even retirement.

The following week, Paul asked Cliff to meet him on another matter. At the end of that meeting, Paul asked Cliff when Cliff would be able to report back to him about the loading dock proposal. Cliff said he could provide an answer at that moment: do not approve the proposal to automate the loading docks! Paul gasped a bit at that response, and then mimicked in astonishment, "What are you saying I should do?"

Cliff's nonchalant response was, "Sell the twenty-four warehouses and ship directly from factory floor to customers." Now Paul was really aghast, but Cliff quickly explained that selling all the warehouses was the future solution that served as the guide for developing the recommendation of selling twenty warehouses and keeping four for low-volume dealers. Cliff suggested that a meeting the next day would give the group the opportunity to explain what led to this recommendation and what they proposed to do in the next six to twelve months to develop the next changes to move the solution closer to the future solution, and even to the "next" future solution of option 4 of developing alliances with other distributors.

The meeting the next day enabled Paul to grasp the significance and workability of the recommendation and what was coming in the future. He then put Cliff in charge of another group to complete the installation plans and put them into action. The first of the four remaining warehouses was set up within three months to serve as a pilot for the other three. The other warehouses went operational around one month after the bugs were worked out.

Selling the other warehouses was done on a pilot basis and then phased out full scale as the direct shipping system to be installed in each manufacturing facility was set up and adjusted, with people involved from each one to handle the uniqueness of their facility. In addition, over a period of eight months to work out the details, arrange the operations of the four remaining warehouses, install the direct shipping systems, and sell the twenty warehouses, this second group started investigating the possibilities of eventually selling the four remaining warehouses in favor of an alliance or partnership with other companies for the distribution of products to dealers.

Results

The systems worked very well when installed in the four remaining warehouses and the factories, although each one needed its own adaptations (remember the uniqueness question). The financial results and increased productivity were impressive—far better than what would have occurred if the loading dock automation had been installed.

Notice that although the automation of the loading docks may have been a creative high-tech solution, it was even clearer with hindsight that it would have been a costly solution to the wrong problem.

More important, this major change in the company's distribution operations became a strategic competitive advantage; none of their competitors were using electronic ordering or direct shipping at that time. Through the use of SQA, the team avoided the trap of making assumptions about the validity and usefulness of the initial data and conclusions to automate, recognizing instead that understanding the larger purposes of what the company needed to accomplish might guide them to other options and breakthrough solutions. Their creative thinking process and creation of many new options paid off, allowing them to develop completely new solutions that eventually proved far more cost-effective, productive, and strategically meaningful for the company. They also fostered a powerful team atmosphere in the company that aided the implementation of the solution and provided a higher-quality environment for all involved.

Here is a speculative question to ponder: What might have happened if Eliot had taken the assignment and used SQA? What is the likelihood that Eliot and whatever group he set up would have proposed the same kind of solution? We have no way of knowing the answers, nor do you, but Eliot would have had a far greater likelihood, than with the approach he used, of developing a much more innovative recommendation, even a similar one of reducing the number of warehouses, than automating the current loading docks.

Postscript

As the group continued to try to find a way of moving the system to the future solution with no warehouses through alliances or partnerships, an interesting turn of events occurred that kept the four warehouses in the living solution in existence and even expanded. Discussions with several other companies with semiperishable products in noncompetitive fields led Cliff to apply SQA with them, and the living solution they developed and implemented was to use the expanded four warehouses as the place from which the other companies' products would be shipped. This agreement opened up yet another profit center for Cliff's company.

This case illustrates a major benefit of SQA thinking: using SQA for every problem-solving, planning, and system development situation provides an opportunity for a potential breakthrough in results and impact on the organization's strategy. The SQA benefit of providing an opportunity for getting powerful results applies at all levels, even when doing strategic planning for the whole organization, as cases in previous chapters showed.

THE GYPSY MOTH PEST MANAGEMENT SYSTEM

This case exemplifies how SQA can be applied to nearly any social, environmental, or political problem in which many different opinions, egos, and societal repercussions are at stake rather than simply profits. These types of problems frequently involve many government regulations and social and political or legal issues, and as a result, they often suffer from bureaucratic paralysis, wherein defining solutions and selecting one can literally be a nightmare.

Background

The gypsy moth pest, imported into the United States in 1869, goes through population explosions approximately every ten years. The pest was becoming increasingly destructive because in years of population explosions, the millions of caterpillars that hatch out of cocoons (before they become gypsy moths) eat the leaves completely off hard-wood trees (primarily oak) in which the larvae had been nesting. The moth was especially rampant in thirteen states in the Northeast, denud-ing and killing millions of acres of valuable forest at an alarming rate.

To resolve the problem before the "ungreening" of the country became a national crisis, around 1974 Congress appropriated $50 million for a five-year program. Three agencies in the U.S. Department of Agriculture (USDA) were charged with the assignment. Govern-ments in the thirteen states, as well as industry and environmental groups, also joined the effort.

For three and a half years, the groups gathered huge amounts of data about the characteristics, biology, and behavior of the moth; forecasts of its spread and impact; information about potential control methods and their environmental impacts; and so on. *(Are you starting to see any red flags raised by their approach?)* High-paid consultants submitted reports proposing pest management systems. The result of this effort was that numerous factions developed among all the participants, each supporting a different eradication proposal while lobbying strongly against the others. In attempts to resolve these conflicts, more studies and data collection were requested. The groups became completely stalemated in analysis paralysis and ego defensiveness, and the country was left with no national gypsy moth pest management system.

I was called by one of the participants, Dan, who knew about my research and consulting work in the field of methods, to create solu-tions. Dan asked me what I thought they should do. I pleaded igno-rance about the gypsy moth problem (even more than I usually do about any situation for which an organization calls me because I don't pretend to be an expert in any of *their* problems, only an expert on the processes they are using to create a solution).

Dan convinced me to help work on this project, which was enor-mous in scope and contained many smaller problems and pieces. To report the entire story would virtually replicate a four-inch-thick final report that summarized all details of the Gypsy Moth Pest Management System. This report of the case where SQA was followed for all aspects covers only four of the pieces needed to develop the GMPMS solutions:

Issue A—to plan a systematic approach to formulate a living solution

Issue B—to create a plan for the living solution: a national com-prehensive gypsy moth pest management system (CGMPMS)

Issue C—to create living solutions for each of the components of the CGMPMS

Issue D—to design a project wrap-up and installation plan

Since each piece of this large puzzle was a little different, we will review only some of the SQA phases for each whole solution to illustrate how a complex system design project is handled.

Issue A: Planning a Systematic Approach to Formulate a Solution

The one condition of this situation that is similar to many I am asked to work on is that the people who are already at loggerheads about the issue are the same as those who must be involved in using SQA. One way that works to defuse the difficulties is what I did here: follow SQA to plan how to do the creation of a solution. In this case, I suggested that the groups shift their attention from the actual gypsy moth problem to the issue of how to organize themselves for planning how to create a CGMPMS solution. Because this is such a neutral-sounding request, this group, similar to those in all the other cases, readily agreed.

PHASE 1: PEOPLE INVOLVEMENT. This phase begins a series of steps to get the groups to let go of their fixation on the problem itself in order to focus on the process of creating a solution. We began here by focusing on people and how they could work together. We needed to create an organizational system before we could even approach designing the CGMPMS. In other words, we needed to plan for how to plan.

Notice that in some instances, it is more important to focus initially on the methods of meeting and planning rather than the content of the issue. When people first come together to work on solution creation, their interrelationships and organizational roles are often not defined or are at odds. They do not yet have a shared language or a shared definition of what needs to be accomplished. It is therefore useful to spend time creating agreement on how the group will work, what the issues are, and what they need to do.

With this organizational planning in mind, Dan and his colleagues invited eighteen people representing key constituencies from among the larger groups to meet for a day as the first step in forming the future task force whose charter would be to design a CGMPMS. This group would figure out how to form a future task force, to be called the Gypsy Moth Planning Task Force (GMPTF), that would create the actual CGMPMS. The day-long meeting was designed to permit the people involved to set aside existing biases and differences so they could concentrate on how to plan the CGMPMS.

Notice that the People Involvement Phase was accomplished quite informally, without completing the Smart Questions People Involvement Worksheet. However, I used the same topics (who, purposes of their involvement, and how to involve them) throughout my discussions with Dan and the group.

PHASE 2: PURPOSES. One of my colleagues and I facilitated an all-day meeting. To open the session, Dan explained who we were, what our roles were, and what he perceived was to be the outcome of the day's work: a framework of operation for how a gypsy moth planning task force would approach the development of a CGMPMS.

What Dan called a "framework of operation" was in effect very similar to the Smart Questions People Involvement Worksheet for the GMPTF. From his point of view, the outcome of the meeting that day was to identify which people should be on the GMPTF, for what purposes, how and when they were going to accomplish those purposes, and what the ideal and potential operating methods would be for the task force. Dan began to create a common language for the group to discuss the solution. At that time, I did not try to explain the entire SQA vocabulary to the group, since Dan's statements were based on the several conversations he and I had had leading up to this meeting.

After Dan's introduction, I made a few remarks about how my colleague and I understood the urgency of doing something about the devastation caused by the gypsy moth and how pleased we were that they were participating in this plan-the-action-plan session. After this, I let the participants vent their frustrations about the past three and a half years for around twenty minutes (the catharsis that is so common in initial meetings like this). I then explained that we were going to use an approach much different from what they had been following in the past, and I asked the group to list—individually and silently and then through round-robin presentation—as many purposes as they could think of that the GMPTF might achieve. The group ended

Small

1. To hold a national meeting on the gypsy moth

2. To clarify the cooperative federal and state roles in gypsy moth pest management

3. To identify areas for further research

4. To develop a gypsy moth pest management system compatible with the missions of state agencies

5. To develop a comprehensive gypsy moth pest management system (CGMPMS) and a continuing planning committee *

6. To provide feedback on ideas and current developments to agencies and groups represented on the Gypsy Moth Planning Task Force and other contacts

7. To implement (or influence the implementation of) a CGMPMS and continuing planning committee

8. To develop educational programs and communication systems that will further the goals of the CGMPMS

9. To investigate the feasibility of transferring components of the CGMPMS approach and technology to other pest management programs

Large

Exhibit 6.2.   Purpose Hierarchy for the Gypsy Moth Planning Task Force

*Purpose level for focus on the Gypsy Moth Planning Task Force.

up with twenty-nine purposes, and its resulting hierarchy is shown in Exhibit 6.2. They then selected Level 5 as the focus purpose.

You may wonder why we bothered going through SQA to arrive at a focus purpose that might be considered obvious. What SQA accomplishes, however, is extremely important because it helps people right away to dwell on what needs to be accomplished rather than on what the problems and issues are. As you will see, most groups will show an enormous amount of interest and intensity in discussing purposes. Furthermore, the Purposes Phase is always desirable because you simply cannot assume that an "obvious" purpose exists; this is a common failing of reductionist thinking, as shown by the difficulties the various agencies had over the first three and a half years on the project. Identifying the larger context of purposes was a critical part of the holistic thinking needed in the design of the GMPMS itself. People also grow in their confidence of their purpose, even if it turns out to be obvious.

PHASE 3: FUTURE SOLUTION. As we moved into this phase, the listing of potential future solution ideas and organizing them into viable options to consider in the decide step engaged the group in extensive discussions. With three government agencies, thirteen states, industries, and outside environmental groups to consider, as well as the large numbers of people in those groups who might be candidates to be on the GMPTF, there was extensive debate. Nevertheless, four major alternatives emerged. Two of them included representatives of three midwestern states where some signs of the appearance of gypsy moths had occurred. One option was selected as the future solution, and it remained largely intact as the guiding idea in developing the project plan living solution. As so often happens with using SQA to plan the planning process, the living solution here was quite similar to the future solution.

PHASE 4: LIVING SOLUTION. By the end of the day, the group had identified a list of twenty-two people from all stakeholder interests to serve on the GMPTF. This list included people who were not even present at this initial meeting. It would be this task force that would eventually determine the purposes to be achieved by the CGMPMS along with its responsibilities, detailed planning sequence, budget, expected products, and the overall project time line.

Exhibit 6.3 shows the initial project time line the workshop members projected for the actual GMPTF. As the project was under way, this time line was amended twice and extended to better fit the conditions facing the task force in terms of its collection of purposeful information. A small group of the people in the workshop was then given the responsibility for arranging the initial two-day GMPTF meeting, with its twenty-two people, scheduled for three months from this meeting.

Issue B: To Create a CGMPMS Living Solution

As Exhibit 6.3 notes, this issue is the start of the development of the solution sought originally with the congressional mandate: a comprehensive gypsy moth pest management system.

PHASE 1: PEOPLE INVOLVEMENT. In three months, as planned, the twenty-two people selected to be on the GMPTF in the first SQA workshop met for two days. Since the people aspect of the project planning was already accomplished, the meeting was supposed to start with developing the purposes of the CGMPMS, that is, working on developing solutions for the problem itself.

September 1977	Begin planning and design of Comprehensive Gypsy Moth Management System (CGMPMS)
October 1977 (two-day GMPTF meeting)	Generate purposes for the CGMPMS Identify and define functional components of the CGMPMS Establish organizational framework (committees) of GMPTF Develop alternative gypsy moth pest management systems Establish evaluative criteria for the selection of the target pest management system solution Identify CGMPMS major solution categories Identify most important conditions of the system Consolidate ideas from functional component committees Select target pest management system solution
Late October and November 1977	Meetings with states to exchange information Meetings with federal agencies to obtain feedback Discussion with or distribution of materials to program board about GMPTF activities
December 1977 (two-day GMPTF meeting)	Review details of target pest management system solution and incorporate feedback from state and federal agency meetings
Mid-December 1977	"National Meeting" on the gypsy moth (tentative)
February 1978 (two-day GMPTF meeting)	Identify less important conditions (exceptions) that must be considered in the CGMPMS Identify major categories of the recommended pest management system Define the broad outlines of the recommended CGMPMS

March 1978	Review outline of CGMPMS with state and federal agencies Review outline with program board
April 1978 (two-day GMPTF meeting)	Define in detail the recommended CGMPMS Develop initial structure for Gypsy Moth Continuing Planning Committee (GMCPC)
June 1978	Develop the plan for implementation of the CGMPMS Identify phases of CGMPMS implementation Identify future research needs
July 1978	Discussion of CGMPMS and GMCPC with Combined Forest Pest Program Board
August 1978	Final detailing of the CGMPMS and GMCPC
September 1978	Submittal of CGMPMS and proposal for a GMCPC to Combined Forest Pest Program Board Assist federal and state governments in implementing the CGMPMS and the GMCPC

Exhibit 6.3.   Tasks and Sequence of the Proposed Gypsy Moth Planning Task Force: Initial Version Time Line

(An important illustration of how SQA is used for all types of situations is the way SQA for all of Issue A really did the work of Phase 1 of Issue B.) An interesting note about the opening of this meeting was the nature of the discussion that immediately followed the introductions of all the people there. Almost everyone present had been involved in some way during the previous three and a half years of futile efforts. They had already experienced many frustrations and felt a need to share them with the whole group. It was apparent that this expression of conflict accounted for much of the lost time incurred in all their previous meetings. As in the preceding one-day meeting described in Issue A, I did not try to cut off the cathartic discussion they were now having, but I gradually and firmly shifted the focus of the conversation from past analysis and blame-game talk to discussing the possible purposes of the CGMPMS.

Sometimes it takes time to move people away from their reductionist thinking and blaming. In this case, as the group worked over the course of several meetings, there was less and less catharsis, and by the third meeting, the group no longer had the need for it.

PHASE 2: PURPOSES. Once the group focused on the purposes of controlling the moth on the first day of our meeting, we began to accomplish what we needed to. During the list step, which I conducted using the structured method in which each person records his or her own possible purposes and then shares them round-robin style, the group produced thirty-nine purpose statements. Such a large number was to be expected with so many stakeholder interests represented.

Generating this list took the rest of the first morning of the two-day meeting, and I was becoming concerned about how much time it had taken us to get to this point. (The catharsis time was lengthier than what I would ordinarily prefer. Three and a half years of frustration and finger-pointing is hard to bottle up.) In order to get us as much time as possible for creating the CGMPMS living solution by the end of the two-day meeting, I decided that my colleagues and I would spend the lunch hour developing at least three sample purpose hierarchies to present to the group when it returned rather than having them go through the organize step on their own. This is the artful part of practicing SQA.

The three alternatives we developed led to a healthy discussion in less time and let the group arrive at their own hierarchy, partially shown in Exhibit 6.4.

Small

:

To identify areas of potential infestation

:

To determine course of action regarding the infestation

:

To cope with the gypsy moth at all levels of population[*]

:

To have gypsy moth population exist below an
established socioeconomic threshold[**]

:

To establish a natural balance between
the environment and gypsy moth

:

To have stakeholders obtain benefits of forests and trees

:

Large

**Exhibit 6.4.   Partial Purposes Hierarchy of the Comprehensive
Gypsy Moth Pest Management System**

[*]Initial focus purpose.

[**]Focus purpose selected after review.

*The full hierarchy is too long to include here and not really of value. But
as an example of the extent of changes that can occur in discussions, the
focus purpose chosen during the Purpose Phase—"to cope with gypsy
moths at all levels of their population"—was eleventh in the full hierarchy,
and the final focus purpose determined after discussions during the future
and living solution phases—"to have gypsy moth populations exist below
an established socioeconomic threshold"—was originally nineteenth.*

*Although the whole group was not involved in the organize step, we
followed the basic SQA precept that options should always be available.
Another important benefit of having many options to discuss instead of
just one proposed purpose hierarchy is that it helps avoid the tendency of
people to form sides, with one side picking apart the one option presented
while the other side defends it. Many options give people fodder to think
about and keep them from polarizing around one idea.*

The original focus purpose chosen in the Purposes Phase and the
final one chosen in the Living Solution Phase represented breakthroughs for the entire group. Over the course of the previous three
and a half years, everyone involved in the process had assumed the

purpose of a GMPMS was to *eradicate* the gypsy moth. As we reviewed the three purpose hierarchies my colleagues and I had created during lunch, the discussion took a fascinating direction. People began recognizing for themselves the straitjacket they had put themselves in for three and a half years. As a result, a new level of enthusiasm and commitment surfaced.

Surprisingly, we then next listed twenty-four possible factors for measuring purpose accomplishment, which the group consolidated into six. They also weighted their importance (shown in parentheses below) when they were to be used in selecting the future and living solutions:

- Reduce defoliation, measured as a percentage in the general infested area (29 points)
- Cost of coping, with benefit to cost measured in dollars (23 points)
- Retard defoliation acres on leading front, measured at the spread of gypsy moths in million acres per year (22 points)
- Number of remote infestations per year (18 points)
- Timber loss, measured in dollars per year (14 points)
- Degree of gypsy moth population stabilization, measured in density per acre (14 points)

PHASE 3: FUTURE SOLUTION. We had already made incredible progress, and the group was able to begin developing future solution ideas by the middle of the first afternoon. The complex and highly interdependent nature of a CGMPMS led to many possible ideal concepts, though many of them were influenced by the perspective of each task force member's current organizational affiliation. Unfortunately, some group members immediately tried to translate these future solution ideas into administrative and organizational structures (for example, they began proposing that their agency control X, Y, or Z solution). There was thus little consensus on many of these premature proposals, as some members began to feel threatened and became defensive.

To counteract the meeting from deteriorating, I reminded everyone that the group needed to concentrate first on the purposes of the components of an ideal future solution and on how those purposes would best be carried out in an ideal way. Precisely which people and agencies would be responsible for what purposes and the accompanying methodologies could be determined during the Living Solution Phase and in the subsequent detailing of the future solution components.

The future solution representing five years from that date is shown in Exhibit 6.5. This solution was selected after the several options from the organize step were reviewed using a rough version of the Smart Questions Decision Worksheet.

The categories listed in the first column are the words the GMPTF adapted from the SQA system elements, and the words used in the first row of Exhibit 6.5 were agreed on. The other elements toward the bottom were less and less known and needed more design and development.

We are not providing further explanations of the future solution LOD steps or the details behind Exhibit 6.5 because the huge amount of details for such a complex system would overwhelm you. Our purpose in presenting this case history is to summarize how the SQA holistic thinking and process lets you wade through the tangled webs of these kinds of projects.

PHASE 4: LIVING SOLUTION. Exhibit 6.5 generally reflects the living solution that the group selected. Of course, the group fleshed out all the systematic issues to create the three parts of a living solution: the details of the first-stage implementation that stay as close as possible to the future solution, the schedule of continuing changes toward the future solution, and the installation action plan for the first stage. These ideas were listed and organized into options that greatly expanded and supplemented the future solution, as well as provided actionable tasks. Because the complexity of these steps would be overwhelming, what follows is a brief description of the selected living solution.

First, the CGMPMS would operate on three levels: Level I would be the local or "firing-line" activities, Level II would be the state and regional requirements, and Level III would be the responsibilities of the national government. Table 6.1 describes the relationship of the activities at these three Levels. The GMPTF decided to make Level III the earliest priority to set up as the first stage to be installed because more details were needed to flesh out Levels I and II. A major aspect of Level III was the creation of the National Gypsy Moth Management Board, whose composition is shown in Exhibit 6.6. This board would have responsibility for overall system evaluation, policy formulation, program coordination, and fundraising. It would have a charter and funding from the USDA, and a federal pest management coordinator would be appointed to integrate all pest management programs as

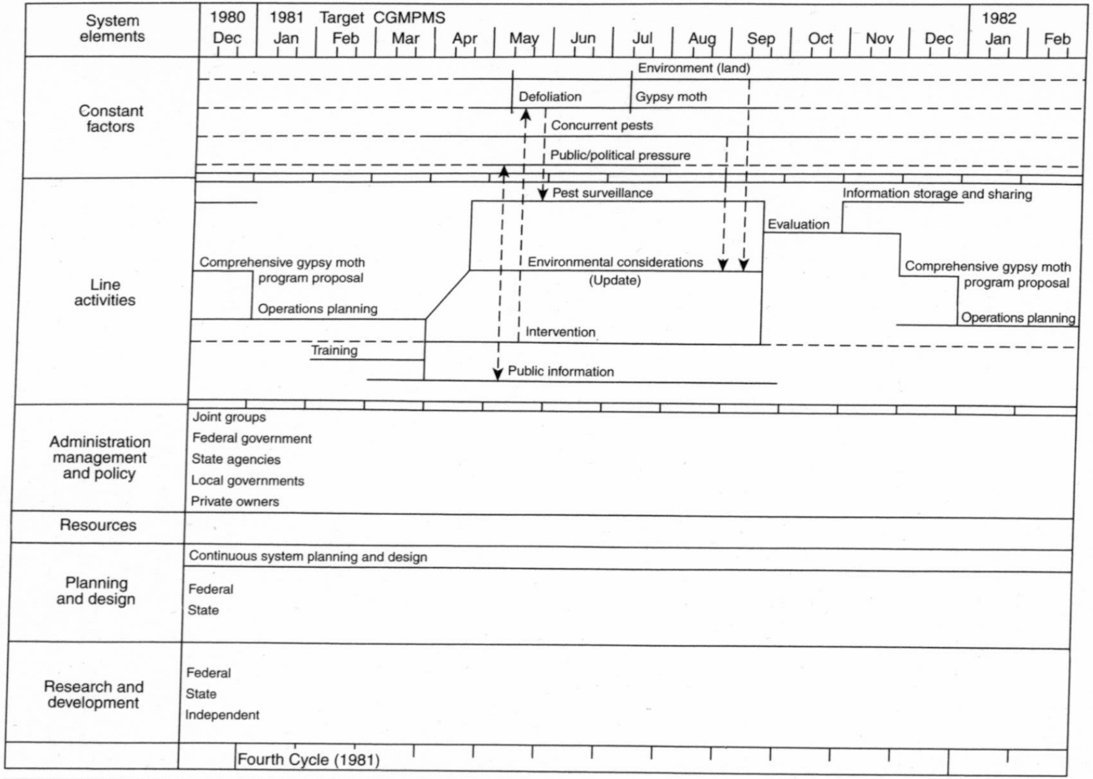

Exhibit 6.5. Future Solution CGMPMS Time Line

Level 1	Level II	Level III
Pest surveillance	Pest surveillance (broad scale)	
Concurrent pests	Concurrent pests (broad scale)	
Intervention	Intervention (broad scale)	
Local operations planning	Regional operations planning	
Local environmental considerations	Environmental considerations	
Logistics	Logistics	
Local public communication	Public communication	Public communication
Local planning and design	State and regional planning and design	National planning and design
	Training	
	Quarantine activities	
	Evaluation and information management	Evaluation and information management
	Research and development	Research and development
	Resources	Resources
		Policy recommendations
		Systemwide coordination

Table 6.1. Relationship of Activities to Structural Levels

much as possible. The planning and design committee would handle the continuing changes outlined by the GMPTF and was especially charged with redesigning the whole future solution every two years to take advantage of emerging technology and the status of gypsy moth infestation.

As the GMPTF was finalizing the living solution, a question arose about the focus purpose. Recall that at this point in the work, the focus purpose was "to cope with gypsy moths at all levels of their population." The group wondered about exactly what the word *cope* meant and how they could translate *coping* into operational procedures. Their questioning was good (they had learned from the SQA process), so as a result, they decided to review the purposes hierarchy, prompting them to select a different focus purpose, "to have gypsy moth populations exist below an established socioeconomic threshold," which they believed was

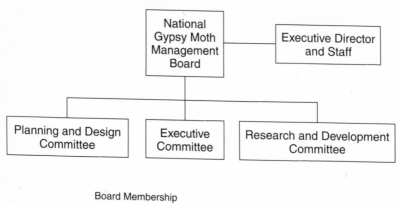

Exhibit 6.6.   National Gypsy Moth Management Board

better. It was both a bigger purpose and had a clearer meaning to the group. ("Socioeconomic threshold" refers to a combination of societal and economic acceptable levels of the six factors to measure purpose accomplishment—in effect, how much "ungreening" would be tolerated by the citizenry before there was a demand for action.)

Notice how the group accepted the fact that the entire SQA process could be iterative. They were not averse to going back two phases to the Purposes Phase and reselecting a new focus purpose from the hierarchy.

This revision of the focus purpose led the task force to establish several stages that the CGMPMS would pass through to control the gypsy moth population during the next three to five years in order to arrive at the future solution. Exhibit 6.7 shows the way the task force implemented the new focus purpose. The near-future stage was expected by eighteen months, the midrange stage by thirty-six months, and the long-range future solution by forty-eight to sixty months.

The GMPTF also set up committees from among its members to create solutions for the line activities identified in Exhibit 6.5: operations planning, pest surveillance, environmental considerations, intervention, public communication, evaluation, information management, training,

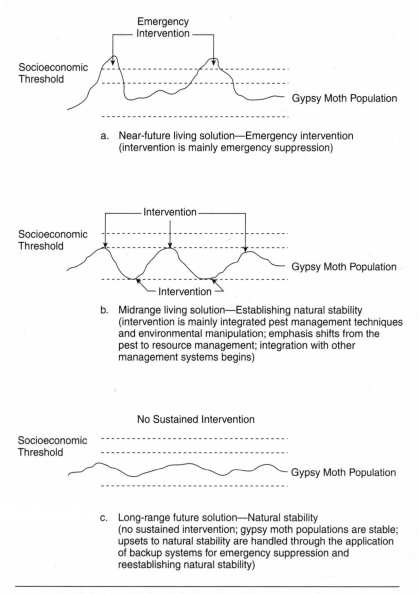

a. Near-future living solution—Emergency intervention
   (intervention is mainly emergency suppression)

b. Midrange living solution—Establishing natural stability
   (intervention is mainly integrated pest management techniques
   and environmental manipulation; emphasis shifts from the
   pest to resource management; integration with other
   management systems begins)

c. Long-range future solution—Natural stability
   (no sustained intervention; gypsy moth populations are stable;
   upsets to natural stability are handled through the application
   of backup systems for emergency suppression and
   reestablishing natural stability)

Exhibit 6.7.   Living Solution Pest Management Systems

and policy formulation. The GMPTF served as the coordinator of the interfaces among all the line activity solutions. The vertical dashed lines in Exhibit 6.5 represent some of the coordination of information among the smaller committees working on the line activity solutions.

Another special group was formed to design a system solution to gain approval of the CGMPMS from the states, U.S. Forest Service, Animal and Plant Health Inspection Services (APHIS), the USDA's Science and Education Administration (SEA), the Secretary of Agriculture's Office, and the various private groups. Finally, a small group was set up to prepare a report on the status and development of the CGMPMS.

Issue C: To Create Plans for the Components of the Living Solution

For this issue, the GMPTF committees and the special group to get the required approvals also used SQA to design the solutions for their assigned responsibilities. The selection of people who would be assigned to these groups was determined during the GMPTF Living Solution Phase. Because there were so many smaller solutions to be created as part of the entire picture, we cannot describe them here through all the phases of each line activity. However, an important benefit resulting from the buy-in of people right from the start in using SQA was getting their support and commitment when difficulties suddenly occurred.

For example, the committee in charge of getting approval developed a serious problem when one of the group members became ill and was not able to conduct a preliminary briefing to the three federal agencies' top managers. Because these agencies did not have this early preview, they became suspicious of the motives of the other agencies and adopted hard-line stances against the proposed CGMPMS. It took the efforts of the chair of GMPTF and other key people over the course of two months to ease these apprehensions and restore trust.

The lesson here is that the implementation of systems must be monitored, even for a system as small and temporary as an approval system, to avoid mistakes and misunderstandings. Generating support for any eventual proposal needs to begin at the start of the process in order to obtain a strong agreement on handling any mistakes and misunderstandings that may arise. This is by far a much more effective way of getting successful results than waiting until you have a recommendation before developing a program to sell the solution.

Issue D: Designing the Project Wrap-Up and Installation Plan

Since you probably have a sense of how the SQA was likely used by each committee and group to undertake its tasks, let's move on to an interesting aspect of this project: designing the project wrap-up and installation plan. This area involved a small group of people to prepare a report on the status and development of the CGMPMS.

PHASE 1: PEOPLE INVOLVEMENT. The GMPTF asked two of its members to serve on this group with four of my colleagues and me as part of setting up the installation time line. We were expected to have a report available in two months.

PHASE 2: PURPOSES. As we developed our list of purposes, as shown in Exhibit 6.8, our group realized, after a meeting with some of the national board members, that the report needed to be addressed to three audiences: policy and resource controllers, field people, and researchers. We therefore prepared three purpose hierarchies—one for each audience. Exhibit 6.9 shows these three hierarchies and the focus purpose chosen for each audience: purposes 4, 7, and 1 from Exhibit 6.8. In addition, supporting purposes in each hierarchy (the dotted circles in Exhibit 6.9) and, in one case, between hierarchies (the dotted arrow), were identified. (Note that statements 12 and 17 in Exhibit 6.8 were not related to audiences and so do not appear in Exhibit 6.9. Statements 19, 20, 21, 23, and 24 were also omitted from the hierarchies.)

Notice that some purpose statements, such as 2, appear at different levels in each of the hierarchies, and that not all the purposes from Exhibit 6.8 appear in a hierarchy. This occurred because each of the three audiences was unique, and so the purpose hierarchies had to be done in a fashion that would reflect that audience's uniqueness. This was done without compromising the intentions of the purposes of the project.

The group also established different factors for measuring purpose accomplishment for each audience. For policy and resource controllers, the measures of purpose accomplishment were the frequency of using or contacting the National Gypsy Moth Management Board, the amount of money and staff allocated, the quality and impact of policy changes, and money for research and for planning and design. For field people, the measures of purpose accomplishment were the ability of a new person to understand CGMPMS, the degree that the document is

Subject: Design of the gypsy moth report

1. Sell ideas developed by the National Gypsy Moth Management Board
2. To give details of techniques for surveillance, intervention, etc.
3. Describe communication channels through which new ideas, policies, etc., can be implemented
4. Plan to get and obtain USDA commitment to utilize the CGMPMS
5. Highlight research needs
6. Propose a target system for gypsy moth activities
7. Act as stimulus for further design efforts
8. Serve as index to all relevant gypsy moth information
9. Make expert recommendations regarding future planning and design
10. To inform those not involved in planning and design about what happened
11. Identify major questions for which information is needed now
12. Serve as first step of our case study
13. Serve as permanent, continuous, updated summary of CGMPMS activities
14. Show how efforts of many agencies can be integrated to accomplish the same goals
15. Establish paths whereby continuous changes can be planned and implemented
16. Justify USDA money allocated for planning and design of GMPMS to encourage future grants
17. Put us in a good light
18. Serve as model for state planning
19. Establish effectiveness of PPFL approach (measure)
20. To be different from the ABC company report (measure)[*]
    —used by people
    —attitude change
21. Serve as a report from the National Gypsy Moth Management Board (solution idea)
22. Highlight effectiveness of National Gypsy Moth Management Board
23. Fulfill terms of USDA grant (measure)
24. Integrate aspects of compendium into report (solution idea)
25. Document whole CGMPMS (without details)
26. Sell researchers on research needs from #5

Exhibit 6.8.   List of Possible Purposes of the Gypsy Moth Report

[*]This is a reference to the company used in the initial three and a half years of the project that had initially been the favorite.

Audiences

	Policy and Resource Controllers	Field People	Researchers
Small	2, 3, 10, 15, 18	3, 8, 10, 15	3, 6, 10, 15, 22
Medium-small	5, 6, 16	1, 11, 13, 22	2
Medium	9, 14, 26	6, 9, 14, 25	5
Medium-large	22, 25	(2) - - - - - - - → (1)	
Large	(1)	(7)	26
Extra large	(4)	18	4

Exhibit 6.9.   Hierarchies of Purposes

Note: The numbers refer to the statements in Exhibit 6.8
The purpose level chosen for each audience is circled, with
supporting purposes circled or connected by the dotted line.

used as reference in planning and design, the comprehensiveness of references, the degree to which future planning and design efforts follow the structure of the report, and the compatibility of various state and federal systems after n years. Finally, for researchers, the measures of purpose accomplishment were the number of research gaps filled after n years, the number of proposals for research funding to close remaining gaps, and the increase in interdisciplinary research (academic and field).

PHASE 3: FUTURE SOLUTION. The list step produced twenty-one ideas, ranging from a slide show summarizing all the content to writing three different reports in loose-leaf notebooks. The organize step arrived at three major alternatives: three reports for the three audiences, a visual and graphic presentation of all content, and a large loose-leaf notebook with multiple color pages containing text on the odd-numbered pages and any related graphics and illustrations on the facing even-numbered pages (or left blank if none).

The decide step was performed rather intuitively in just a short time with the measures of purpose accomplishment as the main guides, but also considering the time constraints for producing the final product. The third major alternative, the loose-leaf notebook, was selected.

PHASE 4: LIVING SOLUTION. Many ideas were listed to keep the living solution as close as possible to the future solution. A few of them included using five colors of paper representing the levels of design specificity (summary, concepts, details, more details, opportunities); using a three-digit number for each section with the page number following (for example 110–1, 110–2, 110–3) while dating each sheet of paper so that new developments and future changes could easily be substituted for the original sheet; having each illustration and graphic contain a full and self-contained explanation; and including an introduction explaining how to use the report.

The organize step narrowed the ideas down to two major alternatives: the loose-leaf report and a bound report with colored pages without the dating.

The decide step was almost completely intuitive. The loose-leaf format was selected because it effectively captured the living solution concept. Each report would start with an outline of the report sections: transmittal or cover letter; annotated contents; list of illustrations; time line perspective of past, present, and future; how to use the report (levels of policy considerations, system concepts, system descriptions, specific details, needs and opportunities, illustrations); followed by issues in gypsy moth pest management based on the six system element levels shown in the left column of Exhibit 6.5, recommendations in terms of six levels, the complete CGMPMS, national level of CGMPMS, and so on; it concluded with eleven appendixes. In the action plan to develop the report, the group assigned one of the group members to each major section and followed up with the first draft being reviewed successively within the group, then with four to six key people, some of the committee members, and then a final report written for submission.

The loose-leaf format was always up to date because it had the built-in capability of being changed as continuing changes were being made toward installing the future solution.

Within a week of receiving the report, Dan talked to several key people involved with CGMPMS who had also received the report, all reporting they were "very pleased with it from both an appearance and content point of view. The overall reaction was very favorable, with many people saying that they knew of no other report like it."

Results

The three federal agencies that had been involved for over three and a half years since the gypsy moth program began were now coordinating their activities for the first time. Past antagonisms among the federal, state, industry, and environmental constituencies were sharply minimized. The board started to operate, and responses from all the groups involved were generally favorable as the board began making decisions. Many positive results began to appear just fourteen months after my initial plan-the-planning session. The field people reported they had a good description of their responsibilities and how what they were doing fit within the bigger picture. Additional talks were started to find ways of integrating the various pest management systems so that overlapping field visits for different pests did not occur, and a common basis for reporting activities was established.

At the completion of the project, I asked the participants how much of all the data they had collected in the first three and a half years they thought they had used in arriving at the proposal. The consensus was just 3 to 5 percent at most.

Postscript

This case was done some time ago, using the foundations of the SQA process created by that time. As a follow-up on the status of the project, the current gypsy moth pest management system provided updated information.

The infestations have become so stabilized that major outbreaks such as what occurred in the 1970s (and which was the motivation for the project) have not reoccurred, despite the fact that the gypsy moth population has spread south and west from the thirteen states that were initially involved. In addition, the USDA's latest *Gypsy Moth Program Manual* (2001) contains many comparable or exactly the same policy statements and responsibilities for the Forest Service (the lead agency) and APHIS, as well as calls for cooperative research with the states and the agriculture research services as the initial CGMPMS report we helped develop twenty-five years ago.

CHAPTER SEVEN

SQA in Organizations and Society

—◦◦◦— D oes the organization where you work or the various associations, community groups, and government or political groups in which you take part need to become SQA users? Is SQA just another change management or planning technique fad that will fade with time?

These are all reasonable questions to ask. We ask these types of questions whenever we read books about problem solving, planning, design, and creating solutions. But obviously we think that the Smart Questions Approach is a sound one for you and any organization. The ideas in this book are based on how leading creators of solutions deal with problems, issues, and opportunities and the constant need for change in their organizations and in their lives. In our more than fifty combined years of research, we have seen people and organizations achieve dramatic breakthroughs using SQA. We know it works. You have to decide for yourself. Is it worth trying the approach?

The best way to answer this is to ask yourself whether you are satisfied with the results you are currently getting in your efforts to create solutions. If you are, great; keep doing what you are doing. If you are not, you and your organization may have reached the point where the way you cope with problems and issues is clearly not effective and you need to try something new. That, we recommend, should be SQA.

BECOMING AN SQA ORGANIZATION

Successful organizations in the twenty-first century need to develop a new mind-set for developing and installing solutions. We especially argue that a key core competency of organizations needs to become the ability to ask questions intelligently to create solutions. As more and more work within organizations revolves around complex problems, it makes sense that the most successful organizations will be those that do not crumble under the weight of their own issues, but rather are equipped to develop solutions that give them a strategic edge. Systems need to change instead of blaming failures on people.

Successful organizations will be those that learn to adapt SQA into their core philosophy and use it to plan, design, develop, implement, create, and improve their solutions and systems. They will incorporate the mental model of the foundation questions and the four phases into all of their planning, communications, financial, and operations actions.

Becoming a smart questions organization is the best way to turn a traditional bureaucracy into an empowered organization—one that supports its employees, customers, and other stakeholders; seeks financial and moral betterment for itself and the world; recognizes that its stakeholders have a variety of learning styles; and understands that each person has, as Alan Rowe notes in his book *Creative Intelligence* (2004), creative potential that, in our way of looking at it, is "free" and aims to take responsibility for advancing change rather than simply perpetuating the status quo. Organizations like this can achieve purposes far greater than any single individual can accomplish, but this achievement requires creating unique, holistic solutions for all issues.

Thousands of corporate failures and flops over the past decade illustrate the results of organizations that fail to recognize the importance of strategic thinking, planning, and execution through a creative solution development process. Many of these organizations operate using only narrow and visible performance factors, such as short-term profits. They tend to stress individual effort over teamwork. Ultimately, myopic reductionist approaches such as these fail, as discussed in the many traps and blunders cited in Ohio State University professor Paul Nutt's book, *Why Decisions Fail* (2002).

To begin the journey to becoming an SQA organization, you need to address two central questions. First, how can everyone in the organization learn to think and act powerfully? Becoming a successful SQA practitioner requires the ability to think powerfully and the ability to take actions that result in the outcomes that you desire. Neither thinking nor action alone is sufficient; you need to do both powerfully. The second question is: How can everyone do this *together*? It is one thing to be an individual SQA practitioner. It is quite another to enroll others in the approach as you work. The key challenges are to master the method yourself and to develop the skills and knowledge to teach others how to use SQA to develop solutions. This is not to say that everyone needs to become an expert in or facilitator for SQA, but they should at least understand the process and know its power.

THE THREE BENEFITS OF BEING AN SQ ORGANIZATION

There are three valuable benefits that SQA will bring you if you decide to take the journey to become a Smart Questions Organization:

• An enabling language for inquiring, thinking, and innovating
• A systems perceptiveness
• An empowering culture

These are core benefits that any modern organization needs to incorporate into its fiber in order to survive. Clearly, there are other factors or dynamics that can affect an organization's success, such as work flow, strategy, cultural history, values, processes, practices, customers, competitors, and government. However, we argue that without having an enabling language of thinking, systems perceptiveness, and an empowering culture, no organization can be positioned for long-term success or establish an effective psychological contract and cultivate employee citizenship in the twenty-first century. In this sense, adopting SQA is almost a requirement for all people and not just managers to handle two organizational lives simultaneously: operating the present for continuity and planning the changes for the future or handling the chaos of doing today and thinking tomorrow.

SQA can become such a platform for innovation related to the reality of the present because its thinking and approach provide the language for effective communication among all parts of an organization. The result is a pervasive organizational capability, culture, and behavior for creativity in operations as well as for innovation that empowers everyone within a system perspective.

A Language for Inquiring, Thinking, and Innovating

All organizations have a language—words they use and words they do not use. To varying degrees, organizations are enabled or disabled by their vocabulary. In our experience, organizations that do not learn well and do not advance themselves are those that do not have a tolerance for inquiring or a vocabulary for thinking innovatively. Literally, they cannot conceive of ways of reflecting, thinking, and communicating, in general and in teams, that allow their people to be creative, inspired, and open to new ideas.

Although having the rich vocabulary that SQA inspires does not guarantee an enabled organization, it helps put you in a much better position to innovate, learn, and grow. As you have seen in this book, SQA offers a holistic process and a new shared language (*purposes, future solutions, living solutions, list, organize, decide, systems*) that helps people focus on creating powerful solutions.

In addition, SQA is "agnostic," or neutral, when it comes to working with any of the many trends, philosophies, and tools from the various management movements (such as emotional intelligence, Six Sigma, lean management, 360-degree feedback, total quality, strategic planning) that your organization may be using. In fact, SQA can help you determine if one of these particular trends will be truly useful to your organization whether you are already using it or contemplating using it. None of these management fads is a solution for an organization; at best, each one may provide some concepts or technology that might be used to help develop your solutions.

Here is a case that illustrates how one organization benefited from using SQA to assess how to install the management movement called strategic planning into its processes. The situation began with an SQA consultant, Lou, who received a phone call from a company intending to "force" strategic planning into its executive core:

LOU: Hello, this is Lou Neptune of Planning Associates.

MARIE [WHO PLACED THE CALL]: Hi. I'm glad I reached you. You were recommended to me. I'm Marie Goodrich, CEO of the Medical Forensics Company. We have eighteen hundred employees, and I want to grow the company. The market prospects look very good, but I don't think our company is prepared to take advantage of the potential. I've talked to several executives at other companies, and they are unanimous in saying that we need to do strategic planning to position ourselves effectively. Several of them gave me your name as one well versed in strategic planning. Would you be willing to come to my office and talk with me about developing a strategic plan?

LOU: Of course. How about next week on Wednesday afternoon?

MARIE: Good. Let's plan on two o'clock.

Lou is impressed with the posters, photographs, and charts on the walls of the MFC office. The company has been a pioneer in developing forensic tools, and its growth has been quite good. When Lou enters Marie's office, he congratulates her on the progress of the company, and she tells him how delighted she is to have the strategic planning consultant so strongly recommended to her visit her company about its needs.

MARIE: Perhaps you could sense from the materials you've seen how proud we are of our developments. The problem I sense is that our growth has been based more on being at the right place at the right time than on knowingly plotting a path to achieve better results. We've done very well in the past, but our future is more uncertain and I want to be sure we continue to grow and develop new services. A lot of companies are using the Internet. We don't have a strategy for that. From what I've learned about strategic planning, I have concluded that we should use it to become more proactive in knowing where we should be going. I returned a couple of weeks ago from a conference where a speaker defined his model of strategic planning. I'd like to use it here. Can you help us?

LOU: Setting up a strategic planning process is very desirable for your company, and the sooner the better. I have had quite a few assignments to do this, so I think I can be of significant help.

MARIE: Good. I'll send a memo to my eight executives telling them we are going to start a strategic planning process in a couple of weeks, and you will be setting up appointments with them to let them know what is going to happen.

Immediately, Lou thought about the impact on each of the executives confronted with the memo Marie wanted to send out. He immediately recognized a reductionist thinking flaw that says to the executives, "Here is an expert who will guide us." Each executive would be likely to wonder if his or her job was in jeopardy, would defend his or her own "planning" actions, would call for more data about why strategic planning was needed, would protect his or her turf in all activities, would curse the CEO for forcing another one of her "programs" down their throats, would question why an outsider was being brought in, and would otherwise behave in a negative way. Lou therefore told Marie:

LOU: Getting the executives involved is essential. Based on my experience with getting organizations to use strategic planning, I'd like to suggest your memo only invite them to a meeting where the issue of strategic planning, and not the problems you face, will be discussed. I would be glad to facilitate a meeting where our expected outcome would be just a plan of action on how to do strategic planning in the company.

Marie agreed to Lou's idea, and they set up a meeting for two to two-and-a-half hours one morning a week later. At the meeting, the executives, including the CEO, sat around a conference table. After being introduced by the CEO, Lou began:

LOU: Strategic planning is a technique that all of you have probably heard about. However, that doesn't mean that everyone agrees on what it is supposed to accomplish. So let's start by having each of you record individually as many purposes as you can think of for strategic planning.

Thirty-six purpose statements were identified by the group. Lou asked them to arrange the purposes from small to large scope, and then select the focus purpose to be achieved by strategic planning in their company.

LOU: Now let's develop some ideal ways the company should organize efforts to achieve the focus and larger strategic planning purposes.

From them, we will set up a plan of action that stays as close as possible to what you select as a good future target way of doing strategic planning.

In about three hours, the group had determined the specifics of the plan of action to do strategic planning (the purposes of the strategic plan, where to start, the form of the outcomes, a time schedule, a series of steps to follow, questions to ask, who would be involved, and what type of resources and computer systems would be needed) and what each person's responsibilities were.

This meeting was a success. Each executive saw an opportunity to contribute, found a sense of meaning in what was to be done, was challenged to be creative, became willing to implement the solution (developed a buy-in to action), understood that change is always going to occur, was motivated, developed trust in the process, saw the whole picture, and found a way to communicate easily with others. Many future organizational concerns and issues would be significantly minimized as a result. The next week, Marie and Lou reviewed the outcomes of the meeting:

MARIE: Lou, now I understand why you are so highly recommended. The strategic planning framework we will be using is not the same as the model I heard about; it fits us better. And your insights about my executives were right on target. Getting our top people together with the agenda you had in developing a plan of action was much better than telling them that strategic planning was going to start in two weeks.

We do not suggest that you simply adopt the SQA language verbatim as we have presented it in this book. Every organization has its own system of language and symbols in place (including history, culture, stories, metaphors, and physical objects that have particular meanings). You need to invent or create a dialect of SQA that works in your organization while not throwing out the underlying fundamental questions and process that we have presented. For instance, one organization I consulted could not use the SQA word *purpose* because it had a religious connotation to its members, so we used the word *objective* for SQA's meaning of purpose.

In developing your own SQA language, we suggest that you begin by finding a department, group, project, or individuals you think have a need and may be most receptive to thinking and acting in new ways.

Introduce them to the Smart Questions Approach. Then use SQA itself with them to develop a plan of thinking and action for developing your own language and approach to SQA.

Begin with the foundation questions and four phases we have presented in this book. Then find out what works and what does not, and begin your creative process of finding your own language and processes for using SQA to your advantage. Your task is to form questions based on SQA and to create a language that works in your organization. Adopting a common language and process is essential to establish a community with a common vocabulary and set of rules that spark mutual understanding and an open, accepting, patient environment that fosters creativity and innovation.

As you go about developing your own SQA language, keep in mind these questions from Chapter One to help you determine if the questions you ask and the language you use are right:

- Does the question I'm asking align with the three foundation questions?
- Does the question I'm asking open and expand look-to-the-future responses and possibilities?
- Does the question I'm asking create new smart question–type metaphors and information sources?
- Does the question I'm asking feel like an interesting question or one that enhances perceptiveness on the part of others?
- Does the question I'm asking spark creative responses (in the sense that the question can yield many options), or other smart question–type questions?
- Is the question I'm asking likely to provide a way to empower individuals to use smart questions for creating solutions on their own?
- Is the question I'm asking likely to bring people together enthusiastically and with commitment to focus on building a desired future and getting results?

Systems Perceptiveness

To work effectively in the new organizations of the twenty-first century, employees must learn to be more perceptive. By *perceptiveness,* we refer to the ability to think about issues in holistic terms that encompass all the systems involved. Everyone needs to be able to understand that whatever action they take or question they ask must be considered in terms of all the systems on which it has an impact.

For example, a customer service representative on the phone with a customer who has a problem needs to have knowledge, before responding, about the purposes the customer seeks to achieve, the purposes of his or her organization, its range of products or services, the environment the customer is dealing with, the nature of the customer's inputs as well as his own, and so on. This is the type of systems perceptiveness that allows people to provide the right level of creative solution finding.

Perceptiveness, or systems consciousness, especially helps keep the uniqueness principle in mind. Having a systems consciousness allows you to alert everyone to the pitfalls of trying to copy a solution from somewhere else; your system elements and dimensions are not the same as those in the other organization. It helps you avoid falling into the technological imperative trap, thinking that you must use the latest technology rather than asking the appropriate element and dimension questions to fashion the right living solution, with or without new technology.

Another reason behind the need for systems perceptiveness is that the new organization is more complex, fluid, and spread out than traditional organizations. The introduction of computer and communications technology has created new relationships and ways for people to work together that require communicating and sharing knowledge across large distances. The customer service representative, for example, has access to a lot more information than ever before, and, just as important, the customer calling has similar resources that allow the two to exchange information quickly and systematically. People now function more in networks or spider webs of formal and informal relationships across boundaries of geography, organization, time, role, authority, and even companies. These networks need to be more in tune with each other than their industrial era predecessors were.

Here is an example of what we mean by systems perceptiveness as it relates to the new organizational work environment. Imagine you are asked to do a simple task for a colleague in another department. He e-mails you a request, asking you to evaluate a report he has written. You give your response, but he is unhappy: you did not note critical mistakes in the report that got him into trouble. The point is that to the person making the assignment, the other person missed some obvious parts of the task—that is, this person did not see the big picture, his picture. You responded to the request from your perspective, not his.

Systems thinking on the part of both parties in such situations would significantly help eliminate such outcomes. The perceptive requester, armed with a systems consciousness, would have explained, for example, that his or her need is an expansion of purposes of the task, some of the output dimensions, and how the requested output fit within the purposes and environment. The other party, even if the requester did not supply the information, would have asked questions of the same sort to provide a context for the task and would then have done a better job.

How can you train people to see issues in a big picture or systems framework? The task sounds daunting, but the good news is that you already have access to the key tools that build perceptiveness when you use SQA. Every aspect of SQA is designed to help you think with systems perceptiveness. However, as with incorporating the language of SQA, we recommend that you follow the same approach in order to customize it to meet the needs of your organization. First, find a department, a particular group, a project, or particular individuals you think have a need and may be most receptive to thinking and acting in new ways about the whole system. Introduce them to SQA. Then use SQA, particularly the systems matrix, to develop a plan of thinking and acting for developing greater systems perceptiveness in everyone.

The main test of whether the perceptiveness level is increasing is the extent to which your people begin to see the totality of an organization and its interconnections between the various systems of your organization and those of the outside world. Are they beginning to see the systems that they operate and those that affect them? Do they realize that there are always many interconnections between all the elements and dimensions of their solutions?

In addition, you can often assess increased perceptiveness when you notice fewer negative workplace actions, such as resentment, lack of teamwork, and water-cooler bad-mouthing. When you see more dialogue, interconnections, diversity of options, ethical considerations being discussed, and conscious choice, you can be assured you are on the right path for more effective thinking and performance.

Instilling an Empowerment Culture

Empowerment is a word that has been overused in the business literature in the sense of its dictionary definition: "vesting power, authority, or license in some person or group of people to take action." In business, this is interpreted as meaning sharing information with employees while giving them task autonomy and self-management. Management typically hopes that "lowering of the levels of decision making" will enrich jobs and improve job satisfaction and morale. Although such empowerment is quite worthwhile, in our experience and others, most such talk is lip-service (Argyris, 1998). Thus, many organizations have abandoned the word *empowerment*. It seems to have too much baggage.

For us, however, *empowerment* is much more concrete and measurable. We use the term to refer to people's ability to think and design from a systems perspective and take action that leads to the attainment of desirable results. It is not only about pushing decision making to lower levels. It is about having the appropriate people in various roles collaboratively develop and install solutions that work now and in the future. This type of empowerment reflects a positive power, in which each individual accepts change and is willing to take risks in trying something new. This view of empowerment provides a way for people to have a sense of meaning and shared purpose, to become self-leaders, to feel significant, to be excited about their work, to be part of a community, and to participate on powerful teams.

Getting people to feel empowered can be visualized in several ways. One model we like is shown in the following progression:

New ways of thinking → learning and growth → increased self-confidence → empowerment of self and others → new experiences and perspectives → redefinition of self and role → new patterns of actions → innovation outcomes → reinforcement → learning and growth → more empowerment

There are three prerequisite notions to consider in order to empower people. First, recognize that very few jobs, if any, exist in isolation. Work has really become cooperative-intellectual work, so organizational solutions today need to begin by getting the right people involved (which is why SQA begins with the People Involvement Phase).

Second, recognize that people seek career growth, learning, and development; exciting work and challenges; meaningful work to make a difference and a contribution; being part of a team; autonomy or sense of control over the job; flexibility; and fun, including some celebrations of success. Do that, and you have already gone a major way toward empowering your organization. After all, thinking is the basis of challenging work, the very opposite of rote, mindless work.

Finally, recognize that you need to make it safe for people to minimize or eliminate their anxieties and stress about change. Not every change effort will result in success, but people need to have the freedom to try a new approach without putting their careers on the line.

The approach that we suggest to empowering your organization is similar to the approach that we suggest for developing your own SQA language and increasing systems perceptiveness. First, find a department, a particular group, a project, or particular individuals you think have a need and may be most receptive to thinking and acting in new ways. Introduce them to the SQA. Then use SQA itself with them to develop a plan of thinking and action for empowering your organization.

There are many indicators to assess how well your efforts at empowerment are progressing. These include noticing employees volunteering to take part in more uncertain projects, producing many unsolicited new product and service proposals, coming up with an abundant number of ideas in all settings that frequently have high returns on investment when they are used, talking with pride to others about what is new in their organization, and having customers compliment you frequently on your ability to anticipate their needs. All these are indicators of the release of creativity in the organization.

ADOPTING SQA IN YOUR ORGANIZATION

Adopting SQA is not a rigorous task. You do not need an SQA department, SQA director, SQA budget (except perhaps for training and some facilitators), or any other formal organizational structure. Such a bureaucratic formation may have been necessary in low-technology environments when the pace of change was slow and incremental, but bureaucracies have become dinosaurs when it comes to planning and managing change.

SQA can be easily learned and brought into as many organizational processes, projects, and experiences as possible—in the boardroom, at meetings, in negotiations, writing proposals, solving conflicts, orienting R&D, and improving human resources, among many others. The specialized vocabulary and processes of SQA do not need to be something extra that the organization does on top of your normal procedures, but rather should become the way things are done, that is, part of the organizational culture. In addition, the three benefits of a common language, perceptiveness, and empowerment provide a key ingredient for the transparency all organizations need to have after the corporate debacles of the early twenty-first century.

Be patient as you begin to use SQA because it takes time to embed it into the core of your organization. We know there are many factors that can easily play havoc with your best intentions to use SQA. The politics of power can be a barrier to implementing SQA, and even if it is not blatant, differences in leadership styles and the comprehension abilities of individuals will affect the pace of getting SQA into the whole organization. You need to acknowledge your own uniqueness issues and then adopt an approach that will work in your unique circumstances.

Here is an example of how SQA was introduced into one company we consulted. The leaders of six large, separate organizations within this company had been given a mandate by the chief information officer (CIO) to combine their separate information technology services into a shared services model. This required that they standardize their services across the different groups and manage the services as if they were one organization rather than six. The task was difficult because they did not immediately have the capability to run a shared services model. These managers had always worked autonomously and provided customized and flexible services to their individual clients. There was no one-size-fits-all fix that could be implemented right away.

The worst of it, though, was that the leaders had no intention of making the shared model work. The CIO was new, and they had no confidence in her or in the shared model concept. But their separate services were too expensive to keep separate any longer, so the shared model had to be implemented despite what they thought. The initial team meetings were so disagreeable that they became the topic of hallway gossip, like a soap opera whose daily events are eagerly awaited.

The first thing we did when we began our work with the six leaders was to have the group come up with ground rules to create a safe space in which to get our work done. This included specific policies regarding twice-weekly meeting attendance, participation in meetings, conduct during meetings, decision making, how to handle disagreements, conducting meetings using an impartial facilitator, and keeping minutes and action items of all meetings. We were beginning to create the conditions for empowerment. People cannot be empowered when the environment is not safe.

Each manager was given time to talk about his or her own service. Once that happened, they became relaxed enough to move on to a discussion about purposes and future solution design. We began to introduce the new language of SQA to the group slowly. The shared language allowed them to go off between meetings and come back to present new ideas for everyone to consider rather than returning to their usual reductionist-type data analysis and blame sessions. Although they were beginning to use the language of purposes and future solutions, they were not yet completely aligned. Nevertheless, they were slowly beginning to respect and even appreciate one another. Over the next few weeks, the meetings became increasingly more productive. The soap opera hallway banter faded.

Eventually, to gain deeper alignment, I asked the group to go off site with me for a three-day retreat. I had two main objectives: to gain alignment about their purposes as an organization and to create a first draft of an ideal future solution. The group needed to create a common systems perceptiveness about what might work in terms of a shared services model.

We broke the managers up into small groups to generate ideas, which were then shared in the large group and taken back to small groups to refine. Each of the small groups developed a future solution using components of the systems matrix. The final afternoon was devoted to evaluating each proposed solution and selecting one to recommend to the CIO. They chose an innovative approach based on a franchise model. Each of the units would maintain some autonomy to account for their uniqueness, but elements of the shared services model would also be implemented.

The solution the group developed was eventually put into place and worked. They created a shared services model that still allowed them to maintain their own clients with timely and well-delivered services. In fact, after several months, the new system received higher client satisfaction ratings than the old warlord approach. During the nine-month life of this project, the team members vastly improved their ability to think through their conflicts because they now had a common language, an increased systems perceptiveness, and an empowered approach for working together. Although the early phases of assimilating SQA into this organization were rocky, the group's commitment, along with a good SQA coach, proved that breakthrough results were possible.

An additional point that we need to make about these three benefits of an SQA organization is that they build one upon another. Having a powerful language and systems perceptiveness are empowering in and of themselves. Being empowered then leads to more innovation, refinement of language, and heightened systems perceptiveness. These three benefits thus spiral forward, providing people with new ways of understanding and the ability to play many roles—project leader, facilitator, communicator, scout, ambassador, gatekeeper, idea generator, champion, entrepreneur, translator, strategic linkage, and so on.

Similarly, having an empowered organization whose members can think and act expansively—in effect being leaders in their own situation—creates the conditions for an even greater evolution in the organization's language and perceptiveness. The entire process is like being swept up in a tide as each positive experience helps people grow into more empowered individuals.

Getting to the point where an SQA organization enjoys the full operation of these three interrelated benefits is like an ideal future solution that you might like to have in, say, five years. This means that you need to think in terms of creating a living solution that you install for now, with a plan for additional changes that will get you to the future solution. Backtracking and revisions as you go along are to be expected; you should not be disappointed and abandon your efforts. Changing the culture and thinking process of an organization is daunting and requires patience, courage, persistence, determination, and commitment as you move toward the ideal future solution.

Attaining these benefits in an organization leads to what is, after all, the purpose or mission of an organization: produce the powerful results of ever greater value over the long haul for all stakeholders—customers, employees, shareholders, suppliers, and society.

BRINGING SQA INTO YOUR LIFE

This book has laid out a holistic thinking paradigm and process to address many types of business and organizational problems. But business and organizational issues are only one area in which to apply SQA. We believe the process has relevance in many other aspects of life, including all the areas of your personal life as portrayed in Figure 2.1.

Consider the following two scenarios. (1) You and your significant other are discussing at dinner what movie to see tonight. (2) Your car sustained expensive major damage in an accident around noon, and since your job requires you to have a car, you have to decide what to do about a car by tomorrow. In these instances, is it worthwhile to think through the four phases of SQA?

The answer is yes; even in personal situations, you might jump to a solution that is not an optimal or creative one, so why not apply SQA? In each of these cases, you could go through the four phases without difficulty to improve your solution creation effort. In the movie situation, you could call someone who has seen several movies recently to get their opinion. In the car situation, you could ask your insurance agent. You could then go through the Purposes Phase of the problem, exploring the purposes of your situation (What do you and your significant other want to accomplish by seeing a movie? What are your total transportation needs?).

Next, you might propose a future solution to accomplish your purposes ideally within the time frame you need. You might decide that the two of you would do best if you could rent a DVD, and you might decide that your best future solution is to lease a car. Finally, you will seek to arrive at a living solution that comes as close as possible to your future solution. For instance, the two of you might go to the movie recommended by a friend who likes some of the same kinds of movies as you do and then rent some DVDs on the way home to achieve other interests you may have. Then you might rent a car for tomorrow.

In these examples, SQA can help you keep the creative space large enough so that your living solution is the best solution possible as you look to the future. In short, SQA—especially the future solution aspect of it—can put you on the road to a creative solution that better prepares you for the continuing changes that you would like to see occurring.

APPLYING SQA TO THE REAL WORLD

Finally, we also want to challenge you to take SQA into every aspect of the real world to make powerful changes for the betterment of all people. There is no shortage of problems where SQA can help. The Union of International Associations (http://www.uia.org/data.htm) tracks over thirty thousand world problems. We have had experiences in using SQA in many of these settings—education, health care systems, regional planning, architecture, engineering, and so on—and the results have been outstanding. You have read about many such cases throughout this book, but there are many, many more.

We want to see SQA applied to the most serious of our national and international problems in education, politics, health care systems and insurance, poverty levels, regional planning, finance, transportation, architecture, defense, and even the development of world peace. Some of the most pressing issues toward which SQA can be applied include reducing nuclear testing, eliminating land mines, creating an international criminal court, reducing global climate change, minimizing oil usage per capita in industrialized countries (especially in the United States), making health care available for everyone, reducing the availability of chemical and biological weapons, and boosting children's rights to life and health.

The pages of newspapers, magazines, and journals are packed with so-called expert opinions about how to solve many of these problems. But the questions and answers put forward by such experts are often too narrow minded or faddish or are based on short-term fixes reflecting traditional reductionist approaches. In our view, only by constructing a conceptual framework within which to ask smart questions and propose unique innovative solutions can we come closer to having living solutions for these serious problems.

We have had many consulting assignments with large and small businesses, hospitals, schools, government agencies, and nonprofit charities where a faddish program was initially adopted, and we were then called in when such programs did not produce results. In every case, our clients cited that these other management approaches led to analysis paralysis: large amounts of data had been collected, but no one knew what to do with the information. Given what you have read about in this book, consider what smart questions could accomplish if they were applied to many of our nation's and the world's major issues. Laws, regulations, policies, speeches, and decisions that result from SQA are far more likely to be creative and effective and to achieve beneficial results.

SQA is especially useful for very large, complex governmental problems. For example, Los Angeles County, larger than forty-two of the states (10 million residents, ninety thousand employees, $16 billion budget) and comprising eighty-eight incorporated cities plus many unincorporated areas, set up a Quality and Productivity Commission with the charge to help the thirty-eight county departments be more creative and effective. SQA was used to help this commission determine how it should proceed in accomplishing its work.

In particular, the concepts were intuitively applied in one very large case involving building codes. Although California has its state-level minimum building code standards, there were well over a thousand additional code regulations added by the various cities as well as the county of Los Angeles. This hodge-podge made it very difficult and costly for builders to develop plans that could be used in more than one jurisdiction. Imagine trying to change and improve this mess by approaching it in a reductionist approach, and you can guess at the tremendous defensiveness each of the entities would have about its particular extra regulations.

Representatives from the various entities identified the real purposes to be achieved (to have safe buildings, to develop economic growth in the county, to facilitate builders in developing proposals for multiple jurisdictions, and others). This led them to realize that the future solution for the county is really the same as the state codes. The living solution they developed and implemented had only forty-four additions to the state codes. They were needed by a few entities to handle specific environmental conditions, such as very hilly terrain, drainage details, forest proximity, and desert conditions.

Most major national and world problems admittedly do not have easy living solutions that can be implemented quickly. But that is why SQA is so important to creating solutions for them. Getting started on these problems using SQA is at least more likely to produce a variety of intelligent options for consideration, while an effort can at least be made to begin implementing a solid living solution for today with an eye toward change and improvement for the future.

THE EVOLUTION OF SQA

Are the smart questions we present in this book going to be the same in twenty years? Fifty years? Not surprisingly, we would not be using the concepts of smart questions if we said yes. SQA can be thought of as a contrarian way of thinking—as we said, only 8 percent of people intuitively think this way. (For another perspective on different ways of thinking, see Sample, 2001.) Our goals are to change this percentage, so that SQA becomes the standard way of creating solutions that 100 percent of people begin using. (This is our future solution—our fantasy ideal solution that serves as our continuing guide.) In a sense, the SQA as we have taught you in this book is itself just a living solution that we hope to be able to continue developing, along with other people, such that over the course of the next ten or twenty years, we can continue to improve the Smart Questions Approach to a point where everyone in the world will want to learn and use it.

One of our goals is to encourage many others to do research into ways of making SQA even better. To achieve this, we have founded the Center for Breakthrough Thinking (www.breakthroughthinking.com), designed to support SQA and apply it to many endeavors. Our organization is intended to be a repository of data on SQA applications and to enable practitioners to pool their knowledge. We are also considering software to facilitate the SQA decision-making process. Especially useful for a geographically dispersed or a virtual organization, the software would enable participants to share questions and responses, build their list of options, obtain links to sources of information that the questions need, maintain records of options selected, and identify those options not used for later reference.

Before closing, we would like to cite the comments that were made to us about the benefits of SQA from the superintendent of a school district with 230,000 students in 650 schools:

Our staff thinks of work achievements in terms of "end results" rather than inputs and efforts, budgets, and manpower. However, our new way of thinking is changing our culture by focusing us on accountability and measures of success in achieving purposes. Our discussions are now very intense and conducted in a positive atmosphere. The level of cooperation within the organization is constantly increasing. The Smart Questions process is indeed a conceptually different thinking approach that has created major changes in the way our supervisors, principals, teachers, and even pupils go about planning and solving problems.

We began the Smart Questions journey in Chapter One by emphasizing that people need to move beyond problem solving into creating solutions by asking the right questions and incorporating a new framework into their thinking. We hope that by now you know how to do that, as Figure 7.1 reminds you.

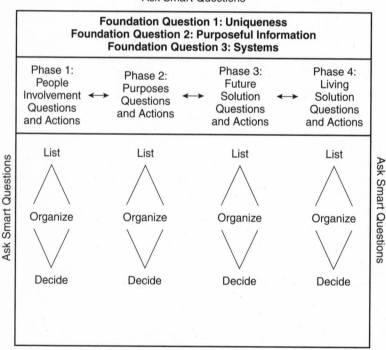

Figure 7.1.   The Smart Questions Approach for Creating Solutions

—⁓— References

Adams, J. *The Care and Feeding of Ideas.* New York: Perseus Publishing, 1979.

Argyris, C. "Empowerment: The Emperor's New Clothes." *Harvard Business Review,* 1998, *76*(3), 98–105.

Bossidy, L., and Charan, R. *Execution: The Discipline of Getting Things Done.* New York: Crown Business, 2002.

Brown, J. S., and Duguid, P. *The Social Life of Information.* Boston: Harvard Business School Press, 2000.

Drazin, R., Glynn, M., and Kazanjian, R. "Multilevel Theorizing About Creativity in Organizations: A Sensemaking Perspective." *Academy of Management Review,* 1999, *24*(2), 286–307.

Gardner, H. *Frames of Mind: The Theory of Multiple Intelligences.* New York: Basic Books, 1993.

George, W. *Authentic Leadership: Rediscovering the Secrets to Creating Lasting Value.* San Francisco: Jossey-Bass, 2003.

Kegan, R. *In over Our Heads: The Mental Demands of the Modern Workplace.* Cambridge, Mass.: Harvard University Press, 1994.

Kegan, R., and Laskow Lahey, L. "The Real Reason People Won't Change." *Harvard Business Review,* 2001, *79*(10), 84–92.

McGregor, D. *The Human Side of Enterprise.* New York: McGraw-Hill, 1960.

Nadler, G., and Hibino, S. *Creative Solution Finding: The Triumph of Breakthrough Thinking Over Conventional Problem Solving.* Rocklin, Calif.: Prima Publishing, 1995.

Nisbet, R. *History of the Idea of Progress.* New York: Basic Books, 1980.

Nutt, P. *Why Decisions Fail: Avoiding the Blunders and Traps That Lead to Debacles.* San Francisco: Berrett-Koehler, 2002.

Perlow, L. *When You Say Yes But Mean No: How Silencing Conflict Wrecks Relationships and Companies . . . and What You Can Do About It.* New York: Crown Business, 2003.

Rowe, A. *Creative Intelligence: Our Hidden Potential.* Upper Saddle River, N.J.: Prentice Hall, 2004.

Sample, S. B. *The Contrarian's Guide to Leadership.* San Francisco: Jossey-Bass, 2001.

Tucker, R. *Driving Growth Through Innovation: How Leading Firms Are Transforming Their Futures.* San Francisco: Berrett-Koehler, 2002.

Van de Ven, A. "The Process of Adopting Innovations in Organizations." In E. Laumann, G. Nadler, and R. O'Farrell (eds.), *People and Technology in the Workplace.* Washington, D.C.: National Academy Press, 1991.

⟿ Acknowledgments

Although the basic concepts in this book were identified from our research and practice over thirty years ago and have been refined since then, we are always trying to put them into a framework that is easily understood and usable by as many people as possible. Each framework that was presented in previous books has benefited from the editorial advice of writing experts, and each book was, in our minds and those of the many readers of those books, an improved way of explaining the concepts. Our previous book, aided in significant ways by Thomas Dworetzky in editorially shaping an engaging manuscript, dwelled on our belief that the concepts were best presented for learning and application in the form of questions. This book goes much further in organizing the idea of the questions format, and we are sure you will learn a great deal from it.

For developing the new framework of questions, we owe thanks to our Jossey-Bass editor, Kathe Sweeney, who suggested we use the services of developmental editor Rick Benzel. And to Rick, we are very thankful you pushed, cajoled, and otherwise stimulated us to probe deeply into how we could reorganize and present the concepts so they are crisp and usable. We very much appreciate your willingness to work closely with us and help in making our writing clear.

A book that presents a synthesis of a lot of research and practice has an extremely large number of people to thank, primarily all those who let us study how they approached their assignments and from whom the concepts of this book were synthesized. You know who you are (we promised them anonymity), and we express our appreciation to you. Our practice of the ideas has been facilitated by many adventurous executives who were willing to try this different approach to planning, design, development, improving, and creating solutions. The outstanding results of such applications have been one payback for their willingness to experiment, and we offer the payback of sincerest thanks. Many of these projects are reported in this book.

It would take many pages to list all of these people plus students doing research, representatives of funding agencies, and assistants in copyediting and formatting. Because you would probably not read all the pages and we are almost certain to omit several important names, we offer to every one of these people, as well as the authors of other articles and books we read and often quoted, sincere appreciation for your help.

G.N.
W.C.

—⁓— The Authors

GERALD NADLER is IBM Chair Emeritus in Engineering Management and Professor Emeritus of Industrial and Systems Engineering at the University of Southern California. He was previously on the faculties of the University of Wisconsin–Madison, Washington University in St. Louis, and Purdue University (where he received his undergraduate and Ph.D. degrees), and accepted five invited visiting professorships, four of them abroad. His industrial experience started with industrial jobs and extends through a vice presidency of general operations for a 400-employee manufacturing company and a sixteen-year stint on the board of directors of a $300 million manufacturing company. He is president of the Center for Breakthrough Thinking, an international firm of consulting affiliates with clients in all sectors of society and a think tank for the application of transformational thinking approaches to achieve business and personal breakthroughs. He has written or coauthored over two hundred published articles and fifteen books, several of them translated into eight other languages. He serves on the Los Angeles County Quality and Productivity Commission and on the board of directors of the University of Southern California Credit Union and previously was an elected member of a board of education for a midsized school district in the St. Louis area. He has received over twenty-five national and international awards for his work.

WILLIAM J. CHANDON is a vice president of the Center for Breakthrough Thinking. He has over fifteen years of experience in the fields of organizational development and business transformation. He has consulted with many and varied government, nonprofit, and commercial businesses from many industries. He also teaches management courses at St. Mary's College of California. Chandon received a B.S. from Washington State University, an M.A. from California State University, and a Ph.D. from the Fielding Graduate Institute.

Index

A

Adams, D., 132

Antagonists, foes, enemies, 70–71

APHIS, 263

Asking questions: creativity fueled by, 17–19, 155–157; as fundamental premise of SQA, 16; reductionist thinking about, 17; Socratic method of thinking and, 16. *See also* Purposeful information questions; SQA foundation questions; SQA Smart Questions; Systems questions; Uniqueness questions

Authentic Leadership (George), 91

B

Bacon, Sir F., 3, 10

Betterment, 94

Biographical method, 154

Bossidy, L., 91, 201

Brown, J. S., 56

C

The Care and Feeding of Ideas (Adams), 6–7

Cartesian scientific thinking paradigm: fallacies in implementation of, 4–7; four principles of, 3; origins of, 2–3; testing your own use of, 3–4

Change: people's reaction to, 52–53; social science research on resistance to, 46; SQA recognition regarding people and, 46

Charan, R., 92, 201

Churchill, W., 230

Convergent thinking, 34–35

Copernicus, 17

Creative Intelligence: Our Hidden Potential (Rowe), 50

Creative Solution Finding (Nadler and Hibino), 7, 12

Creative space expansion, 88

Creativity: asking questions to fuel, 17–19, 155–157; divergent/convergent thinking and, 34–35; of holistic problem solvers, 13–15; inspiring, 152–155; People involvement foundation question 1 on, 50–53; unique qualities of, 51–53; "virtuous" spiral facilitating, 143

D

"Daily swing thought," 130

Data: biased nature of, 23; raw, 23–24; real information from, 24–25

Decide step: future solution phase, 167–174; living solution phase, 219–221; people involvement phase, 79–82; selecting focus purpose phase, 118–128

Decision making: intuitive method of, 124; logical method of, 119, 121–124; other possible techniques for, 125

Descartes, R., 2, 3, 6, 10

Different interpretations/perspectives, 55